# THE RIGHT FREQUENCY

# THE RIGHT FREQUENCY

## THE TALK RADIO GIANTS WHO SHOOK UP THE POLITICAL AND MEDIA ESTABLISHMENT

FRED V. LUCAS

History Publishing Company
Palisades, New York

Lucas, Fred V.
    The right frequency : the story of the talk radio
  giants who shook up the political and media
  establishment / Fred V. Lucas.
    p. cm.
    Includes bibliographical references and index.
    LCCN 2012941696
    ISBN 9781933909431 (hc)
    ISBN 9781933909172 (pbk.)
    ISBN 9781933909165 (ebk)


    1. Radio in politics--United States.  2. Right and
  left (Political science)--United States.  3. Radio talk
  show hosts--United States.  4. Radio talk shows--United
  States.    I. Title.

  HE8697.85.U6L83 2012            384.54'55'0973
                          QBI12-600137


Published in the United States by
History Publishing Company LLC
Palisades, NY
www.historypublishingco.com

To my wife Basia, whose love, support and encouragement made
this book possible

# Table of Contents

## Leaders(s) of the Republican Party?

## Early Voices
H.V. Kaltenborn: Dean of Commentators
Boake Carter: Far and Away the Most Daring
Father Charles Coughlin: Right Wing Radio Priest?
Fulton Lewis Jr.: Combating the 'Ultra Liberal Eastern Crowd'
Walter Winchell: Inventing Infotainment

## Lonely Voices
Clarence Manion: Taking Bipartisan Aim
Dan Smoot: Fighting Invisible Government
Rev. Carl McIntyre: Crushed by the Fairness Doctrine
Rev. Billy James Hargis: Catalyst to the Red Lion Ruling

## Game Changers
Joe Pyne: 'Father of In Your Face Talk'
Bob Grant: 'Perfecting Anger'
Barry Farber: 'Publicist of Ultra Conservative Outlooks'
Marlin Maddoux's Point of View
George Putnam: 'Greatest Voice in Radio'
Dr. Dobson: Changing America's Focus
Libertarian Chatter with Neal Boortz

# FOREWORD BY MARTHA ZOLLER

I've been in the talk radio business since 1994. All of us in the business owe our jobs to Rush Limbaugh. Without him, there was no resurgence of AM Radio or the movement to FM Talk that's happening today. But Talk Radio is and always has been about content. It's individual and it's personal. When you hear a presidential candidate talking to your local radio host and then you see that host somewhere, you feel connected to that experience. The guests, the content, bring the listener and the host closer together.

While content is delivered through many formats today, essentially, radio is the American experience. And that experience is epitomized by the independence of riding in your car to work and play and everything in between, with the radio on. In the early days, we were listening to "Top 40" with our parents, but then as we matured, we started listening to Talk Radio.

Fred Lucas is a reporter for CNSNews.com (Cybercast News Service) and a contributing editor to *Townhall Magazine*. He's one of the great providers of content in what Michael Harrison of *Talkers Magazine* calls "New Media." It's media outside the mainstream. I would argue, it is mainstream, but the terminology hasn't caught up yet.

In "The Right Frequency" By Fred V. Lucas, he traces the history of Talk Radio as a mover of conservative thought throughout most of the last century in to this one. "The powers that be" keep predicting the demise of radio, but they can't replace the personal nature of the interaction. In the 21st century, we see our growth in listenership to our own local stations through apps on smart phones. But it is still personal, it is still a relationship.

At the core, Talk Radio is a relationship between the host, the guest and the listener. Callers make it interesting, but most people don't call, so the ultimate relationship is a personal one. Americans are independent and the ability to travel independently on the road throughout this great nation, or just back and forth to work is the American frontier in its most current form.

People have tried to duplicate the talk radio format throughout the world, but it's never as good as it is right here in America. From the big, national syndicated shows hosted by Rush or Hannity, to the regional shows like "Rick and Bubba," to the local shows like mine, listeners to talk radio are coming home to the format that is most like them: opinionated, smart and fiercely patriotic.

Lucas in "The Right Frequency" will remind you why you love Talk Radio if you are a fan and will make you curious about the medium if you are not. And if you are one of the Mainstream Media and you dare to pick up a copy, you will wonder why you can't create that kind of relationship with your viewers/listeners. Talkers have replaced the anchors of the early days of Television as the most trusted people in America and the Left hates it.

Talk Radio will be here now, and in the future, and Fred V. Lucas tells you why in "The Right Frequency."

*Martha Zoller has been a talk radio host since 1996. She retired from her radio program in May of 2012 to pursue a run for Congress in Georgia's new 9th Congressional District.*

# INTRODUCTION

When President Barack Obama made a personal phone call to Georgetown law student Sandra Fluke, it served two purposes in the 2012 election cycle: shore up support among women voters and once again make Rush Limbaugh an issue.

Democratic operatives hit the airwaves criticizing Mitt Romney for not criticizing Rush Limbaugh. In echoes of a 2009 strategy, the head of Obama's super PAC Bill Burton said Limbaugh was "the de facto leader of the Republican Party."

The controversy began in February when Fluke, speaking to a House panel, expressed support for the government mandate that employers cover contraception—even at religious-affiliated institutions such as Georgetown, which did not cover the cost for conscience reasons. "Forty percent of the female students at Georgetown Law reported to us that they struggled financially as a result of this policy," Fluke said. On the radio, Limbaugh questioned why Fluke or anyone else is entitled to have their safe sex paid for by someone else. He jokingly said, "What would you call someone who wants us to pay for her to have sex? What would you call that woman? You'd call them a slut, a prostitute or whatever."

This prompted a loss of sponsors and days of onslaughts, after which Rush apologized. "For over 20 years, I have illustrated the absurd with absurdity, three hours a day, five days a week. In this instance, I chose the wrong words in my analogy of the situation. ... I sincerely apologize to Ms. Fluke for the insulting word choices."

Despite the apology, the desire for the Democrats to target Limbaugh as a part of the reelection strategy shows that Limbaugh, and other hosts, are still a thorn in their side, and occasionally a strategic tool.

While researching for this book, I learned about voices that helped plant the seeds of today's cultural phenomenon. To do a book about the history of talk radio would be too broad. It would necessarily have to profile Howard Stern, Larry King and Don Imus. The focus is rather on conservative talk radio, which saved the AM dial after Limbaugh spawned an entire industry.

My hope is that this would be both a history book but also be a fun and light read. Each chapter is divided into profiles of major radio personalities who emerged in a particular era, and particular issues that talk radio impacted as it became more influential.

This is not just the story of talk show hosts. It is essentially the history of the United States since the 1920s told through the lens of radio and conservatism.

CHAPTER ONE

# Leader(s) of the Republican Party?

The crowd erupted as Glenn Beck took the stage, throwing an arm around David Keen, the president of the American Conservative Union, before he delivered the keynote address at the 2010 Conservative Political Action Conference, or CPAC, in Washington.

"It is such an honor to be here, it really is," Beck said in opening remarks in the ballroom of the Marriot Wardman Park Hotel in late February. "Last year, I was actually in my car listening to Rush Limbaugh give the keynote."

Beck's mention of Limbaugh prompted another round of cheers from the audience of conservative activists, mostly youth.

"Rush is a hero of mine and I'm listening to him and my producer, I write him a text on my e-mail and he gave it to me just this week; I wrote him last year. Wow! What must that be like to give the keynote at CSPAN, at CPAC," the audience cheered. "Here I am, here I am today, and I can't believe it."

Looking over at a seated Keen, whose organization ACU runs the annual conservative conference, Beck mused, "I mean it's been a tough year for you, if you're down to me it's a tough year." The humility of the joke prompted laughter.

He continued, invoking another broadcasting legend—Ronald

Reagan—who among other lifetime achievements was also inducted into the National Radio Hall of Fame. "It's not just that Rush has done this, one of my other heroes Ronald Reagan, how many times, 12? Because of Ronald Reagan, my grandfather, my father, I have a hope for America. I remember when Ronald Reagan talked about morning in America. I have always believed that. I have always wanted to believe that, that tomorrow is going to be better than it is today. If you ask people now all across the country, if you say, do you think you're children are going to be better off than they are today, the answer is going to be a resounding no and it's not just from Republican or conservatives. It's from the entire, uh, uh, uh, whatever."

The second flub, after first referring to CPAC as CSPAN, less than two minutes into the speech got an endearing laugh from his fans. "It's the entire spectrum. I'm sorry I don't use teleprompters, I speaking from here," Beck said holding his left hand over his heart and taking a jab at President Barack Obama's reliance on reading speeches. An audience member shouted, "We love you Glenn!"[1]

Such minor errors illustrate Beck's popularity—a regular guy—and one contrast he has with Limbaugh, known for his "excellence in broadcasting," who delivered near flawless verbal prose as the 2009 keynote speaker at CPAC. As Beck rolled on, he began to scold the Grand Old Party for betraying its conservative values and buckling to the forces of progressivism.

"One party will tax and spend; one party won't tax but will spend: It's both of them," Beck said.

"All they're talking about is we need a big tent. We need a big tent. Can we get a bigger tent? How can we get a big tent? What is this, a circus?" Beck told the convention hall. Then, the admitted recovering alcoholic said the party must first admit it has a problem. "Hello, my name is the Republican Party and I've got a problem. I'm addicted to spending and big government." He continued, "I'm so sick of hearing people say, 'Oh, Republicans are going to solve it all. Really? It's just progressive-light. ... It's like somebody sticking a screwdriver in your eye and somebody else pulls it out and puts a pin in your eye. I don't want stuff in my eye."[2]

The following Monday after Beck's Saturday speech was as clear a demonstration why talk radio is not an echo chamber parroting Republican Party talking points, as so many critics on the left would insist.

Despite getting kudos early in the speech, Limbaugh was not happy with the content and the volume of criticism leveled against Republicans in the lead off to what could be an important election year.

"I would not have said that the only people who can stop Obama —Republicans—should be excoriated for being just as bad," Limbaugh said on his radio show. "It would never occur to me to say that. I don't know what the objective would be."[3]

It would be a stretch to say that Limbaugh and Beck have a rivalry. If anything, Beck's rivalry is with Mark Levin, who similarly after the speech said "Decide what you are. A circus clown, self-identified, or a thoughtful and wise person. It's hard to be both."[4] Even that rivalry seems to have settled substantially in recent years, as Levin has had high praise for Beck's staunch support for Israel. There is also Michael Savage who attacks Beck, Limbaugh and every other conservative host.

Different hosts take a very different approach on the spectrum of conservatism. Limbaugh, Hannity and Levin take a more traditional Reagan conservative view. Beck leans close to libertarianism, while still holding social conservative views. Savage speaks loudly for the anti-war right. Hosts Bill Bennett, Michael Medved and Dennis Prager offer a reserved and analytical style absent the yelling or name calling of other programs. The bigger picture from this is that conservative talk radio has become such a large universe that different definitions of conservatism and different styles of programming can co-exist on the airwaves.

What Limbaugh and Beck represent is two eras of talk radio. In many ways Beck is to the Obama era what Limbaugh was to the years of President Bill Clinton. Rush still trounces Beck and everyone one else in ratings. Beck is only number three in the number of listeners behind Sean Hannity. The great similarity is that Beck became a cultural phenomenon during the Obama administration, the same way that Limbaugh became a cultural phenomenon in the

Clinton administration. Even in the universe of talk hosts, Beck is the only host that rivals Limbaugh in invoking something akin to hatred from the left.

"Glenn's emergence reminds me of Rush's emergence in the early '90s," nationally syndicated conservative host Mike Gallagher told *Politico* in 2009. "People have asked me, 'Who's the next Rush,' because Rush is the gold standard. ... seems to be Glenn."[5]

The same *Politico* story quoted Levin saying, "Comparing Rush Limbaugh to Glenn Beck is like comparing George Washington to George Jefferson. Beck can be very entertaining and even informative, but he is neither the face nor the voice of the conservative movement. He is one of many."[6]

Nevertheless, the Obama administration never anticipated Beck's rise to prominence, as Democrats initially targeted Limbaugh, with an orchestrated effort, calling him the "Leader of the Republican Party."

During an interview on Fox News and on his radio show, Limbaugh asserted of Obama, "I hope he fails." Democratic strategists James Carville and Paul Begala, along with Democratic pollster Stanley Greenberg, developed a strategy that even brought White House Chief of Staff Rahm Emanuel into the fold. The Democratic party's strategy would be to force Republicans in Congress to either agree with Rush—and alienate independent voters, many who hoped the then popular Obama would succeed even if they voted against him—or disagree with Rush and tick off the conservative base. The Democratic Congressional Campaign Committee, the Center for American Progress, Americans United for Change and others began a full throttled focus on Limbaugh. Politico first reported that this was an elaborate plan, not something spontaneous in response to Limbaugh's "I hope he fails," line, and that it included White House political advisor David Axelrod and Press Secretary Robert Gibbs, who would routinely call Limbaugh the "leader of the Republican Party" during his daily press briefing.[7]

Emanuel said on CBS's Face the Nation that Limbaugh "is the voice and the intellectual force and energy behind the Republican Party. And he has been up front about what he views, and hasn't stepped back from that, which is he hopes for failure. He said it. And I compliment him for his honesty, but that's their philosophy that is enunciated by Rush Limbaugh. And I think that's the wrong philosophy for America."[8]

Days before the *Politico* story, February 28, 2009, Limbaugh was the keynote speaker at CPAC, in what he called, "my first ever address to the nation," as it was aired live on Fox News and C-SPAN. Rush never backed away from his assertion that he hopes President Obama fails, but he did explain, as a reoccurring theme in the speech was he wants the country to succeed.

"We're in the aspects here of an historic presidency. I know that. But let me be honest again. I got over the historical aspects of this in November. President Obama is our president. President Obama stands for certain things. I don't care, he could be a Martian. He could be from Michigan, I don't know—just kidding. Doesn't matter to me what his race is," Limbaugh said. "It doesn't matter. He's liberal is what matters to me. And his articulated—his articulated plans scare me. Now, I understand we can't say we want the President to fail, Mr. Limbaugh. That's like saying—this is the voice of the New Castrati, by the way, guys who have lost their guts. You can't say Mr. Limbaugh that you want the President to fail because that's like saying you want the country to fail. It's the opposite. I want the country to survive. I want the country to succeed."

The CPAC crowd started chanting "USA."

"I want the country to survive as we have known it, as you and I were raised in it, is what I mean. Now, I have been called—and I can take it. Pioneers take the arrows. I don't mind what anybody says about me, any time ever. I don't have time for it. I don't give other people the power to offend me. And you shouldn't either, by the wasted time being offended," Limbaugh said to applause.[9]

As it turned out, the White House's Limbaugh strategy did not work so well for Obama and the Democrats, only serving to elevate Rush, while really only getting the folks who already did not like him bent out of shape. Calling him the leader, by the way, is not entirely original, as a *National Review* cover story on

September 16, 1993 called him, "The Leader of the Opposition."

Limbaugh biographer Zev Chafets said Limbaugh did become the leader of the party, and that was only to the benefit of the GOP. "Democrats responded by branding Limbaugh—whom they considered self-evidently unattractive—as the leader of the opposition. Rahm Emanuel, the White House chief of staff, went on 'Face the Nation' and described Limbaugh as the 'voice and the intellectual force and energy' of the GOP. Limbaugh loved being tossed into this briar patch. He mocked the notion that he was the titular leader of the GOP even as he was becoming the party's top strategist and de facto boss."[10]

After the 2010 primary season, when it appeared Republicans were going to roll on to victory in November, Limbaugh deserved the credit, Chafets wrote.

"The Obama victory in 2008 left Republicans dazed, demoralized and leaderless. Less than six weeks after the inauguration, in a nationally televised keynote address to the annual Conservative Political Action Conference, Limbaugh stepped into the void with a raucous denunciation of the president's agenda and a strategic plan based on his belief that real conservatism wins every time," Chafets said. "He reiterated his famous call for Obama to fail and urged the party faithful to ignore the siren song of bipartisanship and moderation and stay true to the principles of Ronald Reagan."[11]

Chafets continued, "His strategy was simple. With Democrats controlling Congress, Limbaugh saw that there was no way to stop the president's agenda. He dismissed the moderates' notion that compromising with the president would make Republicans look good to independents. Instead he decreed that the GOP must become the party of no, and force Democrats—especially centrists—to go into 2010 with sole responsibility for the Obama program and the state of the economy. And that is what has happened."[12]

As significant as Rush has been to conservatism, one could just as easily say that many talk radio personalities including Hannity, Beck, Levin, Laura Ingraham, Savage and others are the leaders of the Republican Party. They are leaders in the sense that they motivate voters, motivate citizens to be active in the political process through flooding congressional offices with calls and rallying for or against certain legislation.

"Before the Internet came along, talk radio was the most powerful medium for exploring and sharing conservative ideas," said Bill Bennett, host of Bill Bennett's Morning in America, the most prominent national morning program. "The talk radio technology has transformed the arena of public discussion from open air town halls and public forums to millions of listeners in their cars, at work, and at home, all experiencing and participating in discussion and learning.[13]

It is widely believed, but hard to accurately measure, the impact of talk radio on such historical events at the Republican victories in Congress in 1994 and 2010; the recall of California Governor Gray Davis; the Clinton impeachment; the defeat of the immigration reform bill and other public policy issues. Further, they can keep Republican politicians honest, calling them out to a larger audience for abandoning their promises for more limited government. Nobody in the GOP wants Levin to call them a "Repubic" on the air. But other than inspiring Republicans voter, and admonishing politicians, or preaching to the choir, conservative talk radio largely serves as an avenue for listeners to hear their views that are frequently mocked or ignored in the mainstream media. Talk radio can also push stories into the mainstream media, the so called gatekeepers, that might otherwise be ignored. As media critic Howard Kurtz observed the gatekeepers are hardly gatekeepers any longer because in many cases talk radio stories go directly to people and cause an uproar.

"There is a reason that conservative talk radio prospers and liberal talk radio does not. Conservatism thrives on the intelligent exchange of ideas from history to philosophy to economics to the culture," Bennett said. "Talk radio is now one of the primary mediums by which conservatives vet ideas and candidates, meaning that it has enormous impact on American politics. Speaking of the modern conservative movement, I don't think the Tea Party would have the momentum and energy it does without the assistance of talk radio."[14]

In 1980, when Ronald Reagan was elected president, only about 75 all political talk stations existed. With the elimination of the Fairness Doctrine, the emergence of Limbaugh, who spawned an industry for Hannity, Beck, Levin, Bennett and others, the news talk format was the most popular radio format in the United States, surpassing even country music for the first time in 2008, for a total of 2,064 stations carrying all political talkers, up from 1,500 a decade earlier.[15]

In 2006, Senator John Kerry, who was the Democratic presidential nominee two years earlier, spoke at Pasadena College and only one California TV station reported on it. Buried in that TV report was Kerry's assertion that students should get a good education, otherwise they could "get stuck in Iraq." The implication was the U.S. military, which he served in, is made up of undereducated people. John Ziegler, a local host of KFI in Los Angeles picked up the quote and played it over and over. "I predicted my audience would be one of the few to ever hear this," Ziegler said. After he broadcast it, it appeared on Michelle Malkin's popular blog and then on the Drudge Report. "I knew the story was going nuclear." From there, the story dominated cable news for days until Kerry apologized for what he called a "botched joke." Ziegler added, "It never would have happened in the old media age."[16]

It is a great anecdote, one of many, on how talk radio can push a story forward. But it is also an example of how talk radio's clout is limited. Even though Republicans sought to use Kerry as a symbol for comments made just weeks before the election, the Democrats still recaptured control of Congress.

In 2008 Rush Limbaugh's "Operation Chaos" very likely helped prolong the Democratic presidential primary between Barack Obama and Hillary Clinton. With John McCain having wrapped up the GOP nomination early, and an apparent Obama nomination, Limbaugh encouraged his listeners to vote in Democratic primaries, changing their party registration if necessary, to cast a vote for Hillary just to keep the contest rolling along, knowing Hillary would cling to any chance of victory. The idea was to create as much division in the Democratic Party a possible and give Republicans a better chance of winning in November 2008. But in the end, Obama won both the nomination and the election.

The view that conservative talk radio is an all powerful, or as former Republican Senator Trent Lott said, "talk radio is running America," is ridiculously overstated. If that was the case, Obama would have never been elected president. For that matter, John McCain would not have been the GOP nominee in 2008, and the runner up would not have been Mike Huckabee, the two candidates least liked by talk radio hosts.

It is difficult however to deny the influence of talk radio on the political system. Of listeners to the news talk format of radio, 77 percent voted in the 2008 presidential election, according to the 2010 Talk Radio Research Project conducted by *Talkers Magazine*, which covers the talk radio industry.[17]  Compare that to 56.8 percent for the general public. That does not mean Limbaugh, or for that matter Ed Schultz, is the reason certain people vote. It's probably a no-brainer to say a frequent voter is likely more inclined than a non-voter to listen to political radio. Still, it is quite likely that the entertainment value of talk radio—a mixture of satire and commentary—has made ordinary Americans more engaged in politics than they would be if talk radio did not have such a large reach, even if some of those listeners are just tuning in to argue with the host.

"The people who listen to news talk radio, news talk as opposed to all talk radio, have a higher percentage of people who vote than the people who listen to other forms of radio or people that don't listen to radio," said Michael Harrison, editor of *Talkers Magazine*. "That's one of the reasons people consider news talk radio to be politically powerful. It's because it's where the voters are. If you go on a music show and talk about a political cause, the per capita people listening are less likely to vote than the people who are listening to talk radio. Talk radio has a very high concentration of voters in its audience."

Still, Harrison stressed, that's not the purpose of talk radio. He said he often has to explain to politically minded journalists that it is not about politics. It's about ratings and ad revenue.

"The purpose of that show is to get people to listen and to watch and to read. So, what it does is it makes the conversation more palatable and it draws more people into the media," Harrison said. "It

23

does not necessarily draw more people into the political system. It is not about the political system it is about the media system. Entertainment and reality have a very blurry line between them. There's always been an entertaining, sensationalist to the political process. To think that they're separate is to miss the point of what Shakespeare said: 'all the world's a stage.'"

Though, he said there is definitely some level at which talk radio influences people that might not otherwise be politically active or vote to be politically active and vote.

"There's a degree of that. There has to be a degree of that," Harrison said. "Just like sports talk radio might influence people to go to the stadium and buy a ticket or watch a game that they might otherwise not have. Media exposure increases participation to one degree or another."[18]

Bennett disagrees, believing that a significant number of people are drawn to politics through what they hear on the dial.

"Because of the technology and the communal nature of radio communication, I think talk radio engages many people who normally wouldn't participate in political discussions, like parents busy at home, children carpooling to school, and professionals at work," Bennett said. "Conservative talk radio, in particular, fosters a sense of civic duty and participation in our system of government. Politics revolve around the exchange of ideas and policies, and there is no better medium for thoughtful and intelligent political conversation than talk radio. Everyday people from all over the country can engage in political discussion without having to leave their homes or their cars. Again to use the example of the Tea Party, many Americans who had never before attended a townhall or called their Congressman or even voted were motivated in large part by talk radio."

Meanwhile, according to the 2010 Talk Radio Research Project, 81 percent of all news talk radio listeners are 35 years or older. Interestingly, just 28 percent identify themselves as Republican, while 54 percent of the listeners identify themselves as independent. This indicates that voters that do not have their mind made up on an issue could be swayed by radio hosts. On political philosophy, 40 percent identified themselves as either conservative or ultra conservative, while just 15 percent identified themselves as liberal or ultra-liberal. More listeners are men, 57 percent, than women, 43 percent. The bulk of listeners have at least some college education, earn between $30,000 and $69,000 annual and donate $500 to $1,000 in charity each year, according to the survey. Other than talk radio, these listeners by 20 percent said Internet-only sites were their biggest source of news, while Fox News came in at 15 percent and 10 percent turned to MSNBC, while network news, major newspapers and newsweeklies were all in the single digits, making it clear that the talk radio audience favors new media.[19]

Two quasi-conservative commentators, David Frum and David Brooks, who have largely made careers of attacking conservatives, had two differing views on talk radio.

After the Democratic health care bill was passed into law without a single Republican vote, former Bush White House speech writer Frum blamed talk radio and Fox News for Republicans not compromising.

"There were leaders who knew better, who would have liked to deal. But they were trapped. Conservative talkers on Fox and talk radio had whipped the Republican voting base into such a frenzy that deal-making was rendered impossible. How do you negotiate with somebody who wants to murder your grandmother? Or—more exactly—with somebody whom your voters have been persuaded to believe wants to murder their grandmother?" Frum wrote in March 2009. "The real leaders are on TV and radio, and they have very different imperatives from people in government. Talk radio thrives on confrontation and recrimination."[20]

In another anti-talk radio tome, though one grounded more reality than Frum's, *New York Times* columnist Brooks assured that talk radio was not really that invincible.

"Over the past few years the talk jocks have demonstrated their real-world weakness time and again," Brooks wrote. "Over the years, I have asked many politicians what happens when Limbaugh and his colleagues attack. The story is always the same. Hundreds of calls come in. The receptionists are miserable. But the numbers back home do not move. There is no effect on the favorability rating or the re-election prospects. In the media world, he is a giant. In the real world, he's not."[21]

The Frum view that talk radio controls the GOP and the Brooks view that talk radio is irrelevant are neither true, as evidence has show several cases where the GOP did not do exactly what talk radio demanded of them or when talk radio played a significant role in promoting or stopping legislation, a recall, an impeachment and a Supreme Court nominee.

So is talk radio really responsible for the Republican Party moving to the right, as Frum charges? Harrison, of *Talkers*, says no.

"I believe they are reflecting. I believe the cause and effect relationship between the media and reality is fascinating, complex, nuanced in ever changing concepts," Harrison said. "If we understood how it all works, we'd all be media geniuses. We'd all be able to sell out every store that we create ads for and we'd be able to influence people to do whatever we want. The truth of the matter is we've never fully been able to have a handle on the cause and effect relationship between the media and the public. When you get up in the morning and look into the mirror, it reflects you. In that reflection you're able to comb your hair. You're able to brush your teeth. You're able to see how you look. For a woman, she's able to put on her makeup. Not only does it reflect, but that reflection in effect has a causal relationship. That's sort of what happens with the media."

"Rush Limbaugh had influence, as one of many influences, in the process of it becoming more conservative," Harrison continued. "At the same time, much of his success has derived from him being able to speak for and reflect an already pre-determined trend that was in the making with him or without him. It's like a parade. If the parade following a leader or is it following a pre-set course. It looks like the leader of the parade is leading but sometimes the leader of the parade just happens to be standing in the front and if the leader takes the wrong turn, the parade will keep going and goodbye leader. If the leader gets too far ahead of the parade, the parade will go its own way and there will be a new leader."

The problem with the analysis of Frum, Brooks and others is the implication that it is a necessary negative that talk radio would have influence over lawmakers, as if it is not the job of the American media, the free press whether print or electronic, to influence a citizenry and stir people to action.

Talk radio can have its excessive sometimes, but it cannot be blamed for the shooting in Tucson, Arizona in early 2011. It cannot be blamed for the bombing of the Oklahoma federal building in 1995. It certainly is not seditious, as a couple of journalist asserted on the Chris Matthews Show in 2010.

During the Matthews program, *Time* magazine's Joe Klein pulled out a napkin. "I did a little bit of research just before the show on this little napkin here. I looked up the definition of sedition, which is conduct and language inciting rebellion against the authority of the state. And a lot of these statements, especially the ones coming from people like Glenn Beck and, to a certain extent, Sarah Palin, rub right next—right up close to being seditious."

Klein's fellow panelist John Heilemann of *New York Magazine* quickly concurred.

"You know, Joe is right, and I will name another person here, his name Rush Limbaugh, you know, who uses this phrase, talks about the Obama administration as a regime," Heilemann said. "That phrase which has connotations of tyranny."[22]

In 2009, California Assembly Speaker Karen Bass told *The Los Angeles Times*, speaking of conservative on-air personalities, "The Republicans were essentially threatened and terrorized against voting for revenue. Now [some] are facing recalls. They operate under a terrorist threat: 'You vote for revenue and your career is over.' I don't know why we allow that kind of terrorism to exist. I guess it's about free speech, but it's extremely unfair."[23]

To deplore conservative talkers as seditious terrorists that run America is obviously hyperbolic. But frustration from the political and media establishment only represents the power conservative talkers have attained. More than saving the AM dial, these champions of the right have driven political discourse for almost two decades and provided an alternative voice long ignored by the predominantly liberal mainstream media.

It is barely even disputed any longer that the mainstream media leans left. The question is generally how left. The network evening news cast does not celebrate its left leanings as Ed Schultz or Keith Olbermann would, but it is subtle or unstated bias that frustrates the news consumer more than an information source that they know what they're getting.

Whatever verdict is rendered on the influence talk radio has on electoral politics, there is little dispute on what impact it has had on other media, demonstrating a hunger for an alternative news source. After the Rush Limbaugh TV show went off the air in 1996, producer Roger Ailes had another vision. Fox News does not owe all of its success to talk radio, nor is it duplicative of talk radio as many critics allege. But had conservative talk radio not exploded as a huge commercial success, it might have taken much longer for Rupert Murdoch to take a chance on the Fox News style of programming.

"I think talk radio had a tremendous influence on Fox News. I don't know if there would be one. There probably would be in a different form down the road," Harrison said. "Whenever there is a need for something, somebody will eventually fill it. I think, industrially, within the media business, talk radio had a tremendous influence on Fox News becoming what it is today. Fox News is an extension of conservative talk radio. Basically, at this point all of the cable news networks, CNN, C-SPAN, MSNBC, Fox News, are all tremendously influenced by the modern era of commercial talk radio."[24]

It is America's long tradition to criticize leaders, occasionally even in over the top ways, but just as Thomas Jefferson famously said, "If I had to choose between government without newspapers, and newspapers without government, I wouldn't hesitate to choose the latter," the same could be said of talk radio. In many ways talk radio more closely resembles the Founders' vision of the First Amendment's guarantee for a free press than the mainstream media. Like the colonial press, talk radio seeks to stir the public to action, while the MSM is perceived at talking down to its readers, viewers and listeners.

"There are things that talk radio helps catalyze," Harrison said. "If they hadn't done it with talk radio, they might have done it with facebook or they might have done it with telephone calls or they may have done it in newspapers. To give the credit to the medium is to miss the point. There have been issues that have been decided on talk radio. Usually talk radio—and again you're writing about conservative talk radio—usually any kind of politically oriented, opinion oriented talk radio can have influence under two conditions. One, when it's a very, very tight situation and any vote, anybody, any small shift can make the margin of difference. Or, two, when there really is a crazy injustice out there that people know about and care about that the rest of the media is missing. Other than that, you cannot get people to do what they don't have a great disposition to do. You cannot in America get people to change their minds too easily or too readily."

While liberal thought is pervasive in the most dominant media, conservatives are no longer struggling voices in the wilderness relying on *Human Events* and *National Review* to read, or Fulton Lewis Jr. and Clarence Manion to listen to. A hand full of conservative radio host are paid salaries are a par with NFL stars, while many others do very well. Most of those, including Glenn Beck, owe much if not most of their success to Rush Limbaugh for proving the commercial success of talk radio.

But Limbaugh did not invent talk radio, and he stands on the shoulders of many others. Most conservatives know about Bob Grant, a trailblazer in radio that influenced Limbaugh, Hannity, Levin and others. Fewer know about Fulton Lewis Jr., who had a daily program that drew a radio audience on a par with Limbaugh in the 1940s, or of Clarence Manion, whose 15-minute weekly program reached a national audience and had major influence on conservatism.

It is fair to say that modern conservative talk radio began in the 40s and 50s, said Lee Edwards, a historian of the conservative movement.

"Even conservatives are not properly respectful of or interested in history," Edwards, of the Heritage Foundation, said. "It's too bad because they were giants in their time and without them, the movement wouldn't be what it is today."[25]

## CHAPTER TWO

# Early Voices

Radio from 1920 through the mid-1950s came onto the media scene much as the Internet did in the mid 1990s, making a huge impression on the American public and causing anxiety among newspaper publishers. Insecure with the competition, publishers began buying or starting radio stations in the 1920s. After 30 years of dominance, radio eventually lost ground to television, as some of the biggest stars were replaced by more visually appealing celebrities.

The defining political issues of radio's first four decades were the New Deal, World War II, and finally concerns about communist subversion in the federal government, which came to be more broadly known as the Red scare or McCarthyism. Conservative personalities on the air had their gripes with the New Deal, leaned isolationist with regard to World War II—but were quite patriotic when the United States was dragged into the war after Pearl Harbor, and stood firmly behind Senator Joseph McCarthy and other anti-communists.

"Radio, in the days leading up to World War II was more akin to today's television because it was the main living room medium," said Michael Harrison, editor of *Talkers Magazine*. "It was where families gathered and they listened together. It was much more of a mass medium than radio is today. It makes it even more difficult to compare specifics of a medium in the mid-30s and the mid-40s to a medium in the 21st Century because the actual medium of radio played a very different role hierarchy of media."[1]

In 1920, stations could broadcast on any frequency they chose. It is not difficult to see how that created problems, as some stations picked the same dial and multiple frequencies bumped together for various interfering signals. Thus, even small government conservative President Calvin Coolidge saw the need for some government regulation here, signing the Radio Act of 1927, making the airwaves the property of the public that would be licensed by the newly established Federal Radio Commission. The FRC divided the radio spectrum and issued licenses to broadcast on a specific frequency.

Although Franklin D. Roosevelt was famous for his "fireside chats," the first president to use radio as an effective means of political communication was ironically Silent Cal. Coolidge's 1923 State of the Union address was the first broadcast over the radio, and he continued to give at least one radio address per month.[2]

However Roosevelt turned up the volume on radio politicking. Similar to how Barack Obama's extraordinary 2008 campaign effectively used the Internet better than any other national campaign to that point, the charismatic New York governor was able to exploit radio in his 1932 campaign in a way other candidates had not. At the time, America had two radio networks, the liberal CBS and the pro-Hoover NBC. That changed after FDR's smashing victory, as NBC sought to curry favor with the new administration. NBC broadcast 12 hours of speeches and comments from officials in the Roosevelt administration and gave Republicans no time on the air. This was prior to "fairness" rules. In his first year in office, FDR spoke 33 times on NBC radio. In what today might be considered a conflict of interest from both a journalistic and governmental perspective, NBC paid $900 per week to FDR advisor Louis Howe to come on the air and provide analysis on Washington. The network even paid first lady Eleanor Roosevelt $4,000 to host a broadcast in 1934.[3]

Networks never wanted to step too far out of line, as the National Recovery Administration Commissioner Harold Lafount warned stations it was their patriotic duty to refuse advertising time to companies that would not follow the NRA codes. "It is to be hoped that radio stations, using valuable facilities loaned to them temporarily by the government will not unwittingly be placed in embarrassing positions because of greed or lack of patriotism on the part of a few unscrupulous advertisers." Given the government's hand in the airwaves, it seemed a veiled threat, not much of a veil, to revoke a license if a station did not support FDR's policies. By mid-1934, the recovery administration had purchased $20 million worth of advertising time, practically monopolizing public discourse on the airwaves.[4]

That same year, Congress sent President Roosevelt a refined Communications Act of 1934, that broadened the radio commission's powers and renamed it the Federal Communications Commission. During both debates for the Radio Act and the Communications Act, Congress rejected the idea of putting a fairness provision in either law.[5]

*Broadcasting* magazine said in 1939, "Because the bulk of the dailies are predominantly anti-New Deal, it has long been an open secret in Washington that radio more and more was being relied upon to disseminate administration views."[6] Imagine that: talk radio was a liberal balance to the conservative daily metropolitan newspapers.

That said there were certainly some voices very antagonistic to Roosevelt and his agenda. The administration had to deal with radio and for the most part did so very effectively. A *Fortune* magazine opinion poll during the late 1930s found that radio had higher credibility among Americans than the press, as hosts such as H.V. Kaltenborn, Boake Carter and Elmer Davis were more respected than newspaper editors and columnists.[7]

It was in 1930 that the concept of a call-in radio show was adopted, after a disc jockey tried the idea. That year, DJ John J. Anthony—in an apolitical format—took calls and repeated what people told him, but the radio listener didn't hear the caller. After that, the quiz show Vox Pop hosted by Parker Johnson became a popular call-in radio show in the Houston area.[8] Both of these forums were non-political.

It was not until 1945 when Barry Gray of WMCA-AM in New

York was bored playing music that the concept of audience participation in a talk program took hold. Gray laid the groundwork for
the modern talk show, and eventually brought politics into it.
WMCA was reportedly concerned about the technical and legal
issues of using telephone conversations in broadcasts, but Gray did
it anyway, scoring an on-air interview with jazz musician Woody
Herman. The station executives were less concerned once audience
input and phone interviews started drawing a larger audience for
Gray's midnight to 3 a.m. program. So, call-in shows were born.
Gray would become a progressive voice for the air, as he blasted the
red scare in the 1950s.[9] His career includes tales of getting beat up
outside the studio for unpopular comments and being twice dropped
by WMCA for not disclosing an airline provided him with two free
trips to Europe. He continued on the radio in some form until his
death in 1996.[10]

"Barry Gray, although he wasn't a conservative probably influenced conservatives as well," said Harrison of *Talkers Magazine.*
"You've got to remember, conservative talk radio is talk radio. It's
not politics. It's radio that does politics as opposed to politics that
does radio. So, it's very possible that considering it's all radio that an
early liberal talk show host could have had as much influence on
today's conservative talkers as did a conservative one by the very
nature of the style and the system that they operated in."[11]

It was under the Truman administration when the federal government decided on a way to have some control over the political
content of radio—beyond veiled threats and using the most
benevolent phraseology to ensure the public that no First
Amendment freedoms were being infringed. In 1949, the FCC
issued a report titled, "In the Matter of Editorializing by
Broadcast Licensees." From this report the infamous Fairness
Doctrine was established, setting out two basic requirements: 1.)
that every licensee devote a reasonable portion of broadcast time
to the discussion and consideration of controversial issues of public importance; and (2) that in doing so, [the broadcaster must be]
fair—that is, [the broadcaster] must affirmatively endeavor to
make ... facilities available for the expression of contrasting view-

points held by responsible elements with respect to the controversial issues presented.[12]

The FCC established enforcement procedures to allow the listening public to file a complaint to the commission if they felt the matters were not being broadcast fairly. The FCC staff would investigate the matter, and could force the broadcaster to provide equal time, levy a fine or just revoke the broadcast license.[13] There is more on this in later chapters.

Public affairs program had already become popular well before any federal regulation. Many newsmen on the radio would remain newsmen. Some would become just plain old commentators. Most would be a combination. The lines were not as clear in those early days.

"America's Town Meeting of the Air" was among the first public affairs program to really catch on, gaining an audience of 3 million listeners. The program brought in panelists from various sides to debate issues and was hosted by George V. Denny, Jr., associate director of the League for Political Education, the organization that prompted the series. It ran from 1935 to 1956, with the first program titled, "Which Way America? Communism, Fascism, Socialism or Democracy?" with panelists advocating each of those—isms.[14] But this was a talk show notable for the newsmaker guests, akin to Meet the Press or various other Sunday shows. It was not notable for the cult of personalities other hosts would bring to the air.

Another notable radio personality was newsman Elmer Davis, highly popular and trusted. Davis left CBS radio in 1941 to become the head of the U.S. Office of War Information. After the OWI shut down at the end of the war, he returned to the private sector, this time as a radio commentator for ABC radio.[15] It's there he would become a progressive voice and an opponent of sorts to Fulton Lewis Jr.. Davis became so anti-McCarthy that he faded from his reporting duties, and was a subtle on-air supporter of the Adlai Stevens in the 1952 presidential campaign, critiquing the popular Dwight Eisenhower so much that ABC radio feared blowback from their sponsors.[16]

Conservatives such as Boake Carter and Fulton Lewis Jr., and the populist FDR sycophant-turned-raging critic Father Charles

Coughlin managed to thrive during the Roosevelt years. The generally pro-FDR H.V. Kaltenborn—a hybrid of a reporter and commentator—even occasionally critiqued the president. However, Walter Winchell—also a hybrid reporter-commentator but a less reputable one—was enamored with Roosevelt before being enamored by Senator Joe McCarthy.[42]

These and other talk show hosts would become popular, but the all-talk stations that are common today did not exist in those early days, and news talk was mixed with music. A fairly big revolution would have to wait decades later.

Without the proven success stories of the early talk show hosts—including political talk show hosts—a station manager might not have taken that chance.

### H.V. Kaltenborn: Dean of Commentators

In some ways, it is not fair to lump Hans von Kaltenborn in with commentators. The pioneer of radio, better known as H.V. Kaltenborn, was a respected journalist known for his shoe leather reporting in war zones. He was the first true star of news radio, and established an intense level of trust with his listeners.

One anecdote that demonstrates this is a reaction after one of the most noteworthy incidents of early radio. CBS's broadcast of Orson Welles' "War of the Worlds," which was meant to sound like a news report, caused a national panic, with many Americans believing the earth was actually facing a space alien invasion. But one woman reportedly said, "How ridiculous! Anybody should have known it was not a real war. If it had been, the broadcaster would have been Hans."[17]

Nevertheless, he also became known as the "Dean of Commentators." He had become an opinion writer at the time he entered radio when the medium was in its infant stages of news reporting, and most news reports were mere regurgitating of facts. A long time newspaperman with the *Brooklyn Eagle*, Kaltenborn thought newscasters should go beyond the facts and provide their own analysis and insight to get "behind the headlines," a fancy way of saying editorialize.[18]

He was a natural at the medium, and opted not to use a script, but rather speak extemporaneously on the air, and it worked as his audience grew.[19] His notoriety earned him a cameo in the 1939 classic film *Mr. Smith Goes to Washington* and a public mocking by President Harry Truman.

He had a progressive streak. Though it was not necessarily clear cut, as such labels have a different meaning today than in the 1920s. He was not aligned with the Democrats or Republicans. He was critical of organized labor, but was smitten with President Franklin D. Roosevelt. One might also call him hawkish on military intervention—as he wanted to enter World War II well before Pearl Harbor. But the Republican party of that day was largely defined by a strong isolationism.

His reporting on the Spanish Civil War and the Czech Crisis challenged America's predominant isolationist worldview. It was when war engulfed Europe that Kaltenborn would become an aggressive commentator demanding America get involved.

Kaltenborn, born in 1878 in Milwaukee to German immigrants, began his journalism career at the age of 19, becoming a war correspondent after joining the Fourth Wisconsin Volunteers Infantry to cover the Spanish-American War for the *Merrill* (Wisconsin) *Advocate*. He went to work for *Brooklyn Eagle* in 1902 and began taking courses at Harvard's journalism program in 1905.[20]

The *Eagle* helped to promote the opinionated Kaltenborn on the radio. On April 21, 1921 Kaltenborn addressed the Brooklyn Chamber of Commerce speaking from an experimental station in Newark, N.J.[21] He graduated to a larger audience a year later. It was on April 4, 1922 when WVP aired the first current events analysis from the chief editorial writer for the *Eagle*, Kaltenborn. Later that year, he broadcast the news live from the Statue of Liberty for WYCB.[22]

In the early 1920s, the American Telephone & Telegraph Company (known today as AT&T) founded the New York radio station WEAF, which aired the first paid commercial in 1922—a 10 minute ad promoting a housing development in Jackson Heights.[23]

Newspaper publishers became perplexed on how to handle competition from the radio, and began buying radio stations to promote their newspaper, or buying airtime. The *Brooklyn Eagle* did the latter. The newspaper paid WEAF to broadcast its chief editorial writer Kaltenborn for 30 minutes per week. By 1923, Kaltenborn was the first network newscaster when a Washington, D.C. station began to link to his WEAF broadcast. Kaltenborn thought the *Eagle* had censored him from criticizing "sacred cows" of New York society, and expected to have free reign on the airwaves with his own show.

It did not quite turn out that way, however, when Kaltenborn delivered stinging criticism of a judge about to preside over a phone rate case. The AT&T executives called on him to show some prudence. Later, Kaltenborn made some anti-union remarks that caused an uproar in AT&T's labor negotiations. Then, the host turned his guns on Republican Secretary of State Charles Evan Hughes for rejecting diplomatic recognition of the Soviet Union. The politically powerful Hughes, a former GOP presidential nominee and later Chief Justice, heard the broadcast carried on WRC in Washington. The secretary complained to AT&T. Kaltenborn—who would likely seem extremely mild by today's standards—had become too hot for AT&T, which opted not to renew his contract for WEAF. Kaltenborn commented: "Secretary Hughes did not like what I had said, particularly since my opinions were expressed in his own home in the hearing of his guests."[24]

As a possible sign that things have not really changed that much, controversy just made Kaltenborn more sought after. WOR in New York began broadcasting Kaltenborn's Digest. By 1929, he was broadcast on 19 CBS stations.[25]

He abandoned print journalism, resigning from the Eagle to become a full-time broadcaster in 1930. He gained more national exposure in 1932 covering the presidential contest between President Herbert Hoover and New York Governor Franklin D. Roosevelt for his program "Kaltenborn Edits the News," which moved to a coveted Friday evening timeslot by 1935.[26]

During Roosevelt's inauguration in March 1933, Kaltenborn drove up and down Pennsylvania Avenue broadcasting the scene from a two-way radio, and speculating about what the new president's policies would be. A disgusted print journalist reportedly remarked, "I wish I could be as sure of a few things as that guy is about everything."[27]

Roosevelt's Press Secretary Steve Early invited Kaltenborn to visit the White House to observe a typical day by the president's staff. The broadcaster boasted about his ability to "walk in and out of rooms and talk to anyone I please."[28]

It would not be Washington politics that distinguished him, but rather his life as a war correspondent, in Europe and the Far East in the 1930s and then in World War II in the 1940s, even though he was not always accurate at his predictions.

Kaltenborn wrote a dispatch from Germany in 1933 for the highly influential *New Republic* magazine giving his assessment of the political situation there regarding German Chancellor Adolph Hitler.

"He is sworn to obey the Constitution and is likely to do so. The time for a Fascist coup d'etat is past," Kaltenborn wrote. "Hitler himself had definitely lost prestige and power before he won the chancellorship. Whatever the result of the March fifth election, it will not give Adolf Hitler the opportunity to establish his long heralded Drittes Reich."[29]

But his writing is not what he was remembered for.

In 1936, he covered the Battle of Irun in the Spanish Civil War for his radio audience, holding a microphone while hiding in a haystack, he reported on Franco's forces driving loyalists from the battlefield. The report carried the sound of machine gun fire, and continued to air even after exploding shells severed the main cable. He later went on to interview Hitler and Italian Prime Minister Benito Mussolini at the London Economic Conference.[30]

Finally though, it was his reporting on the Munich Crisis in September of 1938 when Germany, England and France negotiated the fate of Czechoslovakia.[31] Hitler's demands threatened to send Europe into war. Kaltenborn spent 18 days in CBS's Studio Nine, making 85 separate broadcasts, to keep Americans informed of every stage of the negotiations, sleeping on a cot, he rushed to the microphone every time a news flash was received, interrupting the regularly scheduled programs on 115 radio stations. He also coordinated the on-air reports from network correspondents in Europe—essentially taking on the role of the modern news anchor—using his German and French language skills; he translated speeches given by Hitler and French Premier Edouard Daladier. He received 50,000 letters and telegrams from listeners praising his work, and he won *Radio Daily's* Most Popular Commentator Award. The clout got him a sponsor, Pure Oil, and a contract giving him something he longed for since the WEAF flaps—complete editorial independence.[32]

Initially, CBS paid him $100 per week for his two broadcasts. He supplemented his income by freelance writing and the public lecture circuit. But his new fame and the addition of a sponsor meant a big pay increase, which also meant he stopped traveling the country as much for public speaking. With this star power, he even played himself in *Mr. Smith Goes to Washington.*

Almost half of American homes tuned into his broadcast in September 1939 as he reported the outbreak of World War II, or the conflict that most Americans insisted was a European matter. Kaltenborn was not most Americans, and in 1940 began demanding the officially neutral United States enter the war to aid Great Britain. CBS news chief Ed Klauber was not happy with this line of commentary, and the two clashed. Klauber asked him to make the commentary less personal. Instead of saying "I think," say, "there are those who believe," or "some experts say." It seemed like a reasonable compromise to Klauber. Kaltenborn found it unacceptable and just went to NBC, a station all too happy to take the competitor's big star.[33] His NBC commentaries in 1941 were almost exclusively about the need for American interventionism, and even warned of an aggressive action by the Japanese before Pearl Harbor.[34]

After America entered the war in response to Pearl Harbor, the then-63-year-old Kaltenborn took a microphone to broadcast from the battlefields in Europe, and interviewed soldiers and politicians. After the war ended, he was recognized with the 1945 DuPont Radio Award, and then with nine other awards the following year.[35]

After the U.S. dropped the atomic bomb on Hiroshima and Nagasaki ending the war, the great World War II correspondent warned, "For all we know, we have created a Frankenstein! We must assume that with the passage of only a little time, an improved form of the new weapon we use today can be turned against us."[36]

In 1948, Kaltenborn was one of the many journalists in both print and broadcast to call the election for Republican nominee Thomas Dewey. The Truman photo holding a copy of the *Chicago Tribune* with a banner headline "Dewey Beats Truman," is legendary. Nearly as well known is Truman's imitating Kaltenborn's "clipped style" in pronouncing Dewey the winner.[37]

On election night 1948, broadcasting from NBC headquarters in Rockefeller Center, Kaltenborn assured the audience that the pollsters were correct even as results began rolling in showing Truman pulling well ahead of his Republican opponent. At midnight, Kaltenborn told America that Truman was 1.2 million votes ahead, but rest assured, Dewey would win. At 4 a.m., Kaltenborn was back on the air to report that Truman was up by 2 million, but explained that Dewey would win.[38]

"It's getting closer and closer on the electoral vote, as one state after another swings from Truman to Dewey, as we get the votes from the country districts. So I still believe that Dewey has the best chance," Kaltenborn said later in the night.[39]

"Now, on the basis of all the polls and everything we know, Dewey has a good chance to add Iowa, 10; Idaho, four; Indiana, 13; Wyoming, three," Kaltenborn said. "What you've got to remember, is that since the big city returns come in earlier than the country returns, and since traditionally the big cities are more Democratic than the country, the total figures are not conclusive ... On a percentage basis, the record still shows that Dewey is going to have more than the number of electoral votes."[40]

The night before his inauguration, Truman delivered a speech doing a comical impression on Kaltenborn.

"Mr. Kaltenborn was saying: The president is a million votes ahead in the popular vote. When the country vote comes in, Mr. Truman will be by another... And I went back to bed and went to sleep."[41]

Kaltenborn continued with NBC until 1953, and even did a few TV reports, but he said he hated the medium of TV. He said the new technology required too much nervous energy "to do anything important in this new form of radio." The novelty of TV reminded him of the excitement of the early days of radio, when he said, "people wrote me letters to say they had actually heard me without troubling to comment on what they heard." But he believed that TV would replace radio because of "the greater advertising impact of the combination of sight and sound."[42]

Kaltenborn died in 1965.

### Boake Carter: 'Far and Away the Most Daring'

Boake Carter's lasting legacy is probably the expression, during the 1930s that "In time of war the first casualty is truth." For a time he had the biggest show on radio, as millions listened for his British accent denouncing President Roosevelt and the New Deal.

Carter was born in 1899 in Baku, Russia to British parents who gave him the name for the city of his birth, where the British Consular Service was located in Russia. He grew up in Great Britain and attended Christ College in Cambridge, and began his journalism career in London. But in 1920, after his diplomat father was reassigned to Mexico, Carter came to the United States. He went to work in Philadelphia for press associations.[43]

He made the transition to radio in March 1932 at the CBS affiliate in Philadelphia WCAU. It was here where he made a national name for himself.

The kidnapping of famed aviator Charles Lindbergh's 20-month old son from their home in Hopewell, New Jersey in March 1932 set off the sensational media firestorm for that era. The investigation involved the New Jersey State Police, the New York City Police and the FBI and lasted more than two years before the kidnapper—who left a dozen ransom notes as he kept upping his ransom—was brought to justice. The body of Charles Lindbergh Jr. was eventually found dead a short distance from the Lindbergh home.[44]

The whole ordeal was a remarkable story. After the kidnapper took $50,000 in ransom money, the FBI was able to track the serial numbers on the ransom money, which led them to Bruno Richard Hauptmann, a German immigrant carpenter. He was arrested outside his Bronx home on September 18, 1934. A retired school principal, who acted as an intermediary between the Lindbergh family and the professed kidnapper, and a taxi cab driver who was pulled into the matter after the kidnapper told him to deliver a ransom note, both identified Hauptmann from their earlier encounter with him.[45]

CBS wanted WCAU to send a mobile unit to cover the trial, and Boake Carter got his chance to provide all of the lurid details, with his accent that became a hit with a national audience. As he became a bigger star, he got his own show, with the Philco Radio Company as his sponsor and he gained a national audience.[46] For several more years, Carter would open his broadcasts with an English sounding, "Hello everyone, Philco radio time, Boake Carter speaking."[47]

The five-week Hauptmann trial concluded on Feb. 13, 1935 when the New Jersey jury found him guilty of first degree murder and sentenced him to death. After his appeal failed, he was to be electrocuted on Jan. 17, 1936. However, that same day New Jersey Governor Harold Giles Hoffman granted a 30-day reprieve. Carter said Governor Hoffman and his administration "turned justice upside down and kicked her in the eye." Hoffman's political backers shot back that Carter "flew through the air with the latest of cheese," and recommended "more ether" for such radio commentators.[48]

On March 30, 1936, the Pardon Court of the State of New Jersey denied Hauptmann's petition for clemency, and he was electrocuted on April 3, 1936.[49]

The case launched the commentary career of Carter. Time magazine commented, "Not only is Boake Carter currently the most popular of Radio's news commentators, with a rating of 12.6 by the Crossley Survey he is also far and away the most daring. His freedom to express any partisan opinion that pops into his curly head is the wonder of a notoriously timid industry. However, while Carter's crusty editorializing delights thousands of listeners, it chagrins thousands more, keeps him in a perpetual controversial stew."[50]

One of his on-air crusades was for the United States to have its own independent air force, as someone who had served in the Royal Air Force. His knowledge of military flight prompted some to suspect he was a British spy, apparently hiding in plain sight. Army and

Navy intelligence operatives combed through information on Carter but did not find evidence he was a traitor to his adopted country.[51]

In 1936, as Roosevelt was running for a second term, Carter assembled a book of letters from his listeners agreeing with his assessment of the nation. The book was titled, "Johnny Q. Public SPEAKS: The Nation Appraises the New Deal."[52] The decidedly negative book about the New Deal lacked punch after Roosevelt swept all but two states that November in his reelection victory over Republican Alf Landon.

As war raged in Europe, Carter wanted the United States to stay out, despite his ties to Britain. CBS became concerned as his isolationist stance became stronger and the network began to get audience complaints that Carter was more cordial about Nazi Germany than the American State Department.[53]

On the home front, one of Carter's biggest targets was organized labor and in particular the Congress of Industrial Organizations (CIO) along with its president John L. Lewis. Carter called Lewis an extremist and obstructionist. So the CIO led a boycott of Carter's sponsor, the Philco Radio Company. The boycott caused Philco to drop Carter's contract in 1938. Organized labor was able to silence its opposition in this case, as Carter's career never recovered.[54] After his sponsor cancelled his contract, he made a comeback to the Mutual Broadcasting System, but never recaptured the influence he once had.[55] He was never to be a star again, but he did return to do a few reports on World War II before his death in 1944.

### Father Charles Coughlin: *Right Wing* Radio Priest?

Just as Rush Limbaugh was becoming a superstar, *U.S. News & World Report* wrote "Some Democrats see Limbaugh as a direct descendant of demagogues like Father Charles Coughlin and Senator Huey Long, who used radio in the 1930s to stir hatred against panoply of enemies, from Big Oil to Jewish bankers."[56]

Limbaugh targets big oil and bankers?

It has been a comparison frequently made throughout Limbaugh's rise to prominence during the Clinton presidency.

Again, in 2009, just months into the Obama presidency the ultra-liberal but often thoughtful media commentator Neal Gabler wrote, "In another era, a vicious blowhard like Limbaugh would have been driven from the air just as Coughlin was because there wouldn't have been sufficient numbers of listeners who would have wanted to continue to identify with him. He would have disgraced them. That Limbaugh, Beck, Sean Hannity, and others remain on the air is partly a testament to how 'nichified' our media have become—how much the mainstream has divided into rivulets."[57]

*Newsweek*, in a 2008 article, referred to Coughlin as a "right-wing radio priest of the 1940s."[58] In 2009, former Clinton White House counsel Lanny Davis wrote about the "1930s right-wing radio commentator, Father Charles Coughlin" in an op-ed on the spat between Obama and Fox News.[59] In 2010, the *Columbia Journalism Review* ran a piece with the headline, "A Distant Echo: What Father Coughlin tells us about Glenn Beck."[60] *The Guardian*, a U.K. newspaper published a piece that said, "It is, in fact, a description of Father Charles Coughlin, the infamous rightwing 'radio priest,' whose broadcasts in the 1930s disturbingly echo those of Beck today. Indeed, some experts see Coughlin as a father figure to the extremist broadcasting Beck has honed so well."[61]

Harrison, of *Talkers Magazine*, considered the comparisons of Coughlin to modern radio show hosts a little ridiculous.

"It's not a good comparison. I think looking at history, Father Coughlin was far more of a negative influence on America and on the decisions facing America at that time than Glenn Beck or Rush Limbaugh could ever be accused of," Harrison said. "The politics was different, and again the role was different. There was a specific anti-Semitism element to what Father Coughlin did that I do not believe exists with a Rush Limbaugh or a Glenn Beck. I do not believe that Rush Limbaugh or Glenn Beck are anywhere near as hateful as their detractors accuse them of being."[62]

Coughlin has so frequently been called "right wing" it became an article of faith despite the fact that nearly all of the policies he advocated were radically progressive. He was a staunch supporter of Franklin Delano Roosevelt, telling his vast audience in the 1932 election it was "Roosevelt or Ruin." When Roosevelt took office, Coughlin insisted that no good Christian could oppose the policies of the New Deal, and he declared an end to capitalism. So how did he earn the label rightwing? He became a virulently anti-Semitic on the airwaves and grew to sympathize with Nazi Germany. It is difficult to understand how either of those would qualify someone as a conservative. But the justification for liberal writers would be that he became just as virulently anti-Roosevelt. Never mind that the anti-Roosevelt tirades were because he thought the New Deal did not go far enough and simply lost patience with the president he so vehemently supported in the 1932 election.

Imagine 40 years or so from today, if media commentators refer to the conservative commentators of that day as the heir to "rightwing filmmaker Michael Moore." Moore has been highly critical of President Obama for the last two years for not going all the way in implementing a single payer health care system and for not abandoning the wars the U.S. first entered in the previous administration and for entering another war in Libya. To say Obama is liberal, Moore criticizes Obama, thus Moore is right wing, is almost the same logic that allows critics of conservative radio today to refer to Coughlin as a man of the right.

Now, in terms of mass audience and political influence, Coughlin was comparable to Rush Limbaugh and Glenn Beck, reaching 40 million listeners per week at his peak. His church even opened its own post office to handle the flow of fan mail. *The Guardian* piece went on to claim that "Coughlin used demagoguery to promote his views, which blended the extremes of left and right into a sort of conservative populism."[63] But, even when his show went into anti-Semitic rants, and blasting FDR, all of the conspiracy theories he touted concerned big corporations and international bankers. He had moved so far out of the realm of reason that he started a third party to challenge Roosevelt in 1936. So he certainly did not lean Republican even though he assuredly was not part of the Democratic establishment towards the later crazier years on the radio.

In that context, it is important to also point out that he was strongly anti-communist and an isolationist, two key traits of the right during that time. Though he sounded like a socialist and was a cohort of Louisiana politician Huey Long, he frequently denounced socialism. As with many progressives of the early 20th Century, much of his support for sweeping egalitarian social and economic reforms was based on the premise that it would halt a Marxist revolution from occurring in the United States. As time went on, several extreme right organizations began to identify with him even though his rigid class warfare never stopped.

Coughlin entered the priesthood in 1916 and in 10 years the Detroit Diocese authorized him to build the Shrine of the Little Flower, meant to serve about two dozen families, Coughlin went overboard, installing theater seating for 600.[64] When the Ku Klux Klan began threatening his church, he decided to combat their threat on the airwaves.[65] In 1927, he offered the first Catholic services on the radio, which began as religious, but soon moved into the political realm.[66]

By the fall of 1930, Coughlin became so popular that CBS picked up his weekly program for national consumption. About 80,000 fans per week wrote him, supporting his crusade for the poor and downtrodden.[67]

Coughlin railed against capitalism and a conservative governing philosophy in an October 1931 speech saying the economic woes wouldn't be solved "by waiting for things to adjust themselves and by eating the airy platitudes of those hundreds of so-called leaders who have been busy assuring us that the bottom has been reached and that prosperity and justice and charity are waiting 'just around the corner.'" The following month, he denounced President Herbert Hoover's belief that economic relief was a local matter.[68]

During the 1932 campaign, he denounced Hoover and praised Roosevelt, getting an invitation to speak at the Democratic National Convention.[69] He called the New Deal "Christ's Deal." In what author Jonah Goldberg described as "grotesquely sycophantic letters" to Roosevelt, the priest vowed to change his own positions on issues for on-air consumption if it would help the campaign.[70]

Roosevelt invited Coughlin to attend the inauguration, and

47

Coughlin praised this "Protestant President who has more courage than 90 percent of the Catholic priests in the country." Coughlin told his listening audience that "Capitalism is doomed and is not worth trying to save," which sounds similar to the title of one of Michael Moore's films.[71]

Coughlin was also a darling for much of the Democratic Party's establishment in the early days of Roosevelt. In 1933, ten U.S. Senators and seventy-five House members, nearly all Democrats, called on the president to include Coughlin in the U.S. delegation to a major economic conference in London because, Coughlin had "the confidence of millions of Americans." Many in the progressive wing of the Democratic Party called for Roosevelt to nominate Coughlin to serve as Treasury Secretary, a push that Roosevelt was wise enough to resist. However, the president's trusted Agriculture Secretary Henry Wallace (later to be FDR's vice president) sought Coughlin's guidance to change the administration's monetary policy.[72]

Sounding almost like a cult leader, Coughlin once declared, "I know Congress will do nothing but say 'Mr. Roosevelt, we follow.'" He continued, "God is directing President Roosevelt," and that "he is the answer to our prayers." He further warned, "If Congress fails to back up the president in his monetary program, I predict a revolution in this country which will make the French Revolution look silly."[73]

Farther Coughlin continued his radio sermons demanding greater government control of national assets, fighting poverty and unemployment and finding villains to blame for these ills such as "the Morgan interests," and the "Tory Press," respectively referring to J.P. Morgan and the big newspaper barons that opposed the New Deal.[74]

But when the New Deal did not cure the nation's ills immediately, and when the Roosevelt administration stopped including him in policymaking decisions, Coughlin turned on the president. In November 1934, the reverend established the National Union for Social Justice. Within two years the organization began publishing a national newspaper, *Social Justice*.[75]

In 1936, fed up with the slow pace of the New Deal, which he began attacking as a tool of banking interests, he helped form the National Union Party—an outgrowth of the National Union for Social Justice. The party ran North Dakota Representative William Lemke for president in 1936. Lemke was a Republican but a member of the National Nonpartisan League, an alliance of farmers that advocated state control of marketing facilities founded by socialist Arthur C. Townley. Coughlin used his show to promote Lemke and predicted he would get 9 million votes. On Election Day, Lemke got fewer than 900,000, and FDR beat Republican Alf Landon in a landslide. The priest bitterly responded to the outcome, "President Roosevelt can be a dictator if he wants," He even vowed to abandon radio, but did not keep that promise.[76] It would have been better for his legacy if he had retired—still holding sway over a significant number of Americans.

He continued to bemoan that New Deal was not doing enough, and one solution, he insisted, was having the government take over the central bank. "Somebody must be blamed, of course. But those in power always forget to blame themselves. They always forget to read the Constitution of the United States of America that says, 'Congress has the power to issue and regulate the value of money.' And blinding their eyes to that as they protect the private issuance of money and the private fixation of money, we are going merrily on our way."[77]

Rallying a populist listenership by blasting the rich and politicians is one thing.

In 1938, *Social Justice*, the newspaper, fed readers a steady diet of pieces on Jewish control of America's financial institutions. He published a version of the Russian diatribe "The Protocols of the Elders of Zion" that accused the Jews of planning to take control of the world.[78]

WMCA, which broadcast Coughlin's show in New York, eventually stopped airing the program. This prompted the Nazi press in Germany to begin praising Coughlin as some sort of truth teller silenced by American propaganda. "America is Not Allowed to Hear the Truth," one headline said. The pro-Coughlin piece said, "Jewish organizations camouflaged as American ... have conducted such a campaign ... that the radio station company has proceeded to muzzle the well-loved Father Coughlin."[79]

In 1940, the Catholic Church, which had already been frustrated with him for some time, silenced him. The Detroit Archbishop Edward Mooney strictly forbade Coughlin from having any ties with his newspaper *Social Justice* or "with any other publication." Faced with the choice of being defrocked or giving up political activity, Coughlin was able to remain at the Shrine of the Little Flower.[80]

By April 1942, Attorney General Francis Biddle ordered a federal grand jury investigation of *Social Justice* because of what he considered its pro-Axis views. Shortly thereafter, the U.S. Postal Service suspended his second class mailing privileges for *Social Justice*.[81] These government actions did not exactly strike a blow for the First Amendment, but it demonstrates how extreme Coughlin had become, as a patriotic country had essentially abandoned him. He died at the age of 88 in 1979.

## Fulton Lewis Jr.: Combating the 'Ultra-Liberal Eastern Crowd'

Nearly 40 years after his death, Fulton Lewis, Jr. was back in the news again. In 2005, Ken Tomlinson, the chief of the Corporation for Public Broadcasting, sought to bring balance to the left-leaning National Public Radio and Public Broadcasting System TV. The move was met with expected resistance, but the liberal online magazine *Salon* determined Tomlinson and William Schulz, the CPB ombudsman, were McCarthy-ite throwbacks. To prove this, *Salon* writer Eric Boehlert looked at a brief association the two men had 40 years ago to discredit whatever point they had to make in 2005, which was sort of, well, a McCarthy-ite move.

*Salon* reported that Tomlinson was once an intern for Lewis—an anti-New Deal, pro-McCarthy radio commentator, while Schulz was once a writer for Lewis.[82]   Retired *New York Times* columnist Anthony Lewis griped, "If both men wrote for Fulton Lewis it means they were dedicated to an extreme-right position that should disqualify them from determining somebody's objectivity."[83]

Politicians and commentators from both sides have often found the best weapon in the public arena against a substantive argument is an ad homonym boogey man. For the left, these boogey men are generally representative figures such as "the wealthy," conjuring up images of a monopoly man in a big hat, "big business," conjuring up an image of a ruthless cigar-chomping man in an expensive suit and the "big oil" image of a J.R. Ewing type figure sticking it to you at the pump. The straw figures are endless. A few real people make the cut, such as Sarah Palin and Rush Limbaugh. But the *Salon* piece going after Tomlinson proved that Fulton Lewis was still a boogey man for the left after all these years, which is quite an accomplishment.

Fulton Lewis, Jr. was definitely part of the extreme right—at least extreme for his time when most Republicans had accepted the premise of the New Deal policies. Lewis railed against the New Deal, supported some discredited communist witch hunts in government, and even lobbed oratorical grenades at Eisenhower Republicans. He was nevertheless very popular at his 7 p.m. weekday broadcast on 550 stations with 16 million listeners per week.[84]

He established the same rights for radio correspondents to cover Capitol Hill that newspaper reporters had. Like others of his era, his star waned with TV—a medium for which he was not well suited.[85]

He introduced such phrases to the political lexicon that would be recycled in some way or another for generations to come such as "The ultra liberal eastern crowd," "the New York Park Avenue Pink Set," "the Left Wing Fund for the Republic," and the "CIO-backed Communist left wing crackpots."[86]

"He would take a position or a stand and people would react to it," said Lee Edwards, a leading historian of the conservative movement, and distinguished fellow at the Heritage Foundation. "He was really as big as, if not bigger than, Rush Limbaugh, in the 1940s."[87]

With a weekly income of $7,000, he was the highest paid broadcaster, and among the highest paid Americans, in the 1940s.[88]

Years before Phyllis Schlafly penned "A Choice Not an Echo," and decades before Ronald Reagan was elected president, Lewis almost prophetically argued that if Americans actually had a choice between conservatism and liberalism, they would vote conservative. The problem, he said, is that moderates had taken over the GOP.

"I said between a clear drawn election between the right, between conservatives—I didn't use the 'right'—between conservatives, conservatism and liberalism, and this is the thing that I have been driving for, for years and years and years, and until we get it the American people are not going to be able to have a free expression," he said in an interview with Mike Wallace in 1958. "If we could get an election between the conservatives and the liberals there is not any question in my mind whatsoever. ... There is no question in my mind whatsoever that the balance would be sixty to seventy-five percent on the conservative side."[89]

Lewis was born in 1903 into a well-to-do family, the son of a prominent Washington attorney. The National Cathedral now sits where his childhood home once stood.[90] He dropped out of the University of Virginia—where he led a dancing orchestra—after three years.[91] He later enrolled in George Washington University School of Law, but his father's footsteps were not for him. He went to work for *The Washington Herald* in 1924, a Hearst-owned morning newspaper and became city editor within three years.[92]

He tried radio in the 1920s, and it didn't work out. So he devoted his life to print journalism and gained a lot of success. He did a major investigative piece on irregularities in the federal payments that airlines got for transporting mail, rooting out huge government overpayments. *The Herald* found it too hot to publish, so Lewis turned his notes over to a congressional committee, which probed the matter and led to the government cancelling all airmail contracts.[93] Such a view of government waste likely led him to lean more to the right.

His journalism career continued to rise when the Hearst Corporation made him the Washington correspondent for Hearst Universal News Service from 1928 to 1937.[94] The news service leaned right, but Lewis really gained bona fides in conservative circles after he married Alice Huston, the daughter of former Republican National Committee Chairman Claudius Hart Huston. The wedding drew 2,000 Washington elites, including First Lady

Lou Henry Hoover.[95] [96] But, Lewis wouldn't always fit in perfect with establishment Washington, as broadcast colleague Wythe Williams would later comment that Lewis was too caustic to be popular with Washington officialdom or other Washington reporters. These same qualities made for high ratings as a broadcaster.[97]

From 1933 to 1936, he had a syndicated column called The Washington Sideshow. Then, in 1937 after a 10-year absence from radio, he substituted for a vacationing radio announcer with Mutual Broadcasting Company. Though he used slang and clichés, he had an excitable voice, he showed up for work on time, and Mutual WOL station manager William Dolph loved the energy and passion. Dolph said, "Announcers who can read the news perfectly are a dime a dozen. I've asked perhaps a hundred announcers to tell me the news after they read it and not one ever came close. They don't know what they're reading. They don't care. Fulton reads from a script, sure, but it's a script he himself has written at the last moment. … He gets excited and loses his place, but you know a guy like that just can't be phony." After Dolph asked him to do commentaries full time for WOL, Lewis dropped his newspaper column with King Features and took a pay cut to do radio full time.[98]

By the end of 1937, Lewis's program was being broadcast nationally, and the Mutual Network, the smallest of all the radio networks, touted him as the only national news commentary originating from Washington. But being a commentator did not mean he was no longer a reporter. He still cozied up to sources on Capitol Hill, and sought to get dirt on the Roosevelt administration. Most of his sources were conservatives from both the Democratic and Republican parties, skeptical of the New Deal. Being a real reporter in Washington means having credentials to cover Capitol Hill, something radio correspondents were not allowed to have then, as the print journalists that ran the press galleries looked down on radio reporters. Lewis leaped into action to crusade for radio as being every bit as legitimate a source for news as newspapers. Newspaper and wire reporters were not considering politicians loved publicity from any medium. Lewis's crusade paid off when Congress voted in 1939 to establish a radio gallery for covering the House and Senate.[99]

He became the first president of the Radio Correspondence Association, today called the Radio and Television Correspondence Association. His office, where he did most of his work, was located in suite 627 of the National Press Building in Washington.[100]

Access in the FDR White House was not a problem for Lewis, though he would sometimes exaggerate his access to the president. During presidential news conferences with Roosevelt, Lewis was known for asking many questions, then reporting on the radio, "The president told me today ..." as if it was an exclusive interview.[101]

However, one major exclusive interview that he scored was with famed aviator Charles A. Lindbergh, who had toured Nazi Germany and was believed to be a sympathizer of National Socialism. Lindbergh, in the interview with Lewis, called for America to stay out of the European war. After the interview, Lindbergh wrote in his diary, "We are disturbed at the amount of Jewish influence. ... Lewis told us of one instance where Jewish advertising firms threatened to remove all their advertising from the Mutual system if a certain feature was permitted to go on the air. The threat was powerful enough to have the feature removed."[102]

At least with regards to the war, Lewis concurred with Lindbergh, taking the opposite approach of H.V. Kaltenborn. He also feared being taken off the air because of the wrath of a few big sponsors, as happened to Boake Carter. So he started to sell cheap advertising time to numerous local businesses, which had the prestige of advertising on a national program even if the commercials were only aired locally.[103]

But, similar to Kaltenborn, Lewis became a war correspondent in 1945—though certainly not as accomplished in this pursuit as Kaltenborn. He also briefly took up another syndicated column, "Fulton Lewis Jr. Says." But the column died out after only a year in syndication.[104]

Lewis would attack the New Deal for its public housing, war time economic restrictions and government price controls. He would step outside the boundaries of a news commentator in 1944. As Coughlin spoke to the Democratic convention in 1932, Lewis spoke at the Republican National Convention in Chicago, which nominated New York Governor Thomas Dewey to challenge Roosevelt. *New York Herald-Tribune* radio columnist John Crosby angrily protested that Lewis "ought to be recognized as a campaigner, not as a commentator, and his national air time be paid for and so listed by the Republican National Committee."[105]

Roosevelt was still a popular war time president and won a fourth term. Lewis was doing OK as well. By the end of World War II, he was aired on more than 150 stations nationally. With one very hot war over, the Cold War had begun and Lewis wanted to do his part in rooting out reds in government. He said the State Department was filled with communists and cheered for the House Un-American Activities Committee investigation into subversives.

In December 1949, Lewis had what he believed to be another big scoop when he brought George Racey Jordan, a 51-year-old major in the U.S. Army, who served in World War II, on to his program to make a strong accusation against Harry L. Hopkins, a long-time advisor to FDR, serving in several White House roles.[106] Jordan told the national audience that when he was stationed in Great Falls, Montana in 1943 and 1944 as a liaison officer with Russian staff headed by Colonel Anatoly Koti-kov, thousands of U.S. war planes were taken to Russia through Alaska. Major Jordan said he became suspicious of black suitcases arriving with armed Russian guards, so he broke open a suitcase and found "a lot of blueprints and maps and engineering drawings and scientific data" that he said were labeled "Oak Ridge, Manhattan Engineering District." Jordan told Lewis and the nation the blueprints said, "Walls five feet thick of lead and water to control flying neutrons." The big scandal though came when he told Lewis he found White House stationary "which impressed me because it had the name of Harry Hopkins printed in the upper left-hand corner. I jotted down part of the message. It said: 'I had a hell of a time getting these away from Groves.' And it was signed with the initials H.H."[107]

General Leslie Groves was then the head of the Manhattan Project, the United States government's operation in developing the atom bomb. Jordan claimed that Hopkins "gave me instructions over the long distance telephone to expedite certain freight shipments ... I was to ... say nothing about them, even to my superior officers." Three shipments came through, of 500, 1,150 and 1,200 pounds, Jordan said, adding, "All I know is that Colonel Kotikov had it listed as uranium."

After the radio program, Lewis set up a press conference with Jordan, who elaborated on the story. "It is now apparent that Harry Hopkins gave Russia the A-bomb on a platter," Jordan told reporters, with Lewis standing by. He said Kotikov would call the Russian embassy and the embassy would "plug in Harry Hopkins at the White House-they had a direct wire ... Hopkins and I got to know each other very well over the phone." The House Un-American Activities Committee opened a hearing into the matter, where Racey testified, but this time said he spoke to Hopkins only once.[108]

"The committee investigator pointed out (and the State Department acknowledged) that export licenses had been granted for shipment of some 1,500 Ibs. of uranium compounds (not the fissionable U-235) to Russia in the spring of 1943 before the Manhattan Project 'cut off all sources of uranium material.' But Jordan's story was of shipments occurring in 1944," *Time* reported.

Lewis added to the story, saying that former Vice President Henry Wallace was the official that overruled the protest by General Groves and insisted the atomic materials be sent to Russia. Wallace called this the "sheerest fabrication."[109]

HUAC actually did verify that the Soviets shipped 1.7 million pounds of documents and small quantities of uranium out of Montana. However, government witnesses said the shipments were done to divert Soviet attention away from the Manhattan Project. While Hopkins did provided classified intelligence information to Soviet intelligence agents, but it was part of a back channel diplomacy effort ordered by the president.[110]

The FBI—J. Edgar Hoover's FBI—dismissed the matter as a fabrication and Jordan as someone simply seeking to draw attention to himself, something he was quite successful at doing thanks to Fulton Lewis. HUAC also lost interest. Since neither Hoover nor HUAC was exactly your typical commie sympathizers inclined to dismiss such accounts, the Jordan story fizzled away. Lewis's credibility was harmed as he came under assault from a gleeful left and establishment media. Edward R. Murrow, *Life* magazine, Eric Sevareid and others denounced Lewis for giving such a discredited story so much attention.[111] *The New Republic* said Lewis's "wild charges were part of his campaign over many years to smear in every way possible the New Deal, the Fair Deal, and everybody not in accord with the most reactionary political beliefs."[112]

However, in the 1990s, former KGB agent Oleg Gordievsky wrote in the book, "KGB: The Inside Story" that Hopkins was an "agent of major significance" for the Soviet government. *The New York Times* later referred to Gordievsky's charge as "generally disbelieved."[113] But it does raise some possibility that Lewis and Jordan were more than just a couple of publicity hungry demagogues.

Despite the Hopkins matter and a brief unsuccessful go at TV in the 1950s, Lewis was not down for the count, and showed he still held sway.

Lewis, like others on the right, had misgivings about Dwight D. Eisenhower's moderate brand of Republicanism. But he was delighted with Eisenhower's choice of a running mate, California Senator Richard Nixon, a man with strong anti-communist credentials from his HUAC days. Lewis had frequently entertained Nixon at his 275-acre Maryland ranch. After Nixon was officially nominated for vice president at the 1952 Republican National Convention in Chicago, he hugged Lewis and said, "Except for you Fulton, it never would have happened."[114]

That may also be true of Nixon remaining on the ticket. Though Nixon helped himself with the famous "Checkers speech," Lewis was also a staunch defender of the VP nominee when Eisenhower considered dropping him from the ticket after revelations that businessmen were financing his personal expenses, which would violate Senate ethics rules on gifts and possibly the law. Lewis urged his listeners to contact Eisenhower's campaign and demand that Nixon remain on the ticket.[115]

His attitude toward Eisenhower: "A man morally fitted for his job, certainly and emotionally in so far that he in—in so far as he intends sincerely to do a good job," compared to enthusiastically saying, "Dick Nixon is a young, very aggressive, probably the best trained man that has ever stood in possible line for the Presidency. A very sincere individual, a very fine, clean, family man and an ardent anti-communist."[116]

Lewis continued on his radio show and had his friend Wisconsin Senator Joseph McCarthy on as a frequent guest.

"When you know an individual to be attempting to do a public service, a patriotic service, and you see him maligned by groups which are not thinking in the public interest, you have a tendency to be a little over-generous with the guy," Fulton Lewis said of Joe McCarthy.[117]

*Look* magazine called Lewis one of McCarthy's "masterminds."[118] Lewis loaned one of his ghostwriters, Ed Nellor to write speeches for McCarthy. McCarthy's office provided Nellor with material about alleged communists in government for Lewis's broadcasts.[119]

The truth is that McCarthy had many friends in the media— Washington reporters hungry for a scoop. But Fulton Lewis was indeed his staunchest advocated on the national scene. And he did not desert McCarthy when he became the most hated senator, censured by his peers—branded as conducting witch hunts.[120] This led to Lewis dwindling in audience, as the public saw McCarthy and those who defended him as discredited, another truism that has been challenged in recent years.

After McCarthy's death, Lewis said, "I think Joseph McCarthy did a great deal of good for the country. I think he was one of the most courageous fighters against Communism that I have ever seen on the national picture. I did not agree with everything that he did and told him so on frequent occasions when I disagreed. I do think, however, that he gave his life for the cause of anti-communism in America and for this I think he deserves great credit."[121]

Lewis once commented that the listeners that remained were too far right even for him, describing his audience as "a very considerable amount of lunatic fringe that adheres like lint to the coattails of the conservative side of the American picture. What can I say? … You cannot control those who follow you down the street."[122] He resumed a column with Hearst's flagship, *The New York Journal-American*, and continued broadcasting to a smaller and smaller audience. After having won several journalism and broadcasting awards, Lewis died in 1966.

### Walter Winchell: Inventing Info-tainment

Walter Winchell's broadcasting career was very political, an ally first for President Roosevelt and later for Senator McCarthy on the radio. However, he rose to prominence digging up dirt on celebrities and various socialites. Like H.V. Kaltenborn, Fulton Lewis, Jr. and Boake Carter, Winchell began his media career as a newspaperman, but in a profoundly different way. He was the first gossip columnist, then radio gossip commentator. He revolutionized the news media, became an unparalleled star across multiple platforms and added many previously non-existing words to the English language along the way.

"Rush Limbaugh flows from Walter Winchell. Walter Winchell was the first heated, irrational, political commentator," liberal media commentator Neal Gabler, a Winchell biographer, said in a 1994 interview with National Public Radio. "In some respects, Howard Stern flows from Walter Winchell, because Walter Winchell was a confessional journalist and really one of the first who talked about his family, talked about his affairs, talked about his relationship to his wife, and did it in the column to a wide public. Entertainment Tonight flows from Walter Winchell. Info-tainment—the whole notion of info-tainment—is really an invention of Walter Winchell's, so, in some ways, when we look at, for better or worse, this media environment in which we live, one can trace its roots to Walter Winchell."[123]

About 50 million Americans out of an adult population of 70 million listened to his radio broadcast, and almost as many read his six-day per week newspaper column syndicated in 2,000 newspapers nationally.[124] He was so much a part of the culture of his day that Burt Lancaster played a Winchell-like character, a ruthless gossip columnist, under the name J.J. Hunesecker, in the 1957 film *Sweet Smell of Success*.[125] His image and phrase "O.K.—America!" were posted on 45,000 billboards across the country to advertising the popular Lucky Strike cigarette brand.[126] In his prime he made $300,000 to $500,000 per year, which would put in on a par with network news anchors when adjusted for inflation.[127]

While Fulton Lewis and Boake Carter can be compared to Rush Limbaugh and Glenn Beck, Winchell most closely resembles Internet mogul Matt Drudge—who would become a media revolutionary in the 1990s. Drudge even wears a fedora to emulate his hero Winchell. Just as much of the establishment press scoffs at Drudge today—though pine to have their story linked on his site—most of the establishment press scorned Winchell in those days, even though he had an unparalleled audience for a newsman of any kind.

He was born in 1897 in East Harlem in New York, the son of Jewish immigrants from Russia. Winchell dropped out of school after the sixth grade.[128] He got a job sending news tidbits to *The Vaudeville News*, then by 1924 secured a gossip column for the sensationalistic tabloid *New York Evening Graphic* called "Your Broadway and Mine." Within 10 years he hit the big leagues getting a job at the *New York Daily Mirror*, a newspaper owned by industry giant William Randolph Hearst.[129]

When one of his editors told him, "You have neither ethics, scruples, decency nor conscience," Winchell responded, "I've got the readers."[130]

His widely read column paved the way for his radio debut in 1930 on CBS's Saks on Broadway, which was a 15-minute feature about show business news. Then in 1932 NBC's "Blue Network," later ABC, hired him to host The Jergens Journal, sponsored by the Jergens lotion, also a 15-minute show about entertainment. Winchell also began talking about national affairs. As we've seen, opinionated radio was nothing new. What was new was Winchell's colorful, fast-paced, staccato style with a telegraph typing in the background.[131] He frequently would say, "I'll be back in a flash with a flash"; "Attention, Commissioner Valentine, please phone—I have an alleged clue;" "Dots and Dashes and Lots of Flashes from Border to Border and Coast to Coast." He still managed to write six columns per week for the *Mirror*. In gossip, he came up with the phrase "main stem" for Broadway, a "keptive" was a mistress and newlyweds were either "lohengrinned" or "welded."[132] A pregnant woman was "infanticipating" and if a famous couple broke up they were "sharing separate tepees."[133]

He would open his shows generally saying, "Good evening, Mr. and Mrs. North and South America and all the ships at sea. Let's go to press."

He would generally end the show saying, "And that, ladies and gentlemen, winds up another *Jergen's Journal* until next Sunday night at the very same time. Until then and with lotions of love, I remain your New York correspondent, Walter Winchell."[134]

After the 1932 presidential race, Roosevelt invited Winchell to the White House and thanked him for his support, even telling him to call whenever he wanted.[135]

"It was in 1933, after the inauguration of Franklin Roosevelt that he really became a political gossip and a commentator, as well just a gossip monger on Broadway and Hollywood and the entertainment circles," said Gabler, author of *Winchell: Gossip, Power and the Culture of Celebrity*. "And that was because Franklin Roosevelt, shortly after that inauguration, invited Walter Winchell to Washington, obviously in the interest of promoting himself and the New Deal, and Winchell was easily courted, becoming really, perhaps, the most prominent cheerleader in all of the media, for FDR, because after 1935, most of the media in this country were arrayed against him. But there was Walter Winchell, a lone and loud voice, promoting the New Deal and FDR."[136]

After the first meeting in 1933, Winchell called FDR, "the nation's new hero."[137]

He should be credited for being among the first pundits to denounce Adolph Hitler, though not always in the most substantive way. In 1933, he said of the German chancellor, "I cannot refrain from flaunting the fact that he is a homo-sexualist."[138] Winchell aggressively called for U.S. intervention into World War II, often ripping into the isolationist's movement demanding the country stay neutral.

Next to Roosevelt, his favorite political figure was FBI Director

61

J. Edgar Hoover. This was despite Winchell's chumminess with organized crime figures. He interviewed Al Capone and was friendly with Frank Costello. In one unusual occurrence, Louis (Lepke) Buchalter—whom Hoover called "the most dangerous criminal in the United States" surrendered to Winchell in 1939.[139]

In 1940, *New Yorker* writer St. Clair McKelway wrote a book scrutinizing Winchell's work, titled "Gossip: The Life and Times of Walter Winchell," and concluded that Winchell's reporters were 41.2 percent completely inaccurate, 18.3 percent partially accurate and 40.5 percent completely accurate.[140] It didn't matter to most of the public. Far more people counted themselves among Winchell's loyal listeners than read the book about him.

Winchell was very forward thinking on civil rights, going with heavyweight fighter Joe Louis to his favorite night spot, the Stork Club. In other cases, he would escort blacks into clubs to integrate them. More importantly, black soldiers would write him about abuses they suffered in the military and Winchell would send a note to President Roosevelt. Roosevelt valued his relationship with Winchell, and had his staff take action.[141] He also escorted Sugar Ray Robinson into a segregated hotel in Miami.[142]

FDR's death was a blow to the country, but particularly one for Winchell.

"Winchell loved FDR and took his political bearings from FDR, so that when FDR dies, Winchell, like most of the country, in point of fact, lost his political bearings, and when one factors that in with the other side, that with the Nazi threat gone, Walter Winchell has no adversary," Gabler said. "And Walter Winchell is a man who lives an adversarial life. Everything in Walter Winchell is predicated on the notion that he is sounding the alarm for Americans."[143]

So that alarm would be the communist threat. Roy Cohn, Sen. Joe McCarthy's chief aid, befriended him and brought him into McCarthy's circle. Like FDR, McCarthy knew how important finessing a giant media personality could be.[144]

In one broadcast Winchell warned Americans, "And now to beat the hand around the clock. International News Service—January 10th is the date for a mass meeting of the communist leaders in

Washington, D.C.—behind closed doors, of course. The real purpose, however, will be to protest the trial of the 12 leading commie chiefs in the United States."[145]

He went on to accuse Lucille Ball of being a communist. Her husband Desi Arnaz responded, "The only thing red about Lucy is her hair, and not even that is real."[146]

After McCarthy became disreputable in the public's mind, so did many who aligned themselves with him. In the case of Winchell, it was McCarthy and a number of other factors that led to his decline. When entertainer Josephine Baker claimed she was discriminated against at the Stork Club for being black, Winchell—who had a good on-air record for civil rights—scorned Baker for attacking his favorite night spot. The public spat made front page news.[147] Also, Winchell—like so many other radio titans—couldn't cut it on the TV age. The staccato-style so popular on the radio caused him to bob, weave and jerk, which was OK before it became visual. On TV it just seemed weird. Also, fedoras were out of fashion by the 1950s. He found a successful TV gig though as the unseen narrator of the crime drama "The Untouchables" from 1959-1964, a fictionalized version of Elliot Ness's book by the same name—not the news commentator he had been used to. *The Daily Mirror* folded in 1963, and Hearst dropped his column from *The World Journal Tribune* in 1967.[148] That year, desperate for work, he took out an ad in Variety asking for someone to hire him, with no luck. Even worse, no publisher was interested in his autobiography.[149]

He also had an incredibly messy personal life. He was a notorious philanderer during his two marriages. Meanwhile, his son committed suicide, and one daughter died of pneumonia. The one-time huge star, Winchell died of cancer in 1972 in Los Angeles, only his daughter Walda attended his funeral.[150]

## CHAPTER THREE

# Lonely Voices

The 1960s was not a good time for conservatives, and particularly not a good time for conservative media. With government regulation, editorial viewpoints could be rare on TV and radio. This chapter looks at key conservative voices in the era from the mid-1950s through the 1960s, a time when the news media's worldview had moved decidedly left and when the Republican Party was hardly a mouthpiece for the right.

After Dwight D. Eisenhower secured the Republican presidential nomination in 1952, the GOP was controlled by the eastern establishment for most of the 1950s. Then there was the news media moving left. As was the pattern with most American post-New Deal, many reporters became Democrats who were not before. Though FDR met much opposition on the editorial pages of the 1930s, things were changing as the pro-New Deal reporters were now editors, publishers and station managers controlling the coverage.

Some of the bias can be traced to the 1930s, with *The New York Times* scandal of Walter Duranty, who won a Pulitzer for coverage he did of the Soviet Union in which he knowingly denied forced famine in the Ukraine.

*The Chicago Tribune* was the nation's largest conservative newspaper, but had little influence outside the Midwest, and was often scoffed at by the Beltway-Manhattan elite. The same was true for *The Manchester* (N.H.) *Union-Leader*, *The Philadelphia Evening-Bulletin*, *The Houston Chronicle* and a few other major metropolitan newspapers with conservative editorial pages, all lacking national influence.[1]

Walter Cronkite—who as the CBS anchorman would call for the U.S. to withdraw from Vietnam—was in the early stages of becoming the most trusted man in America. There was a tri-opoly for national broadcast news—CBS, NBC and ABC—all which leaned left in the 1950s and 1960s. These networks who took their cues on news judgment from *The New York Times* were sympathetic to the Great Society and in opposition to America's involvement in the Vietnam War.

The more conservative *U.S. News & World Report* did not have near the market penetration of its two larger rival news magazines *Time* and *Newsweek*. In the nation's capital in 1955, the liberal *Washington Post* bought the conservative *Washington Times-Herald*. The conservative afternoon *Washington Star* was still around, but by the close of the 1950s, morning newspapers were at a huge advantage over afternoon competitors.[2] The two most influential opinion journals at the time were *The Nation* and *The New Republic*, both liberal. *National Review*, in its earliest stages, and *Human Events*, a conservative opinion newspaper, did not come close to the clout of these publications at the time.

Nevertheless, while several conservative broadcasters managed to emerge from that era, their voices were largely drowned out as the news media was in a transition of moving leftward. According to historian Paul Johnson, "The growth of the TV personality meant that many of those who appeared in front of the cameras, though originally of little account in the official hierarchy of the state, became famous to millions, valuable commodities, and soon earned more than their superiors up the hierarchy and eventually (in some case) as much as station owners. And in time they, rather than the management, let alone the stockholders, began to set the tone of comment and thrust of opinion."

The most clear example of this, according to Johnson, came

with Edward R. Murrow's "See It Now" CBS News program, and his March 9, 1954 documentary on Senator Joseph McCarthy that forever set the frame of reference of the Wisconsin Republican as an irresponsible red baiter, and set an example that journalists wanted to emulate.[3]

"The gradual but cumulatively almost complete transfer of opinion-forming power from the owners and commercial managers of TV stations to the program makers and presenters was one of the great new facts of life, unheard of before the 1950s, axiomatic by the end of the 1960s," Johnson wrote. "And it was gradually paralleled by a similar shift in the newspaper world, especially on the great dailies and magazines of the East Coast, where political power, with few exceptions, passed from proprietors and major stockholders to editors and writers. Owners like [William Randolph] Hearst and [Colonel Robert] McCormick (of *The Chicago Tribune*), [Joseph] Pulitzer and Henry Luce (of Time-Life), who had once decided the political line of their publications in considerable detail, moved out of the picture and their places were taken by the working journalists. Since the latter tended to be overwhelmingly liberal in their views, this was not just a political but a cultural change of considerable importance. Indeed it is likely that nothing did more to cut America loose from its traditional moorings."[4]

The media was particularly hostile to Vice President Richard Nixon in his 1960 campaign for president, holding a grudge over the Alger Hiss matter, and awestruck by the dashing Senator John F. Kennedy. Liberal leanings would assuredly impact the 1964 presidential campaign of Republican nominee Barry Goldwater, but most of all influenced coverage of the Vietnam War throughout the decade.

Cronkite reported after Kennedy's assassination in 1963 that Goldwater's response was "no comment," when Goldwater actually had not been interviewed yet because he was at his mother-in-law's funeral at the time the president was murdered.[5]

A *Columbia Journalism Review* survey in 1962 of 273 Washington correspondents found that 57 percent of those informing the nation of political affairs were liberal while 28 percent defined themselves as conservative. That disparity would widen significantly in similar surveys taken during the 1980s and 1990s.[6]

The earliest and most influential critique of the broadcast news media—affirming what most already knew—came in the early 1970s, evaluating the previous presidential election coverage. TV Guide writer Edith Efron used a grant from the Historical Research Foundation to examine the coverage of the 1968 presidential campaign. Her research turned into a book called "The News Twisters" in 1971, which reported that the network news coverage of Republican Richard Nixon was mostly negative and mostly positive for Democrat Hubert Humphrey. CBS, ABC and NBC also slanted their coverage against U.S. involvement in the Vietnam War, promoted the cause of black militants and ignored the problems caused by black militants. Interestingly, she cited the Fairness Doctrine as a key reason why bias is a problem.[7]

This was the first study to tape, transcribe and analyze every nightly news program on CBS, NBC and ABC during the 1968 race. For an idea of how the study broke down, it found that from September 16 through Election Day 1968, ABC used 7,493 words "against" Nixon and 896 words "for" him, an 8-1 margin. It was doubly worse for Nixon at CBS, where the score was 5,300 words "against" Nixon and 16 words "for" him, a 16-1 bad press ratio.[8]

Thus was the stage at which a hand full of conservatives were on the air, at least in a national forum, some paying for their own time, managing to have an impact even as their voices were generally drowned out.

When conservative radio hosts didn't pay for their commentary time they had to find a sponsor, typically small businesses. Clarence Manion, Dan Smoot and two raucous radio pastors who litigated the Fairness Doctrine became celebrities during the time despite limited resources. Those were the Rev. Carl McIntyre and the Rev. Billy James Hargis, who ran Christian broadcasts with a strong political focus.

"These were two preachers, pastors, I'm not sure whether we'd call them evangelicals in the current sense of it, but they were early day Jerry Falwells who did have a definite pastoral mission but then were also very much involved in the politics of the day," said Lee Edwards, a leading historian of the conservative movement and a distinguished fellow at the Heritage Foundation. "Both, strongly anti-communist, strongly conservative, had many stations, appreciable audiences. If you compare them to the *National Review* approach to conservatism, obviously they were more hard core than say Bill Buckley or somebody like that. ... They were both certainly substantial figures in this early period when we're talking about a conservative movement."

### Clarence Manion: Taking Bipartisan Aim

Clarence Manion, the retired dean of the Notre Dame School of Law, became one of the most thoughtful conservatives from the mid-1950s through the 1970s. While Fulton Lewis Jr. was the more excitable and more remembered for his radio program, Manion had a philosophy fairly in tune with modern conservatism. The "Manion Forum" began broadcasting in 1954 and continued until his death in 1979. It had a national audience, but was not a profitable venture, as he purchased airtime, raised money for the efforts and did not have a salary. He didn't even apply for non-profit status out of fear the Internal Revenue Service might harass him for his content.[9]

"Today's major radio talk shows are ongoing infomercials for political parties, but it hasn't always been that way," his son Christopher Manion wrote in 2009. "The 'Manion Forum,' a national radio show founded by my father in 1954, took bipartisan aim at whoever was in power—Republican or Democrat—on the basis of solid conservative principles."[10]

Early on Manion, a lifelong Democrat, was a huge supporter of FDR and the New Deal, even writing a book endorsing the agenda in 1939. But when FDR began moving toward interventionist policies, Manion joined the America First Committee and began to rally against interventionism and big government.[11]

He retired as the dean at Notre Dame to work full time for Senator Robert Taft's presidential campaign. After Taft fell short of his bid for the Republican nomination in 1952, Manion would head the "Democrats for Eisenhower" organization. President Dwight D.

Eisenhower named him as the chairman of a commission to study how to return to states the power that the federal government had taken away under the Roosevelt and Truman administration. It was "a task taken seriously by Dad but, in short order, not by Eisenhower," his son wrote. What caused Manion's ouster from the administration was his public support for the Bricker Amendment, named for Ohio Senator John Bricker. The proposal sought to eliminate "executive compacts"—such as those made by FDR and Truman with Soviet leader Stalin—if the agreements lacked congressional approval. When Manion did not back away from his support of something the administration opposed, Eisenhower fired him. So he returned to Indiana and began broadcasting the weekly 15-minute program from his home.[12]

The "Manion Forum" was an early victim of the Fairness Doctrine, when in 1957, the Mutual network feared Manion's comments on a strike in the Midwest would prompt union demands for equal time. As a pre-emptive measure, they dropped his program.[13] In other cases, stations warned that in addition to paying for his own time, he would have to pay the cost of the other side's time for balance. He stopped doing business with these stations.[14]

Manion still maintained a national audience that heard him express his anti-communist views, criticize the Earl Warren court, and lambast the amount of deficit spending the government was doing even under a Republican administration. He caused an uproar when he called Social Security a "ponzi scheme." He decried the cost of Eisenhower's interstate highway system. He also spoke up for America's religious traditions. In 1957, Senator Barry Goldwater got welcomed national exposure as a guest on the show.[15]

Manion talked Goldwater into writing a book that the he thought should be titled a *Conscience of a Conservative*. The book was ghost written by L. Brent Bozell II. But the publishing industry was not receptive, so Manion founded Victor Publishing Company, and the book launched Goldwater's forward to the 1964 Republican presidential nomination and influenced the politics for generations.[16]

"Clarence Manion was very important to the conservative movement. His weekly program was very well read and carried on many stations," said Lee Edwards of the Heritage Foundation. "The transcripts of his broadcasts were then reproduced and distributed widely in the conservative movement. It was always regarded as a mark of your standing if you were a guest on the Manion Forum. He was a major player."[17]

Other guests on the show included General Douglas MacArthur, Jesse Helms, Strom Thurmond, Harry Byrd Sr., Henry Regnery, and Stan Evans, all key players in the rise of the conservative movement. Though Manion was on the executive board of the John Birch Society—a group eventually shunned by the conservative movement—Manion would remain a significant voice in the mainstream conservative movement until his death. Though his show did not have the ratings, bombast exposure, or even make money, it did carry forward a purist conservative message in a well reasoned sober way that was important in America's gradual shift to the right.[18]

### Dan Smoot: Fighting Invisible Government

After America's entry into World War II, Dan Smoot decided to give up his teaching fellowship at Harvard and join the military. When all three branches turned him down, he went to work for the Federal Bureau of Investigations, where at one point he was assigned to investigate communism. After a nine-year FBI career, convinced the federal bureaucracy was not sufficiently taking on the communist threat, he did what so many government officials and politicians do today—he became a pundit.[19]

Smoot had a very American story: the son of sharecroppers, orphaned at 11, worked hard to become the salutatorian at his high school, graduated from Southern Methodist University, and earned a teaching fellowship at Harvard on his way to earning a doctorate in American Civilization.[20] While eclipsed by many others, he would become a leading voice of the right through his newsletter, TV exposure, and most of all radio.

Dallas billionaire H.L. Hunt, the richest man in the world according to some reports, met Smoot and decided to make him the host of "Facts Forum," to promote free market economics, which

Hunt believes was disregarded by the liberal establishment press at the time. Hunt's financing helped Smoot's weekly radio program reach more than 300 stations in 48 states by 1952.[21]

In that weekly show, he advanced such views that a bill in Congress to provide community mental health services in Alaska was actually a cover for "the beginning of an American Siberia," where Americans that opposed socialism might be shipped.[22] This is one of the more excessive examples. Smoot was generally on the conservative side of the issues of that day, pro-McCarthy, anti-New Deal and highly skeptical of the Council on Foreign Relations, an organization that even today includes conservative and liberal internationalists. "Facts Forum" provided an opposing viewpoint—as Hunt touted it as an "educational effort to reestablish America as an independent constitutional republic."[23]

Giving equal weight to a point of view that Smoot saw as anti-freedom was not acceptable to him, so he ventured out to make his own program in 1955. He was successful in publishing *The Dan Smoot Report* subscription newsletter.[24] However, he had trouble finding a broadcast outlet. A year of trying to launch his program saw only four radio stations and no TV stations pick up the show. He later wrote about the irony that so many businesses were afraid to air his conservative message because of broadcast regulations at a time in America when the left hysterically complained over "blacklisting" and "McCarthyism."[25]

Businessman D.B. Lewis took up Smoot's cause, deciding to buy time for Smoot to air his TV and radio programs on more markets. This came despite warning from business associates that funding a conservative talk show would harm Lewis's business interests. Smoot later wrote, "D.B. figured they might be right; but, he said, businessmen had sat trembling with cowardice for thirty years while government, often guided by socialists and communists, gradually destroyed our Constitution, eliminating the free market system that made all business possible. He guessed that I might ruin his business, but knew that big government was ruining all businesses anyhow .... If the business he had built was to be ruined, he wanted to choose his own method of ruining it."[26]

Because of Lewis's risk, Smoot's program reached 150 stations and gained 50 sponsors by 1957, with about 16 million listeners. That is impressive by any standard, but still a smaller reach than he had working with Hunt, as Smoot was now limited almost entirely to the western United States.[27]

In 1962, he wrote *The Invisible Government*, which accuses the federal government and college campuses of destroying the country from within. Supporters say it sold 2 million copies despite being ignored by the establishment press.[28] Just a few years later, in the midst of the Vietnam War, the countercultural revolutions of the 1960s happened on some of the most elite colleges. However, the book also contained warnings about plans for a "one-world government."[29] In 1973, he wrote another popular book titled "The Business End of Government" that made the case federal policies undermined the free enterprise system, blaming voter apathy in part for not keeping power grabbing politicians accountable. "The goose that laid the golden eggs (free enterprise) is in trouble," he wrote. "She may not be in the oven yet; but the poor creature, already severely plucked by government, is cornered, menaced by many foes with sharp and gleaming axes. Rescuing her will take courage, as well as effort."[30]

Smoot's brush with the Fairness Doctrine began during the 1964 Democratic National Convention that nominated President Lyndon B. Johnson. Smoot said the convention resembled a "Munich beer hall coup." Smoot criticized Johnson, the Social Security program and the civil rights movement. He also said Johnson "would do anything to help his election this fall—even contrive a war if necessary." The Democratic National Committee requested free time to respond on several of the stations carrying Smoot's show, and many provided the time.[31]

His broadcasting career came to an end after his desire to present—what from his perspective the only truth—prompted fairness complaints as the FCC began mandating equal time for all sides. In 1971, he closed up shop.[32] He would continue as an author and lecturer, affiliated with the ultra-right John Birch Society that was not part of the mainstream conservative movement as leaders such as

William F. Buckley and most Republican politicians repudiated the organization. Smoot died in 2003 at the age of 89.

### Rev. Carl McIntire: Crushed by the Fairness Doctrine

The Rev. Carl McIntire was a conservative Christian broadcaster that held views outside mainstream of even conservative Christianity and to the right of most of the conservative movement. Nevertheless, he had a strong following, as he was carried on 600 stations, mostly in the South and Midwest.[33]

He is also an example of how the Fairness Doctrine could be used as a weapon by political opponents to destroy what had been a successful program called the "Twentieth Century Reformation Hour," which began airing in March 1955. The show's name derived from his belief that too many churches had become overly liberal. That criticism was lobbed at all the mainline Protestant denominations as leaning toward communism; but he also lambasted the Roman Catholic Church as "fascist," the Southern Baptist Convention as "soggy compromisers" and even the Rev. Billy Graham "a cover for the apostates."[34]

"We found a way we could reach the public under the liberty we have in our Constitution. I found we could not get our story before the public through the networks, and the press was generally blocked against us," McIntire said. He said most Americans were "prisoners of the liberal media" and believed using small radio stations across the country to reach people, "we could get on and talk about those matter in a free exercise of religion and reach millions of people."

While he managed to alienate plenty of Christians, his primary audience, he still had influence over a broad audience. That was evident from his ability to get 14,000 people marching down Pennsylvania Avenue to demand U.S. victory in Vietnam—counter to the usual protests of the day, as the reverend declared, "We are going to keep this country from falling to the communists."[35] He also could prompt people to send money, raising $50,000 for his church over the air and $6,000 for Israel during the Six Day War.[36]

He weighed in mostly on political issues of a moral nature, such as opposing gambling, sex education, and even expressed his opposition to fluoridation of water. His program included a colleague named Charles Richter, known to listeners as "Amen Charlie," because often when McIntire would make a point, he would pause to ask "Isn't that right, Charlie?" Charlie would respond, "Amen. You're right, Dr. McIntire!"[37]

McIntire picketed meetings of the World Council of Churches to protest appearances in the United States of religious leaders from the Soviet Union who he said were KGB agents.[38] "These are agents of the Communist government, folks!" It prompted mostly eye rolls. However, after the fall of the Soviet Union, new information surfaced. Christianity Today's Richard J. Mouw wrote: "I did not take this kind of thing very seriously. Like the ecumenical leaders McIntire was criticizing, I dismissed his accusations as fanatical rantings. We have learned a lot about Soviet Communism since those days. Things were much worse than many of us wanted to admit at the time. We also know now that many of those Russian Orthodox leaders were indeed conscious agents of their Marxist government. On this subject at least, Carl McIntire was issuing some legitimate warnings."[39]

By the late 1960s, McIntire's troubles with the FCC began when civic and religious groups the reverend had been flailing away at complained to the commission about WXUR in Media, Pa., owned by McIntire's Faith Theological Seminary under the corporate name Brandywine Main Line Radio Inc. One clergyman denounced the station for its "highly racist, anti-Semitic, anti-Negro, anti-Roman Catholic" sentiments. McIntire indeed had powerful enemies. The National Council of Churches and the Urban League joined forces in their complaints to the FCC. The Pennsylvania House of Representatives actually passed a resolution calling for the FCC to investigate WXUR and McIntire.[40]

The FCC determined in 1970 that the station had consistently violated the Fairness Doctrine and would not consider the stations license renewal. McIntire was particularly shocked when FCC Chairman Dean Burch, the former Goldwater campaign aid appointed by Nixon, voted against his station. McIntire suspected it had something to do with his commentaries against Nixon's efforts to get out of Vietnam and denunciation of Nixon for opening trade with China. He would later comment without proof it was an operation by White House Counsel Charles Colson. "It was just another one of those dirty tricks from the Watergate gang. That fellow Colson [was] the one to deliver the message to Burch to close us down." [41]

WRIB in Providence, R.I. told McIntire he must not mention any more names if he is to continue broadcasting. WMEN in Tallahassee, Fla. just cancelled his program simply saying they "were afraid to do anything to offend the FCC." Dozens of other stations would cancel, citing the same reluctance to upset the government.[42]

McIntire waged a two-year legal battle with the FCC, which had revoked the station's license. The battle that ended on September 25, 1972 when the U.S. Court of Appeals in Washington, D.C. upheld the FCC's ruling. Appeals Court Judge Edward A Tamm wrote in the court's opinion, "At best, Brandywine's record is indicative of a lack of regard for fairness principles; at worst, it shows an utter disdain for Commission rulings and ignores its own responsibilities as a broadcaster and it's representation to the Commission." However, in the dissenting opinion, Chief Judge David A. Bazelon expressed grave concerns about the use of federal power. "In silencing WXUR, the Commission has dealt a death blow to the licensee's freedom of speech and press. Furthermore, it has denied the listening public access to the expression of many controversial views. ... In the context of broadcasting today, our democratic reliance on a truly informed American public is threatened if the overall effect of the Fairness Doctrine is the very censorship of a controversy which it was promulgated to overcome." Even those who thought McIntire repulsive found it troubling that a small radio station could be snuffed out with a federal order. Senator Sam Ervin, a North Carolina Democrat, said, "When all the legal mumbo jumbo is clear away, the fact remains that the FCC chose to apply highly technical rules to this single station, having been forced by outside political pressure to do so."[43]

After the case, more than 200 stations dropped McIntire's program. The program continued until his death in 2002 at age 95, but in a steady decline.[44] He was heard on only one station in Camden, N.J.[45]

"I was muffled by the Fairness Doctrine. I was crushed by it," the radio preacher said.[46]

McIntire's daughter Marianna Clark said after his death that her father "never criticized anyone else's theological or political opinions without offering them [a chance] to come on his station and reply, but no one would come on to discuss it or debate with him ... the liberal groups that were opposing his conservative views ganged up and went to the FCC and said this radio station is not abiding by the Fairness Doctrine. It was a devastating thing that the FCC did in taking away this man's religious freedom and his freedom of speech."[47]

## Billy James Hargis: Catalyst to Red Lion Ruling

The most significant role the Rev. Billy James Hargis made to talk radio was his role in giving the Fairness Doctrine constitutional credence, though he gained a significant following, reaching 500 radio stations and 250 TV stations at his peak. The Washington Post said, "he was perhaps second only to Carl McIntire in spreading an ultraconservative fundamentalist message to millions."[48] He was known for his strong anti-communist message, but crumbled under the weight of a lurid sex scandal, one which he denied until his death in 2004.

Even the snarky obituary in the Economist magazine credited him for his missions, orphanages and clinics set up in Africa, and sending 100,000 balloons from West Germany into communist East Germany carrying scriptures.[49]

Initially a Disciples of Christ minister, the Disciples dropped him as an accredited minister in 1957 when his radio addresses claimed government, business, labor, entertainment, cultural, charitable and religious organizations were harboring communists.[50] So he started his own Church of the Christian Crusade, devoted to fighting communism. He said his mission was to "to succor the spiritually starved captives of communism." He wrote the book,

"Communist America—Must It Be?" in 1960. He claimed he once wrote speeches for Senator Joseph McCarthy and promoted the candidacy of Senator Barry Goldwater, even though Goldwater was not what we would today consider a religious conservative.[51]

"Write your congressman and your senator," he told a gathering in 1962. "Don't ask them to outlaw the Communist Party. Demand that they outlaw the Communist Party in the U.S.A. Don't ask them to reconsider our affiliation with the United Nations. Demand that they get this country out of the United Nations to reorganize the United Nations against godless anti-Christ communism. You are not working for them. You have nothing to fear. They represent you, and you should make your wishes known."[52]

While he had the right idea about representative government, it is somewhat difficult to imagine talk radio hosts of today that routinely rail against anti-free speech measures such as the fairness doctrine and campaign finance restrictions would support an outright ban of a political party—no matter how extreme the party.

The IRS alleged his tax-exempt church, which went from revenue of $63,000 in 1957 to about $1 million in the early 1960s, was involved in political activities. Christian Crusade lost its tax exempt status in 1964. Hargis said he was being "persecuted" and that "This action doesn't affect our corporation, only the contributors to our cause. And even so, our average contribution is $4. Now what would tax-exempt status mean to these 250,000 people? They are not big-money."[53]

As we will talk about more later, he was the host that figured prominently in legitimizing the Fairness Doctrine as constitutional. After he criticized left wing activist and commentator Fred J. Cook shortly after the 1964 election, Cook demanded that stations that aired the criticism provide free time to respond. Numerous stations turned him down, Cook, at the prodding of the Democratic National Committee, complained to the Federal Communications Commission about a station based in Red Lion, Pa. When the case made it to the Supreme Court in 1969, the justices ruled that the Fairness Doctrine was constitutional.

Two years after losing in the high court, Hargis established

American Christian College in Tulsa, Oklahoma to teach "God, government and Christian action." From the school, he formed a touring musical called "An Evening With Billy James Hargis and His Kids."[54]

Then, in 1974, things really began to fall apart after Time magazine reported that the pastor and president of the college had sexual relationships with five students—four of them male. Hargis first declined to give a specific reply, but through a lawyer said, "I have made more than my share of mistakes. I'm not proud of them. Even the Apostle Paul said, 'Christ died to save sinners, of whom I am chief.' Long ago, I made my peace with God, and my ministry continues."[55]

The students reportedly came forward to school administrators, who confronted Hargis. Hargis would eventually deny the charge, but was pushed out of the school by other administrators. Despite dumping Hargis, American Christian College never recovered from the scandal—with difficulty raising funds and recruiting students, the school folded in the late 1970s.[56]

Hargis remained married to his wife and continued to deny the allegations, and wrote a book, "My Great Mistake," published in 1985 that repeatedly denied the charges. He said in an interview about the book, "I was guilty of sin, but not the sin I was accused of."[57]

## CHAPTER FOUR

# Game Changers

Except for the small cadre of conservatives that paid for their airtime, why was radio almost void of conservative hosts? It wasn't liberal bias. In fact, there weren't many liberals on the air either. There just wasn't a lot of talking and a whole lot of singing.

TV had become the top source for news and entertainment. Station managers in the 1950s felt the best way to get an audience was music, and top 40 was particularly lucrative—not always in the most up and up way. As popular as Winchell and Kaltenborn were in the early years of radio, when TV became the primary medium for news and entertainment, radio became a music medium.

Yes, it was reducing the power of the Federal Communications Commission in that late 1980s that allowed talk radio to explode. Ironically though, it was an emboldened FCC in the early 1960s that allowed the genre to even regain a commercial foothold in the age of TV.

Rock-n-Roll, according to many accounts, was a term coined by disc jockey Alan Freed, one of the most famous disc jockeys of the 1950s. He was at the top of his industry until he became the face of Payola scandal that rocked the radio industry.

In the late 1950s, NBC TV had to confess to rigging "Twenty

One" game show. It was the famous quiz show scandal that became the subject of a major motion picture. This prompted both the Justice Department and Congress to explore the radio industry. Representative Oren Harris, an Arkansas Democrat, completed his oversight investigation into TV game shows and announced that radio would be the next industry to be scrutinized. In radio, they found even more sleaze.[1]

Investigators discovered that record producers would hire "song pluggers" to get radio stations and disc jockeys to play certain songs, and play them often, to increase their exposure and perceived popularity, thus increasing sales. The record companies would routinely provide bribes of cash, booze and women to get prominent play for their songs.[2]

WABC in New York asked all of its disc jockeys to swear under oath they never received payments for playing music and also that they did not own interest in the recording, publishing or merchandising of the music. Freed declined to answer. Feeling the pressure, WABC radio and WNEW-TV, fired him. Freed shrugged it off at the time. "Payola may stink, but it's here, and I didn't start it," he said.[3] The FCC asked Congress to outlaw deception in the public airwaves. Meanwhile, the agency decided to step up its own enforcement of the public service requirements.

Asked by *Time* magazine if he ever accepted payola, Freed said no, but said he had been a "consultant" for "the major record companies." In *Time*, he recalled, "a man said to me, 'If somebody sent you a Cadillac, would you send it back?' I said, 'It depends on the color.'"[4]

It was only after the Payola scandal that talkers began to emerge.

"We got the scraps in talk radio if there were any left over. That's the way it was until 1959 when there was a scandal that made today's talk radio possible," nationally syndicated host Barry Farber said. "A radio station uses public air. They are licensed. If a radio station loses its license, its value goes from $35 million to $35,000 in used electronic equipment. The FCC got completely irate and they started checking which stations were living up to what they promised they would do if they were given a license."[5]

It is worth saluting shows that managed to not only survive but thrive despite the Fairness Doctrine.

Joe Pyne was a major player in radio before switching to TV, and at least stylistically, may have been the father of modern talk. Bob Grant and Barry Farber beginning in the 1960s and continuing today were significant voices for conservatives. During the 1970s two radio personalities would represent Christian conservatives in politics well before they had ever organized sway on public policy, Marlin Maddoux and James Dobson.

A marked difference with these individuals compared to other conservative talkers in the 1960s was they did not have to pay to be on the air. They did not have to find a financier, and then recruit other sponsors. They were on the air five times per week, not once. Their programs were broadcast and the station sold advertising for that programming based on the ratings. That is the way it works today and one can easily take that for granted. Compared to Manion, Smoot and others, it was a privileged position to be in.

While Christian radio tended to be in the smallest radio markets, Maddoux and Dobson managed to gain national audiences. and helped bring evangelical Christians into the political mix who had largely ignored public affairs before. Both Maddoux and Dobson were never in-your-face hosts, and brought a sober—yet sharply principled tone to their religious-political broadcasts.

"The fact is these are trailblazers for conservative and Christian radio," said Bob Dutko, a former press secretary for the Christian Coalition whose national radio show is syndicated through Crawford Broadcasting in Detroit. "They're the ones who let people know you can have religious programming that can be compelling and interesting. I think there was a time when people saw radio as either political in nature, newsy in nature, or religious in nature."

Dobson and Maddoux set the stage for Christian radio to be dynamic and relevant to current issues, Dutko said.

"Talk radio religious in nature was kind of perceived as boring like the country preacher," Dutko continued. "To see talk radio move into an area where Christian talk can be compelling, interesting, culturally relevant, political, on top of what's happening, cutting edge, but also have that flavor of Christianity running through it, that to me has probably been the biggest growth and development in talk radio that Christian radio is not just the country preacher on radio, but you can have strong political and cultural commentary on the radio and interactive, caller driven radio that's also Christian radio at the same time."

Farber and Grant in the early years at least were primarily in the New York market. Farber, who rose to prominence on the late night slot, mellowed a bit as the years went on. Grant, who rose to the drive time 3 p.m. to 7 p.m. slot, became more testy. But both men were the dominant broadcast voices for the right certainly in the 1970s and the 1980s. Because they were doing good business for big New York stations, they were not as easy a target as hosts paying for time on mostly small stations. Thus, a challenge and harass strategy would not have been as easy against the large New York stations. While most radio history was made in New York, it was out west where the all-talk stations began. In 1961, KABC radio in Los Angeles, KMOX in St. Louis and KVOR in Colorado Springs were the first all talk no music stations.[6]   New York's WNBC switched to all talk in 1964, to compete with WOR.[7]

### Joe Pyne: 'Father of In Your Face Talk'

Joe Pyne made his mark in TV, but got his start in radio and had a definite influence on modern talk radio and talk TV. He was among the first talk show hosts on radio or TV to insult guests, and was entertaining aside from that.

"The first real game changer was Joe Pyne," said Farber. "He was a real rough neck; a rude, crude, opinionated and he wasn't as smooth as Rush and wasn't as brilliant as Rush. He was a former Marine. He had lost a leg. He was very good, and he was a game changer."

*Talkers Magazine* called him the "father of in your face talk television."[8]  Before that, he built up quite a reputation on radio. "He was an early conservative groundbreaker," *Talkers* editor Michael Harrison said of Pyne.[9]

Pyne said he originated talk radio in the 1940s, and said his TV and radio shows would be about serious material. "I don't interview movie stars on their last picture," he once said.[10]

The Chester, Pennsylvania native enlisted in the Marines to fight in World War II, where he lost his left leg.[11] He became known for having a wooden leg, a characteristic that some fans of the show doubted, because they thought it could be part of his eccentric act, but it was true.[12]

He began his radio career at WCAM in Camden, New Jersey then moved into a local TV show on a Wilmington, Delaware station.[13]

Pyne was on the right, but had a sense of equal justice when broadcasting in a segregated city. *The News Journal* of Wilmington, Delaware reported that in the 1950s Pyne did his WILM broadcast from the English Grill restaurant in Wilmington. One of the guests he was to have on the show was black, and was denied service at the restaurant. "Pyne, who was setting up for his program, observed the goings-on and began packing up his broadcasting equipment to leave. He said he would do the show from the WILM studio rather than watch the injustice of Morris being refused service," the newspaper said. "The English Grill manager backed off, obviously so he wouldn't lose the publicity his business got through the Pyne show."[14]

Pyne headed west to Los Angeles for a spot on KABC in Los Angeles.

On KABC Pyne railed against communists, the women's movement and President John F. Kennedy. The station even took him off the air temporarily on November 22, 1963, fearing he would say something inappropriate after the assassination.[15]

He would generally say to callers, "It's your nickel," and referred to liberals as "meathead" long before anyone ever heard of the fictional Archie Bunker character.[16] Some of Pyne's favorite lines involved telling callers or guests whom he disagree to "gargle razor blades" or "take your false teeth out, put them in backward and bite yourself in the neck."[17] He would also say, upon becoming exasperated with a guest, "I could make a monkey out of you but why should I take the credit?"[18] He told one caller, "Look lady, every time you open your mouth to speak, nothing but garbage falls out. Get off the line, you creep."[19]

This brought in listeners, but it also brought in angry calls and letters to KABC and the ABC corporate headquarters in New York. The company was not certain how to handle Pyne, who was bringing in good ratings but was unorthodox. When it tried to handle him, Pyne blasted ABC on the air. He was fired, but got a job at rival KLAC the next day. In national syndication, he would air on 254 stations.[20]

He eventually snatched another TV spot on KTLA in Los Angeles.[21] At his height, his syndicated TV show was viewed in 80 cities.[22]

Pyne made clear the successful TV interview had to be confrontational.

"The subject must be visceral," he told *Time* magazine in 1966. "We want emotion, not mental involvement."

He also engaged his studio audience in what was called the "Beef Box." Whenever he disagreed, Pyne would tell the audience member to "take a hike." He ended each broadcast saying, "Good night everybody, straight ahead."[23]

Pyne, a chain smoker, died of lung cancer at the age of 44 in 1970.

### Bob Grant: 'Perfecting Anger'

Before Bob Grant became a real celebrity out of New York, the producer of his Los Angeles program on KABC got a call from public relations firm that wanted to book Ronald Reagan as a guest.

"My producer, a nice young fellow from Inglewood, N.J. as a matter of fact, he said, 'Bob doesn't do show business stuff. We're dealing mostly with politics and current events,'" Grant recalled. The PR guy asserted, "Maybe you don't know, but Ronald Reagan is not going to talk about his latest movie. He doesn't make moves any more. He's running for governor.' When my producer told me I said get him, by all means. Get Ronald Reagan. I was already a fan of Reagan. I had heard several of his speeches or read them."[24]

"So Reagan was booked and it turned out to be his first radio interview as a gubernatorial candidate. I kept him for two hours. He was only supposed to be on for one," Grant said.

Grant said Reagan, seeking his first political office, fumbled on more than a few questions, but Grant, being a fan, covered for him.

"We even had a woman call from Pasadena and say 'You two ought to change places.' She wanted to vote for Governor [Edmund G.] Brown," Grant said. "She didn't like the fact that I was helping Ronald Reagan. When she said, 'You two guys ought to change places,' Ronald Reagan, such a wonderful human being, says, 'You know, you might have a good point there.' That in retrospect has turned out to be my most memorable interview."[25]

That is saying something for a man who has been on the radio for six decades.

More than two decades later, another California radio announcer would travel to New York to be on the same station as Grant. When an upstart Rush Limbaugh left Sacramento to come to WABC in New York, the excitement of the move was soon blunted when seemingly none of his callers wanted to talk about what Rush was talking about.

"I wasn't just going to do a national show. I had to do a local show for two hours a day on WABC as well, because they weren't going to carry the national show at first," Limbaugh explained. "And, folks, I can't tell you how dispirited I got the first month. Here I am doing my show, and I'm doing my thing, and every phone call I got wanted to talk about what Bob Grant had said the day before. I'm on from ten a.m. to noon, and I'm sitting there saying, 'Are you people not listening to me?'"[26]

It was easy to see why conservative listeners would have considered Bob Grant the gold standard at the time. Limbaugh would of course go on to become the household name that Grant, who was primarily a New York personality, was not. The same would be true of various other talkers from WABC such as Sean Hannity and Mark Levin.

"They owned the town, but then FM came long, and music on AM dwindled away and so WABC decided to switch format and go talk," Limbaugh said. "I've always thought that were it not for Bob

Grant when WABC made this format shift, you might not today know what WABC is."[27]

After 60 years in radio, Bob Grant is still heard on WABC in New York, a station that once fired him over his controversial tongue. *Talkers Magazine* said of Grant, "He didn't invent the 'angry talk host' but he damn near perfected it."[28] Grant's bio on his own website says, "the inventor of controversial talk radio." It is perhaps most accurate to say that while he did not invent controversy on the air, he mainstreamed it in the most important media market in the United States.

"Bob Grant is definitely one of the forefathers of today's conservative talk radio. There's no question about it," said Michael Harrison, editor of *Talkers Magazine*. "He created a style that was quite recognizable. He created a tone and a way of performing that many, many emulated. Bob Grant was one of the founders of today's conservative talk radio."[29]

Robert Gigante began his broadcasting career in the 1940s in Chicago, later changing his name to the more marketable and easy to say Grant. Grant graduated from the University of Illinois with a degree in journalism and took his first job at WAOK in Oak Park, Illinois. By 1949, the first year of the Fairness Doctrine, he moved up to WBBM in Chicago reporting the news. Grant had a brief stint as a TV actor in the early days of TV, but returned to radio in 1959 at KNX now as a talk show host. Three years later, the Los Angeles station KABC hired him away to be their sports director. It was at KABC where he met the legendary Joe Pyne.[30][31]

Pyne's departure came in part because he was rabidly anti-John F. Kennedy. KABC thought after the assassination, his brand of talk might not play well.[32][33] So, the logical place to turn was for someone as mellow as Grant.

As Grant's popularity grew, he moved to New York in 1970s to host a show on WMCA-AM.[34] He left WMCA in 1977 for a job at WOR. For a while, he left New York altogether to host a show for WWDB in Philadelphia. But by 1984, he returned to work for the most important news talk station in New York, and probably the country, WABC.[35] He came to dominate the ratings in the afternoon drive time slot, 3 p.m. to 7 p.m.[36]

"That's the only way anybody survives," Grant said. "If you pick up a copy of the *New York Post* in October 1992, there I am on the cover and you read that and you get the clear picture of how important, it's everything ratings. That's how you survive."[37]

The timeslot itself represents the evolution of conservative talk. Clarence Manion had to pay for his time. Barry Farber entertained and informed night owls. Grant reached the most coveted time slot available and soared at it, shouting "get off my phone" whenever liberal callers got on his bad side—a simple phrase that Mark Levin would later adapt to "get off the phone you big dope."[38] Another favorite phrase was "Your influence counts ... use it!"[39]

Today's talk giants owe much to Grant. His wide listenership on WABC established a platform for Limbaugh to draw an even larger audience, and in turn creating an entire media revolution. It was perhaps the explosion of other talkers in the 1990s that allowed Grant to have some of his biggest influence at the time.

Despite being bigger and more influential, he doesn't think talk radio is better.

"I don't know if it's necessarily gotten better. It's different," he said. "When I started, there were very few of us, very few considered worthy to do this type of program. They didn't just let anybody come in and claim to be a so called talk show host. And, I think in that regard, it was better in those days because there are a lot of people who are advertised as talk show hosts but I really think they're very amateurish. In that regard, it hasn't gotten better. What has happened is that people know about it and there are a couple of guys that are constantly quoted as if what they have to say is important. Maybe it is. It's a mixed bag."

He had high praise for some hosts.

"They can't go through a day without quoting Rush. Which is fine with me because Rush has paid me many compliments," Grant said. "What amazes me and annoys me actually is people say, 'do you know Rush?' Of course I know Rush. Just pick up his first book, *The Way Things Ought to Be*. Read page 13. Then you won't ask if I know him or if he knows me."

Limbaugh wrote that Grant was the "king of talk radio in New York since the early 1970s," and wrote that "he is WABC. Bob Grant is a pioneer. He is one of the few talk show hosts who has lasted in combat radio. He defined it and spawned countless imitators all over the country. Nobody does it better than he does and his ratings are proof. He is New York and the tri-state area both in manner and approach. If New York is an argument, and it is, then Bob Grant's show is New York every day."[40]

He has repeatedly been credited with helping Republican Governors George Pataki of New York and Christine Todd Whitman of New Jersey get elected. Pataki stuck with him until the end. Whitman—elected by a smaller margin in her state—threw him under the bus after political pressure.

"I had a huge audience in both New York and in New Jersey and I think people had great respect for me," Grant said. "They valued my opinion. I never really did say go vote for this person. Go vote for that person. But it was very obvious who I was for. And I don't like to be coy or cute."

Grant could be caustic toward other liberal activists or politicians he did not view fondly. He once notably said, "I'd like to get every environmentalist, put them up against a wall and shoot them." He called President Bill Clinton, "the sleazebag in the White House." Commenting on welfare mothers, he said, "The only hope we have is something that we're not brave enough to do. But if there is a brave new world of tomorrow, they will enact the Bob Grant Mandatory Sterilization Act."[41]

It was not until he had a clear impact on political contests that Democrats and Democratic operatives decided to smear him. In 1993, Whitman was running an uphill race against New Jersey Governor Jim Florio. Grant had Whitman on his program numerous times to sell her tax cutting message, while he shouted about "Flim-Flam Florio" and criticized the governor's massive tax hikes. Whitman, a liberal Republican, campaigned as a tax cutter and appeared several times on Grant's show, helping her solidify support among North Jersey conservatives.[42] Whitman won by a slim margin and credited Grant with helping her get elected.[43]

"He said, 'how can I win with Bob Grant beating my brains out every day?' Grant recalled of Florio. "Years later, there was a lunch arranged by mutual friends to have Jim and I set down to have lunch together. We both agreed. I found him to be a delightful person. We enjoyed it because we weren't talking so much about the election. He was a pretty good sport come to think of it."[44]

Senator Frank Lautenberg, the New Jersey Democrat whom Grant regularly called "Senator Lousenberg" became uptight when he was up for reelection in 1994, a year that looked promising for Republican candidates across the country. His GOP opponent Assembly Speaker Garabed "Chuck" Haytaian was getting much attention from Grant's radio show as well. So to take two opponents out with one shot, Lautenberg said Grant was racist and tied the radio host's racially insensitive comments to his Republican opponent. Lautenberg's campaign used this to mobilize black voters in the closing weeks of the campaign.[45]

Calling opponents racist has and will be a de facto position for the left when they run out of arguments. Unfortunately, Grant invited such criticism. Viewing his comments in context, they probably were not racist, but such statements—especially taken collectively—display perhaps an over the top lack of sensitivity.

After the Los Angeles riots of 1992, he said, "I can't take these screaming savages, whether they're in the African Methodist Church, the A.M.E. church, or whether they're in the streets, burning, robbing, looting." A comment he clarified was aimed at violent rioters. Of Haitian boat refugees he said, "If they drowned! Then they would stop coming."[46]

During the campaign, Grant took Lautenberg's attack as a compliment, telling his listeners, "Bob Grant carried Christie in. It's boomeranging," and urged them to vote the incumbent out of office.[47]

But when some of the same Democrats, African American ministers and civil rights groups pushing Lautenberg's campaign shifted pressure to Whitman, even leading a demonstration outside the capitol in Trenton, she almost instantly caved. She went on his show, lectured him, said she was offended, and vowed she would not return to the program.[48]

Grant accused critics of Stalinism, a Pearl Harbor attack and a crucifixion. However, when callers to the show acted in outrage, he simply joked about the entire matter. An angry caller to the program later said of Whitman, "She should fall down on her knees and ask forgiveness." Making fun of the entire matter, Grant said, "WASPs don't do that. They don't fall on their knees. You're thinking Italians or Greeks."[49]

Grant's influence was not waning in New York. Governor Mario Cuomo, a big state governor and master orator, was the Democratic nominee in waiting before he decided to skip the 1992 presidential race against an unbeatable (or so it seemed in late 1991) Republican incumbent George H. W. Bush. Cuomo instead sought a fourth term as governor, which turned out to be just as much of a sure thing as the Bush reelection.

Grant considered Cuomo an enemy since the governor hung up on him during a 1986 radio interview. During 1994, Grant even hit the campaign trail for Pataki, proclaiming, "We get the chance to show Mario the door in '94." He would regularly bring Pataki on the air and introduce him as "the next governor of the state of New York."[50]

Pataki, felt most of the New York media was solidly behind Cuomo, and had already written him off.

"Whenever I wanted to talk to the people, I'd call Bob Grant," Pataki said. One week prior to the November 1994 gubernatorial election, Cuomo led by double digits in most polls. However, Pataki's numerous appearances on Grant's show, and Grant's own crusade against Cuomo—whom he called "Il Supremo" led to a stunning victory for Pataki, who would go on to serve three terms.[51]"You talk about George Pataki. He was running against Mario Cuomo," Grant said in an interview for this book. "I had campaigned against Mario Cuomo. Mario believed if it weren't for me, he would have had a fourth term."[52]

On April 3, 1996, Grant crossed a line that he deeply regrets and still feels he hasn't fully recovered from. When U.S. Commerce Secretary Ron Brown was killed in a plane crash in Bosnia, initial reports said there might be one survivor. Grants response: "My hunch is that he is the one survivor. I just have that hunch. Maybe it's because, at heart, I'm a pessimist."[53]

Grant was obviously not pleased with Brown's death, but making a joke about anyone's death—public or private citizen—is too much.

"Of course I regret that. The way that afternoon went, we had the television set on in the studio, without the sound of course, they had the captions," he said. "I got a caller talking about Ron Brown and the fact that he was on that plane that crashed in Bosnia. At that very moment, I see it's rumored there may be one survivor. Unfortunately, I said to the caller whose name was Carl, I said 'Carl, I see there may be one survivor. And then I made the quote."[54]

Under pressure from the Reverends Jesse Jackson and Al Sharpton—who had sought Grant's scalp for years—Disney, which had recently purchased Capital Cities/ABC, intervened to fire Grant.[55]

"That has really been a terrible incident in my career. I have to be honest and tell you, I think it damaged me irreparably," Grant said.[56]

The left gleefully began to pile on. Cuomo—who got his own WABC show after losing his previous job, said on his show, "I was disgusted by it." Former WABC liberal talk show host Alan M. Dershowitz, fired the previous month for calling Grant a racist, said his own dismissal paved the way to fire Grant. "Until they took my show off the air in New York, they were able to justify Bob Grant on free-speech grounds. And my preference would be for everybody to be on the air, but once they began to exercise some censorship, they couldn't pick and choose, and choose a racist over a non-racist."[57]

The glee would not last long. WOR-AM, Grant's former employer, almost immediately snatched Grant up to air in the same drive time slot. It was with WOR that Grant first went national through the WOR Radio Network.[58] WOR's ratings shot ahead of WABC's almost as soon as the switch was made, from the loyal following listening to the Grant from 3 p.m. to 7 p.m. WABC—formerly the top dog in New York—put Curtis Sliwa, the founder of the Guardian Angels in the interim slot, and were pulling a 2.7 compared to Grant's 4.1 rating on WOR.[59] Eventually, Mike Gallagher got the ABC slot. Gallagher would eventually go onto national syndication.[60] Finally, Sean Hannity got the WABC drivetime spot.

"The WOR format and image was not what WABC's was," Grant said. "It just wasn't the same. I stayed there until January of '06. They treated me very well, threw me a couple of retirement parties. It's just that I can't believe the sequence of events on that fateful day in April 1996."[61]

Grant, WABC and Dershowitz (who managed to get a program on WOR—midnight on Sunday) would be brought together in an awkward way. The National Association of Radio Talk Show Hosts, the country's largest talk show organization, awarded its highest honor, the Free Speech Award, to Grant, Dershowitz and Disney Chief Executive Officer Michael Eisner. The three got their awards in separate presentation at the 1996 Talkers convention.

"Most people think freedom of speech just refers to letting people talk," Harrison said at the time of the announcement. "But the First Amendment does not protect you from the consequences of your speech. So free speech means Bob Grant can make his comments about Ron Brown, and Alan Dershowitz can call Bob Grant a racist, and also that Disney has the right not to allow those comments on its stations. So they were all exercising free speech."[62] Grant joked that the association was "very creative," and said he, Dershowtiz and Eisner should get together before the ceremony to "talk about old times."[63]

Grant, a New Jersey resident, made headlines again in 1999 when he talked about running for the U.S. Senate as a third party candidate when it was widely believed that Governor Whitman would be the Republican candidate for the seat of retiring Senator Lautenberg. When Whitman did not run, there was little incentive for Grant to be a spoiler.

Grant continued on WOR's drive time slot, eventually falling to second after Sean Hannity sailed ahead of his hero with his 3 p.m. to 6 p.m. WABC program. In January 2006, at a time when conservatives and the Republican Party were in disarray, Grant called it quits. His "final" show included a string of famous guests complimenting his tenure in talk. Governor Pataki called to praise Grant for the assist in ousting Cuomo. William F. Buckley, the leading pioneer of the conservative movement, called Grant as a pioneer of radio at a time when few conservatives existed in the media. Former Speaker of the House Newt Gingrich, former Democratic New York Mayor Ed Koch, Shock jock Howard Stern and conservative commentator and author Ann Coulter all called in to wish Grant well.[64]

The retirement turned out to just be a long break. In August 2007 he returned to radio—interestingly enough with WABC. His program was cut to two hours, and from 8 p.m. to 10 p.m. after the Mark Levin Show. WABC made the move after Disney sold the property to Citadel Broadcasting. "I never thought I'd miss this as much as I did," Grant said upon returning to the air. "I thought I'd retire and just do what I wanted. But it turned out what I wanted to do is what I'm going to be doing now."[65]

Another controversy ensued in 2008, when *Radio & Records* magazine revoked its plan to give Grant a Lifetime Industry Achievement Award after pressure from various interest groups. "R&R is sensitive to the diversity of our community and does not want the presentation of an award to Mr. Grant to imply our endorsement of past comments by him that contradict our values and the respect we have for all members of our community," Radio & Records said in a statement. Grant, characteristically, reacted emotionally, saying of the publication, "It's contemptible that they would do such a thing. I smelled a rat right away."[66]

Most of the talk radio community got behind Grant. Limbaugh spoke up for him. Hannity interviewed him. *Radio & Records* came out looking poorly in the matter. Once again, the legendary Grant landed on his feet. Levin said, "I am disgusted with the mistreatment of Bob Grant. I am fed up with the censors, intimidators, and cowards in this business."[67]

Grant left WABC again in November 2008 and began an Internet radio program. But by popular demand, WABC brought him back in September 2009. This time he was in a less prestigious timeslot of noon to 2 p.m. show on Sunday. He has continued to occasionally substitute for hosts such as Hannity, Levin and even Michael Savage and remains able to reach a huge audience even after passing the torch to a new field of conservative talkers.[68]

"I've had the greatest audience a radio person could have," Grant said. "These people have been loyal. They still call me on my 12 p.m. to 2 p.m. show and they send me the most amazing e-mails. They credit me with so much influence in their lives. It's very touching. I'm glad I wound up making an influence doing something that in the beginning I would have done for nothing. It's great to be paid to do something you love to do. And I love that microphone and still do."[69]

Will he ever *really* retire?

"I'm trying to. I've done it twice and the lure of the microphone, some people say, you're not the same without that microphone," he said. "I have a hunch very soon I will do it for good."

## Barry Farber: 'Publicist of Ultraconservative Outlooks'

"Talk show hosts are laid-back people with pretty faces and boyish grins," read a profile by United Press International when Barry Farber got a TV show after more than two decades on the radio. "Farber is craggy, shaggy and intense. He frowns. He ruminates. He interrupts conversations to take notes with a ball point pen that virtually disappears in the great paw at the end of his shirt sleeve. ... He looks more like a hungry bear demolishing a log in search of his dinner, and that's just the way guests in his 'arena' may perceive him before they retire, bathed in sweat and wondering whatever possessed them to take him on in the first place."[70]

As it turned out, Farber—who got his first radio program in New York in 1960—had a short lived TV tenure in the early 1980s, but one need only read this description to understand the impact he had on future talk show hosts in general.

In other venues he has been widely credited for offering reasoned commentary without the bombast so prevalent today. "For the sake of ratings, I will not get into race-baiting and polarization and divisiveness. I will not pretend to be ignorant and stupid," he said in a 1996 interview. "People like me are at a disadvantage today."[71]

Farber remains a longtime staple in the New York market and a national voice. He is widely reported to know 26 languages. But the North Carolina native who kept a slight southern accent even he reached big city radio, is quite modest about his knowledge of languages.

"When I entered the Army, I took tests in 14 languages and I qualified as an interpreter and that's how I spent my time in the Army, translating," Farber said in an interview for this book. "I am a student of as many as 26 languages. Some I know very, very well. Some I know only greetings, and some I can simultaneous translation in. But it would be wrong to give the impression that I'm fluent in 26 languages. I've done broadcast and speeches. I've done speeches in Hungarian, Norwegin, Spanish, and I participated in Spanish broadcast and in French, but not extensively."

He is a self described "Nixon Republican" even after the downfall.[72]

"I was liberal when it came to the issues of racial justice," Farber said, speaking of his early days when civil rights was the defining domestic issue and the Cold War was the defining international issue. "But I had lucked out and visited the communist world on a fluke when I was 21 years old (Yugoslavia) and I saw all the anti-communist stuff I read was true and it was true in big dimensions. I was very, very liberal on the issue of race, very, very rightwing when it came to issues of communism vs. freedom."[73]

William Safire, who would go on to become a Nixon speech writer and then a *New York Times* columnist, gave Farber his first job as a producer for the Tex and Jinx interview program that broadcast over WNBC-AM.[74]

He got his own radio program in 1960 on 1010 WINS-AM, called "Barry Farber's WINS Open Mike." It was the only talk program on what was at the time a rock-n-roll station.[75] Given the time, it never occurred to him that he could play an influential role advancing the conservative movement as current day talk hosts. Instead, 1010 WINS put his show on to fulfill an education requirement and keep the FCC dogs at bay who had grown hungry after the Payola scandal.

"My first job, I was literally skin grafted with a one hour talk show onto a station that didn't want or need a talk show but figured they damn well better start moving in the direction they had promised they would or they would lose their license," Farber said in describing his circumstances. "So I was on WINS when it was a total Rock-n-Roll station, number one in New York, and that's where I got my first job on New York's number one station, Rock-n-Roll. I was the one hour talk show from 11 at night to midnight."[76]

"In those days we didn't think of ourselves as nation-savers, America rescuers, or ralliers of whatever our political opinion was," Farber said. "We didn't know it was possible to criticize politicians," he said. "It occurred to me to get more exciting guests and bigger name guests. It never occurred to me to do what Rush and Sean are doing today. I really wish it had."[77]

Throughout most of the 1960s and 1970s, he became a fixture on WOR.[78] In 1967, he became an all night host. He considered the station a dynastic station, with programs passed from one generation of hosts to the next.

"In 1962, I was invited over to WOR, which was sort of like being invited to the throne room. That was the number one station. I was not part of a dynasty. I was the first Farber there, 8:15 to 9," he said. "Then they added 9:15 to 10. Then they gave me the all night and kept 8:15 to 9 because we were really bringing in good money. I would set with my panel from 11:15 to 2:03 and 30 seconds in the morning. Then they would play that over again, and that would bring them out to 5 a.m. So when you consider, here I am on the air Monday through Friday, 8:15 to 9 and 11:15 to 5 in the morning, plus repeats on the weekends, I was more than 25 percent of WOR's entire work week."

Of the Fairness Doctrine days, Farber said he was glad to see it go, but in all of his broadcast years prior to 1987, he was never personally affected.

"I'll tell you a dirty little secret. We dealt in opinion all the time and the Fairness Doctrine was only invoked upon me once. It was observed in the breach. It was ignored," Farber said. "Now the Fairness Doctrine was worse than a lot of people realize. It didn't merely say we had to grant equal time if somebody felt aggrieved and asked for equal time. If someoobody were mentioned in a negative way under the Fairness Doctrine, we were obliged to seek that victim out and invite him to take equal time."

The only time he was cited for violating the doctrine was in the 1960s when a white supremacist named Richard Cotton, who Farber called "a Louisiana bigot," demanded his time to respond.

"All I owed him was about four seconds," since a guest mentioned him in a roll call of bigots. "But I thought, this is a hoot. This is a new thing for me. Instead of giving him four seconds, whatever that would have done, I invited him on for the whole 11:15 to 2:07 in the morning."

"He said 'Mr. Farber, I'm entitled to be here and I'm entitled to have my say. The first thing I want to say is that America was on the wrong side in two wars: The Civil War and World War II.' I said, 'I beg your pardon.' He said, 'You heard me. America was on the wrong side in the Civil War and World War II," Farber recalled.

"I said, 'I'm from North Carolina, so anyone can argue that. But you mean we should have never fought the late Adolph Hitler?'" he recalled. "He said 'You heard me. We were on the wrong side.' It went like that all the way through."

Farber responded with history, reason and logic and said, "I wiped him out, he was a smoking crater." But, he said the most powerful letter he ever received came after the biggot's appearance. "Dear Mr. Farber, You must be proud of yourself for having destroyed Richard Cotton on the air the other night. Not so fast Mr. Farber. You see, they play by a different rule book. They don't care about coming into radio studios and winning debates. His mission is to recruit 50 other mentally ill haters out there who will write a post card to his P.O. Box and send him $50 for his Christmas hate package." Farber felt horrible, and said the letter was correct. "They don't care about winning arguments. They want to recruit likeminded people and the only way they can do that is to be as extreme as they can possibly sound."

But ultimately, "In my experience, the Fairness Doctrine, was almost never invoked … People were attacked right and left by my guests and we never heard from them again. And I remind you this is WOR this is not some little dinky station somewhere."[79]

Farber believes expanding universe of talk radio, made possible by ditching the Fairness Doctrine, has definitely improved the dial.

"More people with more knowledge are coming on," Farber said.[80]

Covering a quarter of WOR's airtime was enough exposure to give him political aspirations.

He exited radio in 1977 to run for mayor of New York City. He initially sought the Republican nomination, but before the primary, the Conservative Party nominated him, putting him in company with William F. Buckley, the Conservative Party candidate for New York mayor in 1965. The difference is that Buckley famously said the first thing he do if he won was demand a recount. Farber had a strategy for winning.

"There was a real scenario for victory," Farber said. "Let me explain. We could see in the year 1977 that conservatism was rising. Reagan was elected three years later. Our strategy was to pull an insurgency on the very liberal New York City Republican establishment, run against the Republican establishment candidate. Try to get that nomination. Then hope that the Democrats did what they always do and did up until that year. They always, in their primary, had 15 percent of the eligible voters voting and they always voted with the leftmost candidate."

"If that had taken place, then [former U.S. Representative] Bella Abzug would have been the Democratic candidate," Farber continued. "If both parts of the plan had worked-actually neither worked, I got 42 percent for the Republican nomination for mayor—but if I had gotten the Republican nomination and Bella Abzug had been the Democrat, I'd have won. I had the Conservative Party line too. If I had the Conservative and Republican and Bella were the Democrat, that was a real scenario. It was a long shot, but every Sunday long shots are thrown, they call them hail marries and some are caught."[81]

State Senator Roy Goodman won the Republican primary, but Farber did win more than four out of 10 Republican voters over, which was better than expected. The race was tight in most boroughs, but Goodman trounced Farber in Manhattan. Farber continued his fight into November carrying the Conservative banner.[82] Farber opposed racial quotas, gay rights laws and supported stricter laws for school truancy. Farber, by the way did not give an advantage to Democratic nominee Ed Koch, by dividing the Republican ticket. Koch was fending off Liberal Party mayoral nominee Mario Cuomo. Polls eventually showed it was essentially a race between Koch and Cuomo. On Election Day, Koch won the four-man race with 49 percent of the vote. Farber and Goodman got only about 5 percent each.

After losing that campaign to Koch, Farber returned to radio— this time at WMCA for a much improved afternoon drive time show for the next 10 years. That ended when the new owner of WMCA decided to turn it into an all-Christian programming station and fired Farber along with other hosts.[83]

A significant enough a voice on the right, he penned an op-ed in *The New York Times* rallying to the defense of President Reagan by 1987, then embattled by the Iran Contra scandal.

"Harry S. Truman probably could not have identified the six republics that make up Yugoslavia, but his decision to jump to the aid of Marshal Tito accelerated the fragmentation of the Soviet bloc," Farber wrote in the *Times*. "The notion of a President helping a Communist in 1948 makes the sale of arms to Iran today seem like an embassy party cookie push."[84]

"I happen to value Ronald Regan's Kennedy-like ability to inspire, his Ike-like ability to be the genial daddy of the mall, his Trumanesque toughness to tyrants in all words and some deeds, his Nixon-like willingness to try bold foreign policy initiatives and his Rooseveltian knack of remaining popular through it all," Farber wrote. "Call me wrong, even doltish, but I feel a new pride in this country, a new respect for this country, a new hesitancy in Moscow to commit aggression, a welcome paralysis among Moscow's client states to pursue subversion, and economic optimism to match a rising Dow."[85]

Later that same year, the prestigious weekly Soviet newspaper

*Literaturnaya Gazeta* published Farber's denunciation of Soviet communism, and Soviet crimes unedited, but with a response from the newspaper's political editor Alexander Sabov.

The Soviet paper put a preface on the Farber op-ed, warning readers:

> "Our correspondent in the USA has dictated to our editorial office alongside the article of Barry Farber the following note: 'On your request, I am sending to you the article of the zealous advocate of the Truman Doctrine. The author is a well-known publicist of ultraconservative outlooks. On New York radio an announcement on the unprecedented proposal for an adversary of the Soviet Union to write in *Literaturnaya Gazetta* was transmitted. If now the publication does not take place or is printed abridged a scandal would be fanned in the local press (in New York).' We print a word-for-word translation of B. Farber's article not because we fear scandal, of course. It was in the essence of our editorial intention to give our readers a chance to get acquainted in the original with the stereotypes of anti-Sovietism and a concrete proof of the old way of thinking, which is clearly outdated in our time."[86]

Farber wrote that despite U.S. efforts to contain the spread of communism "it is less safe there (in Western Europe) than in 1947 because of the all-powerful Soviet military." He wrote that Soviet control of Eastern Europe and installing Communist dictators in Angola, Mozambique, Ethiopia, Cuba and Nicaragua ended the goodwill the two nations had during World War II. "We loved the Soviet Union when it was our partner in the fight against Hitler. It would be good to love you again," Farber wrote. He added that reforms proposed by Soviet leader Mikhail S. Gorbachev's reform efforts, "gave us, too, a ray of hope and a little warmth in our hearts."[87]

Farber admitted to being impressed the Soviet paper did not censor him.

"I listed every Soviet crime I could fit in. The Berlin blockade, the repression of the Hungarian revolt, the invasion of Czechoslovakia, the downing of KAL flight 007, the refusal to let Jews and others leave the Soviet Union, the invasion of Afghanistan, the takeover of the Baltic states. I called the role of all the Soviet crimes," he said. "I didn't think they would actually print it. Actually, their preface to my article was rather mild. … I am flattered, encouraged and impressed. But I will be more impressed when a Soviet writer can write the *Literary Gazette* and get it printed then get a call from a Politburo member saying 'Your politics are all wet but let me buy you a beer.'"[88]

Farber was on the forefront of ABC Radio's effort in the early 1990s to create a national stable of talkers called Talknet. After that fell apart, Farber joined Michael Castello and Alan Colmes to help form a new network called Daynet. For a while, he co-hosted a debate show with Colmes, pre-Hannity, called "Left to Right." *Talkers Magazine* called Daynet "one of the forerunners of today's independent talk syndication scene." He continues to do a weekend program on Talk Radio Network.[89]

Farber, a household name to New York radio listeners for decades, didn't actually reach a national audience until 1990.[90] But then he was initially heard outside of New York on his one-hour weekend show carried by the Talk Radio Network, and he filled in for other weekday hosts.[91]

### Marlin Maddoux's 'Point of View'

Marlin Maddoux recalled that he grew tired of pounding his fist on the dashboard when he heard things on the radio that were entirely lopsided, even mocking conservative views, particularly on moral issues.

"I got really concerned, this was back in the early 1970s, over what I had seen going on in the country—quite honestly, the burn America down, the war protesters, the flower children, free love, free sex, drugs, the whole bit," Maddoux told the Dallas Morning News in 1994. "I decided either I would shut up or do something about it,"[92]

He started a 30-minute program "Point of View," in 1972 in Dallas. It eventually gained national syndication and commercial success and expanded to two hours. Popular topics were homeschooling, abortion and gay marriage, always expressing the conservative or Biblical view on the matters.[93] The program would eventually run for two hours on 360 stations with 2 million listeners.[94] [95]

"If there is no outrage from the Christian community, who's going to speak out? The idea that if you disagree with something you're being intolerant has basically silenced the voice of righteous outrage in this country," Maddoux once said.

"I know that I'll be accused of saying, Hey, I'm right, and you're wrong," he said. "But again, I have to be judged on my world view, and my world view is Christian."[96]

Maddoux essentially invented Christian news talk radio, at least the commercially viable kind.

"From that standpoint forward, you would see that Marlin had a tremendous impact, I mean just endless radio stations that had the courage to carry Point of View," said economist, longtime religious broadcaster and Maddoux friend Larry Bates in an interview for this book. "Marlin was a real pioneer in talk radio even before Rush Limbaugh as far as conservative talk. Of course it was from a Christian bent. ... Everybody else is a Johnny Come-Lately, including myself."

Before Christian conservatives became a cohesive force in politics in the late 1970s, early 1980s, Maddoux was on the radio talking about morality in public affairs.

"Ever since we had 501(c)3 organizations, you would have a lot of people in churches that would be afraid to give voice or opinions on public policy and I think what Marlin did is he helped people in the church understand that just because you're a Christian, you don't check your brains at the door," said Bates, who founded the Memphis-based Information Radio Network. "He stressed the point that Christians are to be salt and light. What is salt? Salt's a disinfectant and a preservative. In order to be effective on the culture, it's got to be right in the midst of the culture. That's what he taught people to do."

Perhaps the best example of this, Bates said, was bringing the pro-life movement into focus.

"Marlin Maddoux was fearless. As long as he was getting the truth out, he didn't whose feathers he ruffled. That's what I admired about him," Bates said.

"He probably had more influence on the abortion debate. He had probably the clearest message of pro-life initially after the Roe v. Wade situation and a lot of states were debating the issue. I would say he had probably more influence for the pro-life community than any single person."

How did he survive during the time of the Fairness Doctrine? "He was flying under the radar for a long time before people really knew what kind of impact he was having," Bates said.

As "Point of View" grew in popularity, Maddoux founded his own network in 1985, the USA Radio Network, to carry POV as well as other Christian programming, many shows with a political edge. It also established a full-fledged news organization.

In July 1988, after the trial of central Iran Contra figure Oliver North had been scheduled to occur in the midst of an election year, Maddoux had largest daytime radio talk show audience in the United States and sought to interview North. He didn't get the interview, but he did get exclusive rights to record a speech North delivered at a fundraiser for his own legal defense fund.

Maddoux said that North's lawyers said "the give and take [of an interview] would not be advisable," and instead let him tape the 30-minute speech, which Maddoux played it in its entirety yesterday on the 240 radio stations.[97]

The show had a steady growing audience but as rising tides lift all boats, in the 1990s, Maddoux saw a big residual effect from secular conservative shows.

"I think Rush Limbaugh has revolutionized radio. He has brought talk radio to the forefront and has been good for my program, and for others all across America," Maddoux said in 1994. "The major press in this country is liberal, and liberalism does not express the views of the vast majority of American people. So, when someone comes on the radio and begins to say things from a conservative viewpoint, people become excited, saying, At last, somebody is saying what I believe."[98]

Maddoux teamed up with Texas Representative Dick Armey, and a home schooling parent from New Jersey to mount a campaign against a bill in Congress in 1993 to force home school parents to be certified by the state education system. It seemed an odd regulation since it was government schools these parents hoped to keep their children away from.

"I watched our program and others amplify that single parent's call into a political sonic boom felt round the nation, and especially in Washington," Maddoux said of the defeat of the legislation that resulted in part from his sustained effort. "House members phone and fax lines were jammed; some offices reported thousands of calls in one day, and the liberals retreated, leaving the bill to die a violent death. Do I believe talk radio is affecting this nation for the better? Without a doubt."[99]

He also founded the International Christian Media and the National Center for Freedom and Renewal and also wrote several books, including, "America Betrayed," "What Worries Parents Most," "Free Speech or Propaganda?" and "A Christian Agenda: Game Plan for a New Era." In March 2004, he died at the age of 70 after complications with a heart bypass surgery.[100]

"After he passed away, we were approached by the Maddoux family and we acquired the USA Radio Network and merged it with the Information Radio Network," Bates recalled. That was in March 2008.[101]

"We both at that time had about 1,400 affilliates. Neilson, at the time of the merger, said it formed one of the largest news organizations in the country," Bates said.

Point of View still runs, hosted by Kerby Anderson.

### George Putnam: 'Greatest Voice in Radio'
George Putnam started in radio in 1934 and ended in radio with his death in 2008, with a legendary career in TV sandwiched in between. He was also the inspiration for the Ted Baxter character, the anchorman on the "Mary Tyler Moore Show." Ted Knight, who

played Ted Baxter recalled meeting Putnam at a banquet, where Putnam jokingly said, "Hey Ted, why don't you get your own act?"[102]

A Minnesota native, Putnam got his first radio job at age 20 with a Minneapolis station, WDGY. His big break came after he went to New York in the early 1940s when Walter Winchell wrote in his newspaper column that "George Putnam's voice is the greatest in radio." Putnam said after that, "Winchell made my career. I went from $190 a month at NBC to better than $200,000 a year."[103] After serving in World War II, he returned to broadcasting briefly in New York before heading west.

Putnam became a major star on Los Angeles TV in the 1950s, 1960s and 1970s—reportedly the highest paid anchor in the nation at the time. In a 2000 interview, he said he was earning $350,000 at a time when Walter Cronkite was making only $125,000.[104]

He worked for KTTV, KCOP, KTLA and KHJ (now KCAL). His transience was among the reasons he didn't get the call to work for one of the networks, a friend and collegue speculated.

"George didn't want anyone telling him what to do either," said his longtime friend and radio producer Chuck Wilder. "What messed him up is he was always looking for a better deal from each station. It's kind of a joke that they had to put the red lights down in Hollywood because George was speeding from one street to another to get to the next TV station. He was always looking to get a little bit better deal on how much money he was making, even when he was making the highest price."[105]

Wilder added that Putnam wouldn't do anything for money, and unlike many journalists today, declined to take fees for public speaking for ethical reasons.

"He used to say if he really wanted to make money and forget about all his morals, he would have gone into politics or become a religious broadcaster," Wilder recalled. "He was really playing on the fact that with the religious broadcasters, if you had a really strong voice, and if you didn't really care what you were saying, you could make a lot of money."[106]

On-air editorials became part of routine newscast. The editorial segment at the end of the newscast was called "One Reporter's

Opinion." Also, on the program "Talk Back," he would bring on guest including Nazis and anti-war activists and tell them why they were wrong.[107] While working at KCOP, he briefly co-hosted a program called, "Both Sides Now" along with comedian Mort Sahl.[108]

His trademark end to each nightly newscast was, "And that's the up-to-the-minute news, up to the minute, that's all the news. Back at 10, see you then!"[109]

Putnam was credited with reporting and editorializing that helped force the exit of a Los Angeles district attorney, helping to elect L.A. Mayor Sam Yorty, and commentary that brought about property tax saving measure Proposition 13.[110] Of course, as a TV anchor, openly taking sides was not a normal course of action, which subjected him to much criticism. He was nevertheless a decorated journalist, winning three Emmy Awards, six California Associated Press TV and Radio Association awards, and about 300 honors and citations.[111] In 1995, at a local Emmy awards ceremony, Putnam was awarded the Governors Award for career achievement. He also has a star on Hollywood Boulevard.[112]

"On television, whenever you got on there and give you opinion when giving the news, it's different. When you're doing it on a local television station, under the umbrella of today's newscast, they frowned on it," Wilder said. "That's what got him in trouble was whenever Sam Yorty was running for office in Los Angeles, he said something right at the end of the newscast, 'I'm going to tell you I support Sam Yorty for mayor of Los Angeles and if you know what's good for this city you'll go out and vote for him tomorrow.' Bam! The station was threatened and everything else from the FCC."[113]

By 1976, TV was behind him, but he was still a big name in Southern California, which led to him getting a radio program on KIEV-AM, titled "Talk Back." He remained a radio personality for the next three decades. Beginning in 2004, CRN Digital Talk Radio syndicated his program.[114]

Some of the biggest guests he had on his radio program in the early years were comic actress Lucille Ball, comedian Jonathon Winters and science fiction author Ray Bradbury, Wilder recalled. Politics were never the top priority of the show, Wilder said, but

Putnam talked about a political issue if it was the most important matter he felt was in the news.

Putnam frequentlycommented on conservative social issues, opposed to illegal immigration and was opposed to gay marriage, and was known for putting real enthusiasm behind describing a story, saying things like, "amaaaaaazing," when a juicy detail popped up in a story, or a major story broke.

Still, he did not think he could be easily pigeon-holed as a conservative. "I detest labels," Putnam once told *The Los Angeles Times*. "I've been called many things in my career: right-wing extremist, super-patriot, goose-stepping nationalist, jingoistic SOB. And those are some of the nice things! But those people have never bothered to determine my background: Farmer-Labor Party, Socialist Party, lifelong member of the NAACP, member of the Urban League. I went through the Depression, and my father was reduced to selling peanuts door-to-door. Then, because of that, I fell in love with Franklin D. Roosevelt. I've been a lifelong Democrat. I'm a conservative Democrat."

In 1984, KTTV held a roast for Putnam as part of its 35th anniversary on the air, and Putnam's 50 years in broadcasting. During that roast, former President Richard Nixon delivered a videotaped message. "He won the admiration and respect of millions of people in Southern California due to the fact that everybody could count on him to say exactly what he believed, whether it was popular or not. Some people didn't like what he said; some people liked what he said. But everybody listened to George Putnam. That is why he has been one of the most influential commentators of our times."[116]

Putnam also made cameo appearances as an anchorman in several motion pictures, including, the 1996 film "Independence Day," and the 1958 film "I Want to Live."[348]

He died at the age of 94, having continued his broadcasting career to almost the very end, only taking the last few months before his death off the air because of failing health. His friend and producer Chuck Wilder took over the show "Talkback" which is still on the air in California and is heard nationally.

### Dr. Dobson: Changing America's Focus

Dr. James Dobson has been so much more than a broadcaster and his broadcasts have been more than an essential aspect of the conservative movement. Some evangelical leaders such as the Reverends Jerry Falwell and Pat Robertson have—fairly or not—been accused of pushing the Republican Party line. It is tougher to make that charge against Dobson, who had the ear of the GOP but could be annoyingly independent to those in power. A radio show that began in 1978 went on to gain 200 million listeners worldwide in 27 languages in 160 countries.[117]

During the late 1960s, he was speaking to churches and teacher conference decrying the lack of discipline in schools and homes.

Dobson, the son of a Nazarene preacher, was a child psychologist at the University of Southern California School of Medicine when he wrote "Dare to Discipline," a book that became popular for advocating tough love such as spanking in 1970 when the dominant view was moving against traditional discipline. After gaining national prominence and writing two more books, Dobson in 1977 started a non-profit group called Focus on the Family "to address the breakdown of the traditional family." It was headquartered in Arcadia, California. A year after the organization started, the radio program began.[118] The Focus on the Family 30-minute radio broadcast began, addressing a mix of Christian living advice, Bible scholarship, family advice and politics. He maintained ties with USC until 1983 as an associate clinical professor of pediatrics.[119]

At a time when evangelical loyalties were up for grabs—the Reverend Pat Robertson endorsed Jimmy Carter for president in 1976—Dobson was appointed to a roundtable on family life by the Democratic president from Georgia in 1980. It might have been one of the more popular things Carter did, as the White House got 80,000 letters of support for the Dobson appointment. He held advisory roles during administrations of Ronald Reagan and George H.W. Bush.[120] Dobson served on the Justice Department's commission on pornography during the Reagan administration, as well as other advisory boards.[121]

By 1987, the organization demonstrated a greater commitment

to public affairs by starting Citizen, a magazine on social and political issues. The next year—in the midst of a presidential campaign, the one-to-five-minute "Family News in Focus" began airing on commercial radio stations. This was the first attempt to reach a secular audience, as the regular "Focus on the Family" show aired only on Christian stations.[122]

In one of Dobson's more famous moments, he interviewed serial killer Ted Bundy on death row. Bundy had claimed to have had a religious conversion before his execution. He told Dobson that pornography influenced his murderous life.[123] Focus marketed a videotape of the interview, with the proceeds going to anti-porn groups.[124]

As the organization grew, costs increased in the expensive southern California area. So Focus relocated in 1991 to Colorado Springs, Colorado. The organization was welcomed by local government economic development officials seeking jobs for the area and a $4 million grant from the El Pomar Foundation.[125]

In 1992, during another presidential year, Dobson got a syndicated question and answer newspaper column.[126]

As the organization and Dobson gained even more influence, several Republican presidential candidates visited the Colorado headquarters in 1996, such as Pat Buchanan, Lamar Alexander, Alan Keyes and Phil Gramm.[127] "I will not be making statements as we get closer to the election," Dobson told reporters that year, but he said Republicans cannot shy away from moral issues "as if the only thing Americans care about is money," adding, "The first politician who articulates that [moral] concern is going to have more support than he knows what to do with."[128]

During 1998, Dobson caused a stir when he threatened to lead an exodus from the Republican Party, which he asserted was not living up to its promises to social conservatives. The February 7 speech given to a gathering of 450 conservative and religious leaders denounced even conservatives such as Senator Jesse Helms, a North Carolina Republican and chairman of the Foreign Relations Committee, for not stopping foreign aid subsidies to family planning. He also criticized social conservative Senator Rick Santorum of Pennsylvania for supporting New Jersey's liberal Republican

Governor Christine Todd Whitman's 1997 reelection campaign. The speech landed him on the cover of *U.S. News & World Report*, and interviews on Larry King Live and Meet the Press.[129]

In October 1998, Focus sounded the alarm over comments made on Katie Couric on NBC's Today show after the brutal murder of Matthew Shepard, a 21-year-old gay man and University of Wyoming student beaten to death outside a bar. Couric and NBC reporter Geoffrey Dickens linked several conservative Christian groups by name to the murder, even though there was no evidence Shepard's murder was motivated by religion. "Some gay-rights activists have said that some conservative Christian political organizations, like the Christian Coalition, the Family Research Council and Focus on the Family are contributing to this anti-homosexual atmosphere by having an ad campaign saying: If you're a homosexual, you can change your orientation. That prompts people to say: If I meet someone who's homosexual, I'm going to take action and try to convince them or try to harm them. Do you believe that such groups are contributing to this climate?"[130]

Couric was talking about a full-page newspaper ad that ran in newspapers across the country that July sponsored by 15 Christian organizations, including Focus on the Family. The ads said, "We're standing for the truth that homosexuals can change." During his broadcast, Dobson demanded an apology. "That Couric would repeat such a ridiculous accusation on a national TV show only serves to perpetuate twisted stereotypes of Christian people. Ms. Couric was highly irresponsible and potentially libelous." NBC got so many calls, letters and e-mails demanding an apology, that they contacted Focus and asked them to desist talking about the matter. Neither side backed down and the matter eventually faded.[131]

During the chorus of conservative radio hosts opposed to the President Bush's nomination of Harriet Miers to serve on the U.S. Supreme Court, Dobson supported her. He came under fire, as did the Bush White House, after he announced on the October 5, 2005 Focus radio program that he spoke to Bush political advisor Karl Rove about the nomination. Democratic senators such as Pat Leahy of Vermont and Ken Salazar of Colorado as well as a few liberal interest groups such as American United for the Separation of Church and State demanded records of the communications.

"The issue is whether the White House is giving information to Dr. Dobson that it's not giving to senators and the American public," said Salazar spokesman Cody Wertz said at the time.[132]

Recalling the Rove conversation to his listeners, Dobson said that "Harriet Miers was at the top of the short list," and that "What Karl told me is that some of those individuals took themselves off that list. They would not allow their names to be considered because the process has become so vicious and so vitriolic and so bitter that they didn't want to subject themselves or the members of their families to it."[133]

That wasn't the last Supreme Court "scandal" tied to Dobson. Again, it was largely irrelevant. After the Miers nomination died, and Samuel Alito was nominated to fill the seat vacated by retiring Sandra Day O'Connor. Dobson endorsed the nomination as well. One of the many "thank you" notes Alito wrote was to Dobson after the confirmation. On his program, Dobson read that the letter said, "the prayers of so many people from around the country were a palpable and powerful force. As long as I serve on the Supreme Court, I will keep in mind the trust that has been placed in me." A Supreme Court spokeswoman said Alito's note responded to a Dobson letter the new justice and the pledge to "keep in mind the trust that has been placed in me" was included in numerous replies to congratulatory letters.[134]

In 2008, the Focus on the Family program was inducted into the National Radio Hall of Fame, which said, "The show's host, Dr. James Dobson, is perhaps the most influential conservative Christian leader in the country."[135]

Dobson stepped down as chairman of Focus on the Family in February 2009 at the age of 72, though he continued doing the radio show for a time. One year later, after 33 years on the air, he signed off from the radio, but Focus on the Family has continued.

### Libertarian Chatter with Neal Boortz
Still a fixture in Atlanta radio, though he does many of his

broadcasts out of Naples, Florida, Neal Boortz has probably the only full-fledged libertarian on the air, registered with the Libertarian Party. He even said that once he retires from radio—should that ever happen—he might run for president under the Libertarian Party banner "just for the hell of it." He would pick the most capable vice presidential candidate he can find, should he accidently win, but would "hang around long enough to sign an executive order requiring all airport screeners to have graduated in the top one-half of their high school class," and "free all non-violent drug offenders and take a few spins in Air Force One."[136]

Like other talk show hosts, much of his popularity stems from a brutal pull-no-punches honesty, along with biting humor. But his humor is of a uniquely dry and cynical, and nevertheless contagious. Two of his guests hosts have been Newt Gingrich and Herman Cain, both who sought the Republican presidential nomination in 2012. Boortz helped propel the Fair Tax—essentially a national sales tax to replace the income tax—onto the national agenda that became the centerpiece of Mike Huckabee's 2008 presidential campaign. Further, it was Boortz move to a bigger station that provided the vacancy for Sean Hannity to be propelled into a major market.

Boortz has identified his nine pet peeves over the years. They are 1.Children in first class on airline flights—or children in bars. 2. Hyphenated Americans. 3.Dealer stickers on the back of cars. 4.Minivans in the fast lane. 5.Fat men in tank tops. 6.Fat people on scooters. 7.People who smoke in their car with children. 8.Restaurants that automatically include the gratuity on the bill. 9.Customer cards at grocery stores.[137]

Before he was heard across the country on 230 stations with 5 million listeners, Boortz lived across much of the country, growing up learning the country well as a Marine brat.[138] He was born in Bryn Mawr, Pennsylvania in 1945 and lived in Honolulu, Hawaii; Laguna Beach, California; Morehead City, North Carolina; Virginia Beach, Virginia and Pensacola, Florida.[139]

In college, he became an on-air personality with the campus radio station WTAW-AM at Texas A&M. His on-air name was Randy Neal.[140] Then after graduating in 1967, he moved to Atlanta.

He became frequent caller to the program hosted by Herb Elfman for the morning drive. When Elfman died, Boortz got a two-week trial run before taking over the spot in 1969.[141]

In a self-written bio posted on his Web site, written in the third person, he recalls that those first years of radio were not that lucrative, so he supplemented his income by at different times working at a jewelry store, selling life and casualty insurance, loading trucks, working for the U.S. Postal Service, working in an employment office and even writing speeches for Georgia Governor Lester Maddox.[142] He said he was 47 before he ever had one job, and at his peak he had six.[143] In 1973, he enrolled in John Marshall Law School, and after graduating in 1977 practiced law and kept his radio program.

The status as an attorney provided extra credibility as he called for eliminating the war on drugs, lowering taxes, ending welfare, and distrust of organized religion, once saying he'd rather live under a communist dictatorship than a Baptist one because, "Baptists claim a divine right and communists don't, so they'd be easier to overthrow."[144] So he is very much an equal opportunity offender.

However, he is not entirely a libertarian in the Ron Paul mold. He has been a staunch supporter of America's war on terror, and advocated going into Iraq, defending preemptive war. He also opposes unrestricted immigration even though open borders is a policy of the Libertarian Party.[145]

He debated the Iraq war during the 2008 campaign with Libertarian Party Presidential nominee Bob Barr, a former Georgia Republican congressman, saying, "I would call them a liberating force, and I have a problem with someone who refers to these men and women in our armed forces as an occupying force in a foreign country."

Barr argued. "Neal, they've been there five years now. When do you cross the line from basically protecting a domestic regime over there, propping it so that we provide the security blanket in terms of their economic system, their political system and their security system—I don't think it's an insult to the troops. I don't think it's an insult to the troops. It's a fact. We're occupying the country. We're basically providing the mechanism whereby the country runs itself."

To which Boortz replied, "Look, there is no time limit on trying to liberate a nation."

Barr said, "That's what McCain says, too, I guess....There's no despot or dictator over there. What are we liberating them from?"

Boortz retorted, "Bob, an occupying army does not train the locals to replace them. A liberating army does. An occupying army does not."[146]

As a local host some of the blunt comments included, "A woman with a cigarette in her mouth looks like a whore," and "Uninformed buttheads should not be allowed to vote."[147] He also referred to homeless people as "urban outdoorsmen."[148]

The son of a Marine pilot, Boortz was a recreational pilot, and talked about flying frequently on his show. It helped convince his listeners he would go through with a prank in 1988 when he said he would drop a live cat from an airplane at 12,000 feet, then parachute after it and catch it before it hit the ground. The stations phone lines were flooded with angry cat lovers. The American Humane Society filed a complaint with the Federal Aviation Administration, while almost as many drove around town hoping to see the stunt that Boortz had no intention of going through with. "That's what I wanted," he said. "To absolutely nail these [cat lovers] to the wall."[149]

When liberal TV talk show host Phil Donohue had several talk show hosts on his program, he asserted "there is a little bit of superficiality," in talk radio compared to talk TV, which is more substantive. Boortz shot back, "We're superficial? I have never once in 25 years ever done a talk radio show on blind transvestite lesbians having an affair with their plumber's wives. We're superficial? Hey Phil, I've never dressed up as a woman to do a radio show. I'm superficial?"[150]

In 1992, he left his longtime job with WGST and took a job with 750 WSB, a bigger station in Atlanta.

WGST sued Boortz, asserting his contract allows them the opportunity to match the pay from a competitor.[151] He was also not allowed to compete with WGST for another six months, which meant he was off the air long enough to allow his replacement, an upstart Sean Hannity, gain an audience.

The 1990s were fat years for talk radio, enough to make big stars of both men. In 1999, Boortz beat Hannity into national syndication, made available throughout the country by Cox media, the owner of WSB.[152]

"That's the big question," Boortz said about going national, "Next year, I have been doing this nonsense 30 years in Atlanta. These people (in Atlanta) are used to me. I can commit all sorts of high crimes and misdemeanors, and they say 'that's just Boortz.' But in Duluth, stations might want to take out an insurance policy."[153]

He parlayed the national exposure on radio, along with appearances on Fox News, CNN and MSNBC, into becoming a best-selling author. He co-authored two books, "The Fair Tax Book" in 2006, and "Fair Tax: The Truth" in 2008. He was the solo author of "The Terrible Truth About Liberals" in 2001 that went through six different printing, "Somebody's Gotta Say It" in 2008 which debut at number two on *The New York Times* best seller list. He also wrote, "The Commencement Speech You Need to Hear," in 1997.

He won the Newstalk Personality of the Year award from Radio and Records Magazine in 2002. He was nominated for a Marconi Award, the top honor for a radio host from the National Association of Broadcasters that same year, but the award went to Hanniy, who went into national syndication the previous year.

In late June 2005, a mental patient from Texas called into Boortz show and confessed to the 1994 murder of a store clerk. He only talked to the executive producer Belinda Skelton, so the call was not aired. "I get crazy people all the time, but this guy started rattling off all the details," said Skelton. The show's producers called the police, who arrested the man. Police brought murder charges against Cheo Kasimu Ash after matching his statement with evidence from the crime scene.[154]

After the April 16, 2007 Virginia Tech University shooting that left 32 dead, Boortz questioned why students did not do more to stop shooter Seung-Hui Cho. "How in the hell do you line students up against a wall (if that's the way it played out) and start picking them off one by one without the students turning on you? You have a choice. Try to rush the killer and get his gun, or stand there and wait to be shot," Boortz says in the April 17 program notes on his Web site. This prompted Democrats from the Virginia House of Delegates to write letters to stations across the commonwealth that carried the Boortz show. "Mr. Boortz's hateful comments should have no place in this Commonwealth, particularly at this trying time," said the letter that Democratic Delegates Jim Shuler, Steve Shannon and Chuck Caputo sent to the eight Virginia stations that carry Boortz.[155]

After a decade in national syndication, Boortz was inducted into the National Radio Hall of Fame in Chicago. Rush Limbaugh made the announcement.[156]

"People outside our industry have no idea how big a deal this is," Boortz said of the honor in 2009. "It's bigger than an Academy Award would be for an actor. Instead of honoring one piece of work, it honors a lifetime. ... I was almost in tears. What could be better than to be in the Hall of Fame?"[157]

## CHAPTER FIVE

# Challenge and Harass

Dan Smoot and the Rev. Carl McIntire certainly saw firsthand how full weight of the federal government can quash a talk show host's message to the public, as it was pressure brought about by the Fairness Doctrine that knocked them off the air. Ultimately it would be the Billy James Hargis's program that would be in the eye of the storm on the constitutionality of the FCC rule.

Did the Fairness Doctrine violate the First Amendment?

The answer is more complicated than it might seem.

Was the Fairness Doctrine government censorship?

That's not complicated. It absolutely was government censorship.

The reason there is no contradiction to those two answers is because the airwaves belong to the public, as established law going back to 1927. A station owner owns the station but he or she does not own the frequency. As touched on in a previous chapter, that is because when radio was new, programming frequencies began to bump into other program. A broadcast license gives a station the right to broadcast on a particular frequency, with licenses doled out by the Federal Communications Commission (formerly the Federal Radio Commission). Since there are a limited number of frequencies—thus licenses—the FCC expects some responsibility on the part of the licensee. The same is true of TV.

Cable TV and satellite radio are not subject to FCC oversight because these stations are not part of the public airwaves.

So, from a First Amendment standpoint, anyone with the resources to do so can start a newspaper, magazine, cable TV or satellite radio station and print or broadcast whatever they want under the Constitution. Not everyone can get a frequency to broadcast on the public airwaves because there is not an infinite number of frequencies, or so the argument goes. Despite that supposed scarcity, there has been a proliferation of stations. When the Fairness Doctrine was adopted in 1949, there were 2,881 radio stations. By 1960, there were 4,309 radio stations. By 2008 there were 4,776 AM stations and 6,309 FM stations and another 2,892 educational FM stations.[1]

President Calvin Coolidge signed the Radio Act of 1927 establishing the Federal Radio Commission, which became the Federal Communications Commission after FDR signed the 1934 Communications Act. When both bills were debated, Congress considered a fairness provision, but that never made it into the final legislation.[2]

In 1949, the FCC established fairness rules in the backdrop of a pending case before the commission of George A. Richards, owner of WJR in Detroit, WGAR in Cleveland, and KMPC in Los Angeles. These stations flagrantly crusaded for Republican political candidates. The report essentially required licensees operate in the public interest and "devote a reasonable amount of time to the coverage of controversial issues of public importance." Further, the report called for licensees "to do so fairly by affording a reasonable opportunity for contrasting viewpoints to be voiced on these issues."[3]

It sounds innocent enough—a responsibility on the public's airwaves to provide public service broadcasting and present all sides when doing so. A mechanism was in place for the public to make a complaint if it felt radio or TV was unfair in its coverage of a controversial event. The FCC staff would investigate the complaint and present its findings to the Commission which would make a ruling. This could involve ordering a broadcaster to give equal time to the complainant all the way to revocation of license, as well see. Jim McKinney, a former head of the FCC's Mass Media Bureau recalled to *National Review* how the investigation process worked. The FCC staff would "pull out a stopwatch," said McKinney, who worked for the FCC in the 1960s. "They would get out the tapes, and they would start timing how many minutes and seconds a broadcaster had devoted to the issue of public importance. And then, depending on how that came out, they would either close the investigation, or they would prepare an item for the commission to take an enforcement action."[4]

It was not enough to grant airtime to those who requested response time. To be in full compliance with federal regulations, the station had the affirmative duty to determine what the appropriate opposing viewpoints were on the controversial issue and who was best suited to present it. If that person could not be sponsored, then the station was required to provide the broadcast time at its own expense. The personal attack rule—providing free response to anyone personally attacked on the airwaves, and the equal time rule, exclusively for political candidates, were also adopted by the Commission.[5]

Congress, in 1959, gave a stamp of approval to the FCC fairness rules—but left an unclear picture as to whether it had codified the rules as law or simply approved the Commission's enforcement of them, in its amendment to Section 315 of the Communications Act of 1934.

Section 315 imposes requirements on broadcasters to grant equal broadcasting time to political candidates. With respect to the Fairness Doctrine, the amendment said, "Nothing in the foregoing sentence [creating exemptions from the equal time requirements] shall be construed as relieving broadcasters, in connection with the presentation of newscasts, news interviews, news documentaries, and on-the-spot, from the obligation imposed upon them under this chapter to operate in the public interest and to afford reasonable opportunity for the discussion of conflicting views on issues of public importance." In its report on the amendment, the House explained that this provision "is a restatement of the basic policy of the 'standard of fairness' which is imposed on broadcasters under the Communications Act of 1934." Debate erupted in the coming decades on whether the vague language codified the Fairness Doctrine as law, or just stated Congress's intent to avoid interference with the FCC's enforcement of the Fairness Doctrine. Despite all the overarching matters of whether the doctrine violated the First Amendment and regarding the scarcity matter, it would be the narrow issue of whether it was a law or a rule that would determine its continued existence.[6]

The rule was presumably implemented with the best of intentions, even though today one might easily see how politicians would use the rule as a blunt weapon to silence political enemies. That is what happened. The story of how the Nixon administration tried to bully TV stations over their broadcast licenses has been told and retold. What is less talked about was the organized strategy by the Democratic National Committee (DNC), with the approval of President Lyndon B. Johnson that eventually led to the U.S. Supreme Court ruling on the fairness regulation. What would have been a major scandal had it been discovered, was revealed in former CBS News president Fred Friendly's book "The Good Guys, the Bad Guys and the First Amendment."

The story of how Democrats used Nixonian tactics before Nixon was ever elected president began in the fall of 1963 when President John F. Kennedy wanted to get the Nuclear Test Ban Treaty with the Soviet Union approved by the U.S. Senate. The treaty had bipartisan support and bipartisan opposition, thus was expected to be a close vote. A big concern was criticism of the treaty by the Revs. McIntire and Hargis.[7]

Kenneth O'Donnell, the appointment secretary for President Kennedy sought the advice of former *New York Times* reporter Wayne Phillips on forcing stations to provide equal time. A behind the scenes effort prompted the front group Citizens Committee for a Nuclear Test Ban Treaty, which targeted talk radio. The Rudder & Finn public relations firm, which coincidently is the same PR firm

122

the DNC used, did publicity for the committee. Each time McIntire or Hargis took a swing at the treaty, the committee sent letters to the stations that carried their programs. States where these show aired that had senators on the fence were specifically targeted. A special program was taped specifically for responding in each of those stations. When the Senate ratified the treaty by a surprising 80-19 vote on September 24, 1963, the administration saw how the Fairness Doctrine can be used for high priority legislation.[8]

In January 1964, after Johnson had taken office, Phillips began monitoring conservative radio. "It soon became apparent to me that the extreme right-wing broadcasting was exceptionally heavy on particular stations and in particular areas of the country, and that the content of these broadcasts was irrationally hostile to the president and his programs." Phillips eventually came on board in a more formal role as the Director of News and Information for the DNC. He hired Wesley McCune, head of Group Research Inc., which did research for the DNC, to help him with full time listening duties. The DNC prepared a kit that it delivered to voters and activist explaining, "how to demand time under the Fairness Doctrine." Phillips also brought Fred J. Cook, a friend from his journalism days, into the fold to write a piece for *The Nation* magazine lashing out against conservative talk radio. Cook had just finished a book "Barry Goldwater: Extremist on the Right."[9]

The talk radio piece in *The Nation* ran in the May 25, 1964 issue with the headline, "Hate Clubs of the Air." It said, "The hate clubs of the air are spewing out a minimum of 6,600 broadcasts a week, carried by more than 1,300 radio and television stations—nearly one out of every five in the nation in a blitz that saturates everyone one of the fifty states with the exception of Maine."[10]

According to Friendly's book, "Because of the close association of James Row with President Johnson and also because of John Bailey's standing as chairman of the Democratic National Committee, there is little doubt that this contrived scheme had White House approval."

Bill Ruder, an Assistant Secretary of Commerce in the Johnson administration recalled, "Our massive strategy was to use the

Fairness Doctrine to challenge and harass right-wing broadcasters and hope that the challenge would be so costly to them that they would be inhibited and decide it was too expensive to continue."[11]

The DNC mailed out thousands of copies of Cook's Nation article to Democratic state and local parties and Democratic officials. The DNC also mailed the article to radio stations, with a letter from DNC counsel Dan Brightman warning that if Democrats are attacked, demands will be made for equal time. When McIntire criticized Brightman for sending the letter, the DNC demanded and got free airtime to respond on about 600 stations. Then, when Dan Smoot assailed LBJ during the Democratic National Convention, the DNC got free airtime to respond on 30 stations, though others declined.[12]

Democrats believed their strategy was successful and decided to accelerate things, setting up another front group called the National Council for Civic Responsibility that took out full page newspaper ads that said, "$10 million is spent on weekly radio and television broadcasts in all 50 states by extremists groups." Picked to head the group was Arthur Larson, a liberal Republican who had served in the Eisenhower administration. Larson insisted at the National Press Club, "The council's formation had nothing to do with the presidential campaign or with the right-wing views of Republican candidate Senator Barry Goldwater." Though, he later came clean that leading the organization was not his proudest moment. "The whole thing was not my idea, but let's face it, we decided to use the Fairness Doctrine to harass the extreme right. In light of Watergate it was wrong. We felt the ends justified the means. They never do." He also added, "As soon as I found out the Democrats were putting money into it, I wanted out."[13]

The Democrats produced their own show called "Spotlight," prepared segments ready to run as response in free airtime. These spots ran on 60 stations and were hosted by an actor employed by Rudder & Finn whose on-air name was William Dennis.[14]

Johnson scored a massive landslide, carrying all but six states. Dirty tricks by the Democrats had no more to do with his ability to beat Goldwater than Watergate had with Nixon's ability to trounce

George McGovern eight years later. Nevertheless, political operatives felt compelled to resort to nefarious deeds to ensure a wipeout on Election Day.

The end result was that stations gave Democrats 1,678 free hours of response time resulting from 1,035 letters of complaints, mostly to programs of Clarence Manion, Dan Smoot and Carl McIntire. A proud Phillips wrote, "Even more important than the free radio time was the effectiveness of this operation in inhibiting the political activity of these right-wing broadcasts." Martin E. Firestone, a former FCC attorney who was brought into the DNC fold as a consultant in the operation, said it should not end with the campaign. "The right-wingers operate on a strictly cash basis and it is for this reason that they are carried by so many small stations. Were our efforts to be continued on a year-round basis, we would find that many of these stations would consider these programs bothersome and burdensome (especially if they are ultimately required to give us free time) and would start dropping the programs from their broadcast schedules."[15]

The political effort was a prelude to the Red Lion case that would be decided by the U.S. Supreme Court.

Conservative hosts were not happy with the tenor of the Johnson campaign, and a few weeks after the election, on November 27, one of those hosts—Hargis—used 2 minutes of his 15-minute "Christian Crusade" program to go after Fred J. Cook for his book.

"Now, this paperback book by Fred J. Cook is entitled, 'Barry Goldwater: Extremist on the Right.' Who is Cook? Cook was fired from the New York World Telegram after he made a false charge publicly on television against an un-named official of the New York City government," Hargis said. "New York publishers and *Newsweek* magazine for December 7, 1959, showed that Fred Cook and his pal, Eugene Gleason, had made up the whole story and this confession was made to New York District Attorney, Frank Hogan. After losing his job, Cook went to work for the left-wing publication The Nation, one of the most scurrilous publications of the left which has championed many communist causes over many years. Its editor, Carry McWilliams, has been affiliated with many communist enterprises, scores of which have been cited as subversive by the Attorney General of the U.S. or by other government agencies. Now, among other things Fred Cook wrote for *The Nation* was an article absolving Alger Hiss of any wrong doing, there was a 208 page attack on the FBI and J. Edgar Hoover; another attack by Mr. Cook was on the Central Intelligence Agency, now this is the man who wrote the book to smear and destroy Barry Goldwater called "Barry Goldwater-Extremist On the Right."[16]

Friendly reported that the DNC—not Cook—was listening to Hargis when he made these comments. The committee encouraged Cook to make a fairness complaint, according to the Friendly book, but the book reports that Cook denied any role in a DNC scheme and said he made the complaint on his own.[17]

Most of Hargis's statement was a matter of fact. Cook indeed attacked Hoover's FBI in his 1964 book, "The FBI Nobody Knows," attacked the military industrial complex in his 1962 book, "The Warfare State," and insisted that former State Department official Alger Hiss was unjustly accused of being a Soviet spy.[18] The problem came in accusing Cook of being fired for making up a false story. Such a charge is defamatory and a potential career ender for any journalist, even an opinion writer.

Of the 200 stations he sent this demand to, fewer than 50 provided free time. Those stations aired a three minute audio tape where Cook said Hargis was guilty of a "smear, innuendo, the discrediting of a man by libel." Cook also read excerpts of a letter to him from Hogan exonerating Cook of responsibility for Gleason's false accusation. "Mr. Gleason not only admitted in our office that the charge was untrue, but also completely exonerated you of all responsibility," said the letter from Hogan to Cook.[19]

WGCB in the small town of Red Lion, Pennsylvania, provided an irksome response to Cook. "Our rate card is enclosed. Your prompt reply will enable us to arrange for the time you may wish to purchase," the Rev. John M. Norris, owner of the station wrote back. Norris offered to let Cook pay the same rate as Hargis, $7.50 per quarter of an hour.[20]

Cook was irate at the suggestion he pay for his response, even though that's what most stations told him. He wrote back, "I submit that the least of your obligation in this matter is to grant me free time for a brief reply. Otherwise, it is conceivable that radio stations might be able to drum up a fairly good business by selling time to persons who have been slandered." Norris shrugged, with another letter, "We are at a loss to understand your statement that we ought not to 'drum up' business—we would ask, 'How else may we be expected to stay in business.'" Then Norris added, "What would happen if General Motors advertised the 'best car' and Ford demanded 'free time' to inform our listeners that they had been slandered? This would of course remove all broadcasting from the realm of free enterprise, leaving only government subsidized and controlled radio. I am sure, Mr. Cook, that you would not wish that to happen."[21]

Cook took his complaint to the FCC, as the DNC wanted him to do. Friendly wrote, "the Democratic National Committee wanted to keep the pressure on and put teeth in the Fairness Doctrine for future elections." The DNC made similar complaints against nine other stations.[22]

On October 6, 1965, the FCC ruled that Cook must have a right to reply, but Norris was not about to comply. He sued to have the Fairness Doctrine found an unconstitutional violation of the First Amendment. In June 1967, the U.S. Court of Appeals in the District of Columbia sided with the FCC. In his opinion Judge Edward A. Tamm ruled, "the American people own the Airwaves," and that, "I find the Fairness Doctrine a vehicle completely legal in its origin with implement by the use of modern technology. The free and general discussion of public matters [which] seems absolutely essential to prepare the people for an intelligent exercise of their rights as a citizen."[23]

That same month, Ted Pierson, representing the Radio-Television News Directors Association (RTNDA) announced plans to enter a fight against the FCC rules meant to clarify a station's obligations to give equal time for personal attacks and political editorializing that were adopted after the Red Lion case commenced. These FCC rules specified that the Fairness Doctrine is applicable,

"When, during the presentation of views on a controversial issue of public importance, an attack is made upon the honesty, character, integrity or like personal qualities of an identified person or group, the licensee shall, within a reasonable time and in no event later than 1 week after the attack, transmit to the person or group attacked (1) notification of the date, time and identification of the broadcast; (2) a script or tape (or an accurate summary if a script or tape is not available ) of the attack, and (3) an offer of a reasonable opportunity to respond over the licensee's facilities."[24]

The RTNDA said these rules inhibited news reporting. NBC and CBS filed separate suits on the same grounds. The NBC brief referenced Benjamin Franklin who said a "newspaper was not a stage coach which seats everyone." The brief explained this meant the Constitution guarantees "a free press, not free access to the press." The U.S. Seventh Circuit in Chicago heard the RTNDA case, and consolidated it with the CBS and NBC cases. In this venue, the broadcasters won a unanimous decision. In the opinion of the court, Judge Luther M. Swygert said the court was not necessarily disagreeing with the D.C. court. "We are not prepared to hold the Fairness Doctrine unconstitutional. Moreover, we do not believe that it is necessary to decide that question in this review. Second, we are in disagreement with the District of Columbia's Circuit holding in Red Lion, sustaining the Commission's order, inasmuch as we think that the order was essentially an anticipation of an aspect of the personal attack rule which are here being challenged."[25]

It was on to the U.S. Supreme Court, which heard arguments on April 2 and 3 of 1969 where the Red Lion case was combined with the RTNDA-CBS-NBC case. All plaintiffs argued the case. Representing RTNDA and the networks was Archibald Cox soon to reach fame as the Watergate special prosecutor. All this happened as neither the justices hearing the case nor the lawyers presenting the case were fully aware of the shenanigans carried on by the Democrats in 1964 that brought the case to this constitutional showdown.[26]

On June 9, 1969, in what today would seem almost shocking lopsided majority, particularly for a free speech case, the court ruled 8-0 that the Fairness Doctrine did not violate the First Amendment primarily because of the scarcity of the airwaves. Associated Justice William O. Douglas did not vote, having not heard the oral arguments.

"Believing that the specific application of the fairness doctrine in Red Lion, and the promulgation of the regulations in RTNDA, are both authorized by Congress and enhance rather than abridge the freedoms of speech and press protected by the First Amendment, we hold them valid and constitutional, reversing the judgment below in RTNDA and affirming the judgment below in Red Lion," said the court's opinion, written by Associate Justice Byron White.[27]

White's opinion went on to explain the scarcity issue.

"[B] ecause the frequencies reserved for public broadcasting were limited in number, it was essential for the Government to tell some applicants that they could not broadcast at all because there was room for only a few," the opinion said. "Where there are substantially more individuals who want to broadcast than there are frequencies to allocate, it is idle to posit an unabridgeable First Amendment right to broadcast comparable to the right of every individual to speak, write, or publish. If 100 persons want broadcast licenses but there are only 10 frequencies to allocate, all of them may have the same 'right' to a license; but if there is to be any effective communication by radio, only a few can be licensed and the rest must be barred from the airwaves."

The opinion further says no one has a constitutional right to a broadcast license.

"Because of the scarcity of radio frequencies, the Government is permitted to put restraints on licensees in favor of others whose views should be expressed on this unique medium. But the people as a whole retain their interest in free speech by radio and their collective right to have the medium function consistently with the ends and purposes of the First Amendment. It is the right of the viewers and listeners, not the right of the broadcasters, which is paramount," White wrote, later adding this should not discourage coverage of controversial issues. "It does not violate the First Amendment to treat licensees given the privilege of using scarce radio frequencies as proxies for the entire community, obligated to give suitable time and attention to matters of great public concern. To condition the granting or renewal of licenses on a willingness to present representative community views on controversial issues is consistent with the ends and purposes of those constitutional provisions forbidding the abridgment of freedom of speech and freedom of the press."[28]

With the green light from the Supreme Court, use of the Fairness Doctrine for political ends became a bipartisan affair after the election of President Richard Nixon, who not only viewed the media as liberally bias, but as his mortal enemy. Deputy Director of White House Communications Jeb Magruder developed the "rifle" strategy of targeting unfriendly media coverage. The strategy involved meetings with White House officials and executives with CBS, NBC and ABC about their TV news coverage of the president, while the Republican National Committee encouraged private citizens to put pressure on TV stations through the Fairness Doctrine. By early January 1970, the White House was orchestrating a media monitoring system for unfriendly coverage. This involved having FCC Chairman Dean Burch "express concern about press objectivity" and organizing "outside groups to petition the FCC and issue public 'statements of concern' over press objectivity."[29]

Charles Colson, special counsel to the president, called and visited all three networks, but put most of his efforts behind remaining in touch with CBS—the premier broadcast news organization at the time. In 1972, Colson informed CBS News President Frank Stanton the administration was considering licensing the actual networks rather than just their affiliate stations. In 1973, the White House achieved some success when CBS announced it would discontinue news analysis of the president's speeches. CBS denied it had been intimidated, insisting it only wanted to present the news fairly. CBS did win a legal victory over the Republican National Committee when the D.C. Circuit court overturned an FCC ruling that the RNC must have the opportunity to respond to the Democratic response to President Nixon.[30]

Besides CBS, the top targets were two Florida TV stations and one Washington TV station owned by *The Washington Post*, which was of course the most aggressive covering Watergate.[31] Nixon was quoted saying, "The main thing is the *Post* is going to have damnable, damnable problems out of this one. They have a television station ... and they're going to have to get it renewed. ... The game has to be played awfully rough."[32]

Media bias is a legitimate concern and something that the journalism community and the public should take seriously. But that is where it should end. The First Amendment does not and should not allow government to weigh in on the matter. The use of the Fairness Doctrine during the Johnson and Nixon administration to attempt—and in some cases succeed—in bludgeoning political opposition puts an overly powerful weapon in the government's arsenal. The scarcity argument is logical, but flawed on many fronts. With more media, such an argument became almost irrelevant in decades to come.

CHAPTER SIX

# Renaissance

Five years after the landmark decision in Red Lion, the U.S. Supreme Court undermined its own ruling parsing in their decision making process but not in a ruling itself the difference between fairness on the air and fairness in print.

Patrick Tornillo, Jr. was the Dade County Teacher's Union executive director running for a seat on the Florida state legislature in 1972. *The Miami Herald* published two scathing editorials against Tornillo making the case it would not be acceptable for someone in his position to serve in the legislature. "We cannot say it would be illegal but certainly it would be inexcusable of voters if they sent Pat Tornillo to Tallahassee." Tornillo went to the *Herald* building, accompanied by his attorney, to hand deliver a letter to the editor. The attorney cited a 50-year-old Florida statute that gave every candidate for political office in the state the right to reply to a newspaper attack. Unimpressed by the candidate's hardball tactics, the Herald editors said no. "I always thought we should have printed the damn letter voluntarily," a *Herald* executive said. "But once the state tried to force us to print it, we had no choice but to fight it out in court."[1]

Regardless of whether the *Herald* editorial was a deciding factor or not, Tornillo lost the primary and sued the newspaper. The Florida Supreme Court upheld the right to respond statute. By 1974, the case moved to the U.S. Supreme Court, and the plaintiff cited FCC rules as precedent. This was a bridge too far for the justices. They were prepared to strike down the Florida law as a violation of freedom of the press, but the Red Lion decision presented some difficulties. The only debate among the jurists was whether the court should explain itself. Chief Justice Warren Burger wanted to include language in the opinion explaining why this was different than Red Lion—because the scarcity argument did not apply, and newspapers were not licensed. However including such language risked losing Justices Potter Stewart and William O. Douglass, who would have written separate concurring opinions. The court believed a unanimous ruling was a paramount concern to the country.[2]

As Fred W. Friendly pointed out, there were two issues that the court did not address. One, while government does not license newspapers (and let us pray it never will), President Richard Nixon had already signed the Newspaper Preservation Act, which was a form of government assistance by allowing one industry to skirt the anti-trust laws that apply to other industries. The preservation law allows newspapers in the same city or town to form joint operating agreements, in which the advertising and business departments of the papers merge, while keeping two separate editorial voices. Thus this special government granted exemption could theoretically carry the same public interest obligations as a broadcast license. Further, with regards to the scarcity argument, "there are far more television and radio stations available in the Red Lion-York market than there are newspapers in Miami," Friendly observed. "In fact, the Miami Herald dominated southern Florida like a colossus, while WGCB is a weak daytime signal, which even its primary Pennsylvania market is but one of a multitude of voices."

For Mark Fowler, there were just too many inconsistencies.

"The electronic press, the press that uses air and electrons should be as free as the press that uses paper and ink," said Fowler, who had been a disc jockey since 1959 when he was 17 years old, first working at a rock-n-roll station in Orlando. "Any reason or justification that is advanced to regulate the electronic press is an excuse to regulate, not a reason. That's just a made up excuse: The airwaves belong to the people. I can say, don't the highways belong to the people. Newspapers use the highways to distribute their product. That's really the same analogy to the airwaves. One is physical delivery. The other is electronic."[3]

Fowler continued to work as a disc jockey through the University of Florida, where he also finished law school, earning an income by playing records and speaking into a microphone. He decided he wanted to combine his two loves, so he went to Washington in 1970s after law school to practice communications law. It's through practicing law that he learned all about the Fairness Doctrine first hand, and became an outspoken critic of the rule, and broadcast deregulation in general. He joined the campaign staff of Ronald Reagan in the 1976 losing bid for president and again in the 1980 winning bid.

With Reagan's election came a "government is the problem" deregulation agenda that included the broadcasting industry. The new president appointed as Fowler to be the FCC chairman. Fowler started an effort to dismantle the doctrine piecemeal. During the 1980s, a huge fight in Washington ensued that engulfed the executive, legislative and judicial branch of government deciding on the matter.

"When Reagan won, he asked me what I'd like to do. I said I'd like to run the FCC because I know something about it and I think we can do a lot to unregulate not deregulate or regulate but unregulate that agency, particularly in the area of content regulation," Fowler said. "I took office in 1981. One of the things I wanted to do, one of the objectives I had, was to try to strike down as much of the content regulation abridging the First Amendment that says Congress shall make no law abridging freedom of speech or of the press, and view the electronic press as co-equal under the constitution to any other medium including the printed press."[4]

On Sept. 17, 1981, the FCC voted 4-2 to ask Congress to repeal the Fairness Doctrine and equal time doctrine, with Commissioner Henry Rivera abstaining. The majority argued that the scarcity argument was outdated because of the burgeoning cable and satellite industry, and an expanding number of radio and TV stations. Fowler called the rule a "large burden on freedom of speech. ... Today we strike a blow in the cause of freedom. This is the time to strike down government's role in determining what the people shall hear and see."[5] The FCC did not move to eliminate the policy itself, because of lingering questions over whether the 1959 amendments that Congress adopted to the Communications Act were statute or simply reinforcing support of the FCC rule.

Though he had the support of President Reagan, Fowler did not necessarily have the support of the rest of the administration, as neither conservatives nor liberals were anxious to dump the rule.

"I remember when we proposed and started talking about tearing down and eliminating the Fairness Doctrine, I got a lot of slack from the White House," Fowler said in an interview for this book. "Not from the president, but people I knew over there who had been colleagues and friends of mine during the two campaigns said: 'Why are you doing this? The Fairness Doctrine is the only thing that protects the president—in this case President Reagan—against the onslaught of the Dan Rathers of the world. ... I felt in a way I was pretty much alone. I didn't get much support from the White House. In fact they thought I was nuts. They thought I was doing the big liberal media's bidding in wanting to get rid of it. And liberals were outraged about turning everything over to the free market."[6]

Without a lot of allies, Fowler's strategy was to lay the intellectual framework for getting rid of it by making speeches on the matter. The second was to launch proceedings at the FCC, compile facts and a record to argue the Fairness Doctrine was not constitutional and didn't enhance public debate.

"At that point, when I started proposing we should get rid of it, to say that it's going to give rise to a thousand new free voices in the market place of ideas was predictable. Right?" Fowler said. "Because at that point all the conservatives and liberals saw were still basically the three television networks that were dominant."[7]

A decade after Red Lion, yet another legal case on broadcast regulation would hit the U.S. Supreme Court, this time regarding *not* the Fairness Doctrine directly, but regulation of non-commercial stations, or stations falling under the umbrellas of the Corporation for Public Broadcasting. Congress passed the Public Broadcasting Act of 1967 establishing the CPB for public radio and TV stations, allowing federal funding for non-commercial stations. An amendment added on the House floor was meant to prevent stations getting tax dollars from pushing its politics. Section 399 of the law said, "No noncommercial educational broadcasting station may engage in editorializing or may support or oppose any candidate for political office."[8] Thus, this went a step further than the Fairness Doctrine by outright banning the station management from giving opinions, rather than simply mandating equal time. The justification for such a law was that these stations were getting public money.

The Pacifica Foundation, a liberal nonprofit corporation operating several noncommercial educational broadcasting stations in five major metropolitan areas, sued to have the editorializing law struck down. The League of Women Voters of California and liberal Democratic Representative Henry Waxman were also plaintiff in the lawsuit. The case was called FCC vs. League of Women Voters of California. Interestingly enough, it was the left litigating this case that would eventually undermine the Fairness Doctrine. The Carter administration opted to stop funding the defense of the case in 1979, but the Reagan Justice Department reversed course and chose to defend the statute.[9]

In a 5-4 decision issued on July 2, 1984, the court struck down the provision banning editorializing.

"First, the restriction imposed by Section 399 is specifically directed at a form of speech—namely the expression of editorial opinion—that lies at the heart of First Amendment protection," Justice William J. Brennan wrote in the majority opinion.[10]

The opinion stressed that the court was not reversing itself on previous ruling that affirmed the federal government's ability to regulat the public airwaves. "But, in sharp contrast to the restrictions upheld in Red Lion or in CBS, Inc. v. FCC, which left room for editorial discretion and simply required broadcast editors to grant others access to the microphone, Section 399 directly prohibits the broadcaster from speaking out on public issues even in a balanced and fair manner," Brennan wrote.[11]

Perhaps most importantly, the Supreme Court opinion went on to express the "scarcity argument," the legal linchpin of the Fairness Doctrine, could be flawed.

"The prevailing rationale for broadcast regulation based on spectrum scarcity has come under increasing criticism in recent years," Brennan wrote. "Critics, including the incumbent Chairman of the FCC, charge that, with the advent of cable and satellite television technology, communities now have access to such a wide variety of stations that the scarcity doctrine is obsolete. We are not prepared, however, to reconsider our longstanding approach without some signal from Congress or the FCC that technological developments have advanced so far that some revision of the system of broadcast regulation may be required."[12]

"Of course, the Commission may, in the exercise of its discretion, decide to modify or abandon these rules, and we express no view on the legality of either course," the opinion said. "As we recognized in Red Lion, however, were it to be shown by the Commission that the fairness doctrine '[has] the net effect of reducing, rather than enhancing,' speech, we would then be forced to reconsider the constitutional basis of our decision in that case."[13]

Thus, without ruling on the Fairness Doctrine, the majority opened the door for other branches of government to give the rule another serious look.

With this thrown in the mix, the FCC took another swing at the doctrine. While not yet ready to void the doctrine given the murkiness of whether it was a law or an administrative rule, the Commission provided a thorough report in August 1985 titled "General Fairness Doctrine Obligations of Broadcast Licensees," explaining why the doctrine was unfair, not constitutional and was not necessary since access to broadcast communications was no longer scarce. The report sought to address three main questions related to the Fairness Doctrine: (1) whether the doctrine was constitutionally permissible under then-current marketplace conditions and First Amendment jurisprudence; 2.) whether the doctrine actually chilled rather than encouraged free speech; and, 3.) whether the doctrine was codified into law by either Section 315 or the general public interest standard in the Communications Act.[14]

The report resulted from investigating the real world effect on broadcasters. FCC commission member Dennis Patrick said, "What we found were broadcasters who said that rather than get into litigious waters, rather than incur expenses and risk losing their licenses, they chose to stay away from controversial issues."[15]

The bulk of fairness actions were "second prong" according to the report, meaning that broadcasters rarely faced enforcement action for failing to address issues of public importance in the first place. Rather, most actions were against broadcasters accused of failing to provide all sides of an issue. This, the report said led to broadcasters avoiding the expense of enforcement actions by refusing to cover issues of public importance.[16] The report talked about a radio station manager in Southern California that cancelled a series of reports on religious cults because of "an assessment of the legal and personnel costs associated with defending a possible Fairness Doctrine complaint." The report further talked about a Nebraska TV executive who didn't run several public affairs programs fearing retaliation.[17]

The FCC did not dispute the Red Lion precedent, but only said the doctrine in the current context is constitutionally dubious in the current communications environment, suggesting that broadcast technological advances could be hampered because of the policy. Given that the courts and Congress were pondering the issue, this executive branch (quasi-judicial) agency did not strike the doctrine down.[18]

Ultimately, the FCC determined there was no longer a public interest argument in favor of the doctrine. The policy "inhibits the presentation of controversial issues," "involves government intimidation of the media in scrutinizing programming" and imposes an "unnecessary cost burden" on the government and broadcasters, the Commission said. In shooting down the scarcity argument, the Commission cited its own statistics that found since the Red Lion case, the number of radio stations increased by 48 percent to 9,766 in 1985 from 6,595 in 1969. The number of TV stations increased by 44 percent to 1,208, along with a 195 percent increase in cable stations in the years since Red Lion with a 975 percent increase in cable subscribers.[19] [20]

Of great significance, Exhibit A in the report was the testimony of CBS anchorman Dan Rather, the guy some White House officials wanted to protect Reagan from, whose prominence added significant gravitas to the debate, moving out of the ideological realm.

"When I was a young reporter, I worked briefly for wire services, small radio stations, and newspapers, and I finally settled into a job at a large radio station owned by the Houston Chronicle," Rather said. "Almost immediately on starting work in that station's newsroom, I became aware of a concern which I had previously barely known existed—the FCC. The journalists at *The Chronicle* did not worry about it; those at the radio station did. Not only the station manager but the newspeople as well were very much aware of this government presence looking over their shoulders. I can recall newsroom conversations about what the FCC implications of broadcasting a particular report would be. Once a newsperson has to stop and consider what a government agency will think of something he or she wants to put on the air, an invaluable element of freedom has been lost."[21]

The only other journalist of any prominence quoted by the FCC in support of free speech was Bill Monroe of NBC's Meet the Press. With this scant support, the Reagan FCC ventured forth.

As strong a case as the Commission made against the Fairness Doctrine, like the 1981 decision, it left the policy in place, punting the matter to Congress. It was nothing but a recommendation.

Oddly enough, in 1982, Fowler's FCC upheld the Fairness Doctrine, knowing the matter would eventually be decided by the courts. The ruling created what *The New York Times* called a test case. Ironically, it was two court decisions that went against the FCC rulings that allowed the Commission to put the final nail in the coffin of the outdated doctrine.

WTRH in Syracuse, N.Y., owned by the Iowa-based Meredith Corporation, aired a political advertisement favoring the building of a nuclear power plant. The Syracuse Peace Council, an organization opposed to building the plant, demanded equal time. When it did not get that equal time for free, it filed a Fairness Doctrine complaint. The same Commission that called on Congress to ditch the doctrine was nevertheless obligated to enforce it until the legal matters had been cleared up. Thus, the FCC in 1982 ruled that the doctrine did apply to the Syracuse station. The Meredith Corporation appealed to the U.S. Circuit Court of Appeals in Washington.[22]

But another court ruling unexpectedly came along as well.

The Telecommunications Research and Action Center (TRAC) and the Media Access Project (MAP) argued that teletext—a new technology allowing text to be transmitted through TV, should face the same broadcast regulations as any other broadcast media and challenged the FCC's ruling that the Fairness Doctrine was not applicable in court in 1986. In 1984, the FCC ruled that equal time rules do not apply to teletext because it does not transmit a voice or picture. "We consider teletext clearly as an ancillary service not strictly related to the traditional broadcast mode of mass communication," the FCC decision said.[23]

But, in a 3-2 decision on the same U.S. Court of Appeals for the District of Columbia that would later hear the Meredith case, ruled the Fairness Doctrine should apply to teletext.

"The Commission's attempt to distinguish teletext from traditional broadcasting because of teletext's textual and graphic nature conflicts with the plain intent of Congress ... Teletext and main channel broadcasting are merely different time intervals within the broadcasting spectrum. Teletext is 'ancillary' to main channel broadcasting only in the sense that it will probably not attract as many viewers," the 1986 decision said.

The important part of the ruling was that the court clarified a long standing dispute: The 1959 amendments to the Communications Act did not obligate the FCC to enforce the Fairness Doctrine, which was an administrative rule imposed through the regulatory process not a law enacted by Congress. "The language, by its plain import, neither creates nor imposes any obligation but seeks to make it clear that the statutory amendment does not affect the fairness doctrine obligation as the Commission had previously applied it. The words employed by Congress also demonstrate that the obligation recognized and preserved was an administrative construction, not a binding statutory directive."[24]

On January 16, 1987 two different judges on the same appeals court in Washington ruled in Meredith Corp. vs. FCC that since Congress did not codify the Fairness Doctrine as law, that the FCC must give another hearing to Meredith to determine whether the First Amendment rights of WTRH were violated.[25]

Democrats, realizing the rule was in jeopardy, passed a bill in the House and Senate codifying the Fairness Doctrine as law, sponsored by Representative John Dingell of Michigan in the House and by Senator Fritz Hollings of South Carolina in the Senate. The National Association of Broadcasters lobbied heavily against the legislation on the Hill, making the same arguments as Fowler. But an odd coalition came out in favor of the bill to make it law. Consumer advocate (later perennial presidential candidate) Ralph Nader said without the regulation wealthy corporations would control the political dialogue. Meanwhile, conservative activist Phyllis Schlafly, the legendary conservative activist, recalled her use of the doctrine when fighting the Equal Rights Amendment, and believed it was the only fighting chance conservatives had in the overwhelmingly liberal media.[26] Further, Reed Irvine, founder of Accuracy in Media, reasonably assumed that repealing the doctrine would just move the media further left. "Many [broadcasters] have done no more than pay lip service to fairness even when it was required by law," Irvine wrote in a letter to *The New York Times* in 1987. "It is foolish to think that they would suddenly become addicted to fairness if all legal restraints on their uninhibited exercise of power were removed."[27] Fowler also recalled that other conservative standouts such as former White House staffer Pat Buchanan, who would go on to have a brilliant commentary career and run for president, and Paul Weyrich, the head of the Free Congress Foundation, strongly opposed ending the doctrine.

Both sides of the political class saw too many advantages to keeping the doctrine, Fowler said. "Liberals really loved the idea of putting certain content requirements on broadcasters and I think the dynamic had to do something with this: Liberals didn't like big corporations and felt that this medium, this electronic medium, was incredibly powerful. Any institution that was very, very powerful, and in their view too powerful, had to have certain regulations fastened on it to make sure it served the public interest. That particularly applied, for liberals, to the big corporations called the networks," Fowler said.

Meanwhile, Fowler said, "Conservatives, particularly beginning in the mid-60s to the late 60s, really embraced it more and more because they felt the Fairness Doctrine was the one thing that protected them from what they saw as an increasingly liberal national media, particularly the three networks, whether it was radio or television. It was almost a bipartisan belief that the Fairness Doctrine— for different reason whether you were liberal or a conservative—was a good thing."[28]

The proposal to codify the doctrine as law passed comfortably in both houses of Congress, with bipartisan consensus, by 59-31 in the Senate and by a 302-102 vote in the House on April 21, 1987.

"The debate on the Fairness Doctrine is, at its roots, a debate over government control over a public resource, the spectrum," Hollings said of his proposal. "To balance the limited number of opportunities the public has to become licensees and to provide the public with a greater number of voices, the FCC has required these broadcast licensees act as public trustees."[29]

Not surprisingly President Reagan vetoed the legislation on June 22, 1987, calling it unconstitutional. Fowler, who retired from the Commission after six year as chairman and was replaced by the like-minded Dennis Patrick, said Reagan struck a "huge blow for the First Amendment." Dingell quipped, "President Reagan's veto of the Fairness Doctrine bill flies in the face of urgings from citizens of all political persuasions and from all parts of the political spectrum."[30] Democrats threatened to keep pushing, but did not have the two-thirds needed to override a veto.

"It was just right. It felt right, and even with the slings and arrows from the right and left I persisted and I had colleagues who

I'm indebted to for supporting me like Dennis Patrick who came on board as a commissioner, a good conservative from California," Fowler said. "Ultimately, he succeeded me. There was a conversation. At that point, I'd been there six years. I said Dennis—We worked really hard at it. I could have probably at that point stayed and actually presided at the meeting where we got rid of it. But, I was tired and I asked Dennis if he wanted to be the one to take it over the goal line because I thought we could do it at that point. I thought we built a lot of momentum in some circles through our arguments and he agreed to take that on. And the good news was, he'd be the one to actually preside at the meeting where the commission actually eliminated it. The bad news was he'd still have to suffer some attacks to get that done."[31]

Because the appeals court had sent the Meredith case back to the FCC, it became the test case, which was the idea all along. Ordered to consider the First Amendment rights of WTRH, the Commission considered and determined it was a blatant violation.

It was the fourth of August rather than July in 1987 when America's broadcasters attained independence, or at least a great deal more than they previously had, from the federal government.

In a 4-0 vote, the Commission reversed its previous Syracuse Peace Council ruling, and in the process abolished the Fairness Doctrine. The ruling said, "[T]he intrusion by government into the content of programming occasioned by enforcement of [the Fairness Doctrine] restricts the journalistic freedom of broadcasters … actually inhibits the presentation of controversial issues of public importance to the detriment of the public and the degradation of the editorial prerogative of broadcast journalists." An Appeals Court panel in the District of Columbia upheld the ruling in February 1989.[32]

The move would actually do more than give broadcasters the same freedom as newspapers. It would ring in a new alternative media to compete with the big establishment media. While Schlafly and Irvine were concerned doing away with the doctrine would virtually eliminate conservative arguments, market forces proved the best way to enrich political dialogue for a new renaissance in broadcasting. A 1998 study by communication experts Thomas W. Hazzlett and David W. Sosa found that from 1987 through 1995, the share of "informational" AM programming went from 4.29 percent of all radio programming to 20.89 percent.[33]

"People always say, 'well you got rid of it so the talk radio people could come on and be the big conservative force that they are today.' I had no clue about that," Fowler said. "I don't think talk radio really existed in anybody's mind. It didn't in mine. After we got rid of it, that really enabled talk radio to get underway. Why is that? For the first time broadcasters could put a Rush Limbaugh for three hours, five days a week. They could just basically put different opinionated voices on 24/7 and not have the government looking to see if they had violated this Fairness Doctrine. So it really enabled talk radio to get underway. We did not foresee that. We were just doing it on the basis that it was unconstitutional, that we love the Constitution. The First Amendment is one of the most important pieces of our constitutional rights, and it was being sullied by this noxious Fairness Doctrine and all these other rules that followed from that. It was at the heart of political discourse, the broadcast medium, and there it was being controlled in part by the government. That's what kept us going. We can't take credit for being farsighted enough to say we're part of the reason that talk radio started."[34]

When Democrats captured Congress after the 2006 elections, there was chatter about bringing it back, and even more so once Barack Obama was elected president, giving the Democrats a president to sign such legislation.

"The Fairness Doctrine is coming," Beck warned his audience in December 2008 as if it was a fait acompli. "They are going to do everything they can to silence our voices ... What the hell happened to America? Do we need an alarm clock?" Speaker of the House Nancy Pelosi gave conservatives reason for concern. Responding to a bill that would block funding for the FCC to implement the Fairness Doctrine, Pelosi said, "The interest of my caucus is the reverse." Meanwhile, New York Senator Charles Schumer said, ""I think we should all be fair and balanced, don't you?" California

Senator Dianne Feinstein even threatened to hold a hearing on political imbalance in broadcasting.[35]

However, this never happened and probably won't.

"Personally, I do not think there was a chance in hell the Fairness Doctrine would be reinstated. But having said that, I don't think we should ever drop our vigilance to protect freedom of speech in America and to protect radio from a regulation that is so outdated and so half baked that it would really hurt radio at this point," said Michael Harrison, editor of *Talkers Magazine*. "It would be an existential threat to radio. It could actually put talk radio out of business if there was a Fairness Doctrine. I don't think that the reinstatement of the fairness doctrine was ever a real threat. But then again, just like terrorism, you can't discount any threat. If somebody threatens, you have to close the airplane and everybody has to leave it. Bomb scare, you shut down the building and everyone goes out to the streets. Anytime the word fairness doctrine comes up you've got to fight it. It's unlikely it could pass because it's clearly outdated and clearly unconstitutional."[36]

Further, Harrison is unclear why support and opposition to this seems to go along party lines, referencing the use of the rule by both Johnson and Nixon to target "enemies."

"Politicians will always use any kind of fairness doctrine to further their cause. This is not a liberal nor conservative exclusive deal," Harrison said. "The fairness doctrine cuts both ways. When the conservatives were in power, they would try to shut down the liberals. When the liberals are in power, they try to shut down the conservatives. The fairness doctrine or any regulatory vehicle by government will be used unfairly if it gets in the hands of any political faction."[37]

## CHAPTER SEVEN

# The Rise of Rush

Just before the 1992 presidential election, *Time* magazine asked Rush Limbaugh, "You're unabashedly for Bush and against Clinton. Given 13 million devoted listeners, why is your guy 15 points behind?"

Limbaugh's answer: "I don't say that I have influence. I was totally opposed to the 1990 budget deal, and it still happened. I'm not an activist. I do not give out congressional phone numbers. I do not urge behavior. No tea bags. This is entertainment. And in strict marketing terms, does it hurt me to be the only guy not making Dan Quayle jokes?"[1]

Rush Limbaugh has no influence. Tell that to the Democrats in 1994 who lost their seats en masse in the Republican Revolution that was dubbed the Limbaugh Congress. Tell that to the new majority swept in that year that made Limbaugh an honorary member of their freshman class. Tell that to President Bill Clinton who had public fits during his administration over Limbaugh's commentary. For that matter, tell it to the Obama White House who made it their strategy in early 2009 to call Limbaugh the leader of the Republican Party, a strategy that did nothing to help Obama against the GOP (which was the intent) but tremendously boosted Limbaugh's audience and influence.

To be sure, he does not have unlimited political power. His legions of "ditto-heads" are not mind numb robots marching in lock-step. This is evident during the presidential primary season when callers, who insist they agree with Limbaugh 99 percent of the time, wanted to know why he is so down on Pat Buchanan (1996), John McCain (2000 and 2008), Mike Huckabee (2008) and Mitt Romney (2012) and other GOP hopefuls over the years. The "ditto-heads" are in fact folks who had long sought an advocate who would not mock the views they already held. They found that in Limbaugh.

A month after Republicans faced a beating in the 1992 election, sweeping Bill Clinton into the White House, none other than former President Ronald Reagan wrote a letter to Limbaugh. "Now that I've retired from active politics, I don't mind that you've become the number one voice for conservatism." A remarkable statement from the politician Rush would go on to call Ronaldous Maximus. Reagan's December 1992 letter went on to say, "I know the liberals call you 'the most dangerous man in America,' but don't worry about it, they used to say the same about me. Keep up the good work."[2]

While the left tries to dismiss him, the industry does not, as few people are more decorated than Limbaugh. He was inducted into the National Radio Hall of Fame in 1993, often times a lifetime achievement that comes toward the end of a host's career. Rush was just getting started then. He won a Marconi Award in 1992, 1995, 2000 and 2005, given by the National Association of Broadcasters to the top radio personality. Reflecting his role as a leader in the conservative movement, in March 2007 he accept the inaugural William F. Buckley Jr. Award for Media Excellence, given by the Media Research Center.

Simply put, according to *Talkers Magazine*, the industry bible, "Rush Limbaugh is the greatest radio talk show host of all time."[3] He has not prevented Democrats from ever getting elected again. Nor has he controlled the Republican nomination process—obvious in the 2008 choice of McCain as the GOP standard bearer. He was no cheerleader for Mitt Romney during the 2012 primary either. But he has become in many ways, if not the leader, the inspiration of the conservative movement.

The left has continually gone after him, seeking advertising boy-
cotts, and accusations of various forms of bigotry. The left, which is
often so aghast at casting moral judgment, has repeatedly pounced
on Limbaugh for his being divorced three time and married four—
paying the gay entertainer Sir Elton John $1 million to perform at
his most recent wedding. He was married the first time for 18
months; the second time for five years, the third time for 10 years.
He married Kathryn Rogers in the summer of 2010.[4] Though virtually every bad adjective imaginable has been used to describe him,
Limbaugh has contributed millions from his own pocket and raised
hundreds of millions for leukemia research.

Rush Limbaugh has been a transformative figure in the political,
media and entertainment universe. He was born and grew up in
Cape Girardeau, Missouri, a town he called, "a quintessential
Midwestern small town." He became a fan of radio as a kid, and in
high school was playing records at a station in his hometown.[5]

He became a top 40 deejay in the 1970s, opting against college
to the angst of his father who doubted there was any future for his
son in something like radio. He played music for stations in
Pennsylvania where he became a diehard Pittsburgh Steelers fan. He
came back to Missouri to work in the office of the Kansas City
Royals, but could not stay away from radio. In 1983 he returned to
radio, doing a political commentary show for KMBZ in Kansas City.
He parlayed that into a job in Sacramento in the mid 1984 to do a
pro-Reagan, pro-Republican talk show on KFBK.[6]

The Sacramento show was a success. Limbaugh was becoming a
local star and was very comfortable with where he was. But his friend
and radio consultant Bruce Marr insisted he had what it takes to go
national.[7]

In January 1988, not long after the Fairness Doctrine had been
killed, Limbaugh got a call from a group in San Francisco that wanted to syndicate his show nationally. Rush rejected the idea because,
"the group was too ideologically driven," and they wanted his show
to be about "saving the country from whatever commie-lib evils they
thought existed."[8] It might be tough today to imagine Limbaugh
being repelled by something too ideological.

149

Marr introduced Rush to Ed McLaughlin, former ABC Radio Network president who had recently started his own syndication network. Laughlin was convinced Limbaugh could succeed with a national political show as well.[9] The story of how Limbaugh got his national show is one of conservative principles; of taking a big risk, sacrifice and hard work, and battling odds and the can't-do-that norms of the radio industry at the time.

One of those odds was "The Local, Local, Local" problem. Radio stations wanted all local, at least in peak listening times. National programs were subjected to night hours when advertising was cheap. "We were planning to do what virtually everyone at any meaningful radio station in the country said was impossible: syndicated a controversial, issues-oriented program during the middle of the day. When I say no one gave us a chance, I'm not exaggeration," Limbaugh said in his first book "The Way Things Ought to Be."[10]

The deal that McLaughlin worked out for Limbaugh wasn't that great initially. Limbaugh could have a nationally syndicated show through ABC, but the national show would not be broadcast in New York, the largest media market. He would have broadcast space at WABC in New York. In exchange for using the broadcast space, Limbaugh had to do a two hour Local, Local, Local show on New York issues for two hours—for free. What Limbaugh got from offering his free labor was a guarantee that the ads he sold for his fledgling syndicated show would also be heard on his New York show, giving advertisers exposure in the New York market.[11]

The WABC local show began on July 4, 1988 and the national show started on August 1. After just three months, he was carried in 100 markets, many of them small, such as Lancaster, Pennsylvania, where the local newspaper did a feature on his show. Rush recalls the WABC general manager saying, "Well, what do you want, to be a big guy in Lancaster or a big guy in New York, because you can't do both. You're kidding yourself if you think we'll ever carry your national show here. I don't give a hoot what they think in Lancaster and neither does anyone else in New York. You better figure it out because you can't do both."[12]

Of course, eventually WABC did pick up the show as it just

became too popular for the most powerful talk radio station in the country to not include in their lineup.

Limbaugh, like many conservatives, was enraged by the first President Bush for going back on his no new taxes pledge. Thus, in 1992, Limbaugh threw his support behind Pat Buchanan, a pundit himself turned politician.

"That was my effort to send the President a message," Limbaugh said. "The Republican Party and George Bush got in trouble when they moved to the left, when they signed on with the civil rights bill with its quotas and the tax increases. He let down people who elected him."[13]

It was that election year that Limbaugh got a syndicated TV program, carried on 220 stations, produced by Roger Ailes, a one time Republican Party media advisor.[14]

Among his biggest enemies have been feminists, the more radical brood of which he calls "feminazis," a term that made its way into the political lexicon. He has explained that does not apply to all women. "A Feminazi is a feminist to whom the most important thing in life is ensuring that as many abortions as possible occur. There are fewer than twenty-five known Feminazis in the United States."[15]

Limbaugh became a huge star when the Clintons moved into the White House, eager to point out various Clinton scandals and denounce the Clinton health plan and other policies. In 1993, his second book, "See I Told You So," was released as Bill Clinton was becoming more unpopular during his first year in office. Meanwhile, the radio audience had ballooned to 20 million listeners in more than 600 markets. Remarkably, as more mega-stars burst onto radio getting their own huge ratings largely because Rush proved the commercial viability of conservative radio, Limbaughs ratings have remained steady.

He began doing commercial endorsements, a role usually reserved for professional athletes and actors not political commentators. In early 1994, the Florida Citrus Commission paid Limbaugh $1 million to do commercials for Florida orange juice. Democratic Florida Governor Lawton Chiles was bent out of shape, as was the

National Organization of Women and other liberal groups.[16] NOW led a boycott against Florida orange juice, and the controversy resulted in the citrus group dropping Limbaugh from doing further commercials after August.[17]

No worries. Limbaugh found another product to advertise for, albeit a less healthy product than orange juice. In 1995, Limbaugh was one of many celebrities to do an ad for Pizza Hut's new stuffed crust pizza, which includes a ring of cheese baked into the crust. In the ad, Limbaugh calls for people to eat pizza the "right" way, which means eating pizza crust first. The idea was to market the stuffed crust pizza as edgy and controversial, because eating a slice crust first was not conventional. Other controversial celebs in the series of ads were the divorced Donald and Ivana Trump arguing over how to split the pizza, and an ad with straight-laced NBA star David Robinson telling bad boy teammate Dennis Rodman to be different and eat his crust first.[18]

As a big star now, largely credited with the Republican takeover of Congress in 1994, Limbaugh seemed like a potential kingmaker for the GOP presidential primary in 1996. He actually never endorsed a candidate, other than to express a liking for Steve Forbes. "There's somebody whose closer [to my views],—but he's not all the way there, it's Forbes." He also defended Forbes when all the other Republican candidates ridiculed his flat tax proposal.[19]

But Limbaugh's vocal support for Forbes that year was not nearly as pronounced as his opposition to Pat Buchanan, whom he endorsed for president four years earlier. This time Buchanan had a much stronger support base, winning the caucuses in Louisiana and Alaska, then edging out Bob Dole in the New Hampshire primary. It was a real possibility Buchanan would be the GOP nominee. But Buchanan's stances against the North American Free Trade Agreement and other free trade policies were too much for Limbaugh.

"I'll tell you something, you are being manipulated in a way that I find very bothersome," Limbaugh told Buchanan supporters after the New Hampshire victory. "Pat Buchanan is not a conservative. He's a populist." He also said, "Pat Buchanan wants to engage in policies that expand the role of government in people's lives."[20]

Buchanan supporters made up a big portion of Limbaugh's audience. Talk Daily did an analysis from February 19-23, 1996 and found that pro-Buchanan callers outnumbered by 3-1 pro-Dole, pro-Forbes and pro-Lamar Alexander callers combined. Limbaugh said Buchanan's philosophy did not shrink government. "You are asking government to come in and protect your jobs," Rush told Buchanan supporters. On another occasion he said Buchanan wanted to redefine conservatism. "One of the things that worries me about the redefinition of conservatism is that now there's going to be a sect of the conservative movement which wants government action on its behalf."[21]

Did the sustained attacks impact the primary contest eventually won by Dole? Michael Barone, author of The Almanac of American Politics thinks so. In an interview on Limbaugh's show, Barone said, "One avenue the Republican Party might have taken is the Patrick Buchanan avenue: isolationism, negativism, dislike of other people who are different from you, protectionism," Barone told Limbaugh. "You spoke out consistently against those things to the core audience that Buchanan was aiming at, and he failed completely, and you … play a great role in shaping opinion in the 1990s."[22]

Though, his syndicated TV show went off the air over the summer of 1996, his radio numbers remained stratospheric. His producer Ailes wasted little time in moving toward establishing a little cable product known as Fox News. President Clinton won a second term in November, which meant a stellar four years for Limbaugh's radio ratings.

Limbaugh rallied support for George W. Bush against Al Gore in the 2000 election, and was a fierce advocate for the new president, whom he took a greater liking to than Bush the father. Though he would go on to excoriate Bush over expanding Medicare and increasing federal intervention in schools.

In October 2001, shortly after signing a new deal with Premiere Radio for $31 million annually, Limbaugh revealed to his audience that he was losing his hearing, a big problem for someone who talks for a living.

"I lost hearing every five days, to the point that I'm now totally deaf in my left ear," Limbaugh said. He described that it was gradual, but he really began to notice in late May of that year when he found, "Music was just a mass of noise. I was unable to hear it. I still don't know music. I haven't been able to recognize a song." During one broadcast, he explained that losing hearing made it difficult to speak, since he couldn't hear what he was saying. "To describe for you the way I hear things now: I understand what I'm saying, but I think it's more because I know what I'm going to say rather than I'm actually hearing what I say,"[23] While 100 percent of the hearing in his left ear was gone, 80 percent of the hearing in his right ear had disappeared, and for a time he relied a on teleprompter and staff assistance to understand what callers to the program said.[24]

The House Ear Clinic and Institute in Los Angeles diagnosed Limbaugh with the rare autoimmune inner-ear disease (AIED), an inflammatory inner ear condition that typically begins with sudden loss of hearing in one ear before spreading to the other. Less than 1 percent of the 28 million Americans with hearing loss were affected by AIED. A few days before Christmas—December 21, 2001—he had cochlear-implant surgery, which involved implanting electrodes into his inner ear to replace the lost nerve cells.[25]

In 2003 Limbaugh ran into problems not from his political opinions, but from sports and his personal life. The football lover was offering commentary on ESPN, and had this to say of Philadelphia Eagles quarterback Donovan McNabb. "I think what we've had here is a little social concern in the NFL," Limbaugh said. "The media has been very desirous that a black quarterback do well. They're interested in black coaches and black quarterbacks doing well ... McNabb got a lot of the credit for the performance of the team that he really didn't deserve."[26]

Not surprisingly, folks who already did not like Limbaugh accused him of racism. He resigned from his post on ESPN's "Sunday NFL Countdown."

Peter King, the NFL writer for Sports Illustrated offered what was not full a defense of Limbaugh, but one that seemed to put it in perspective. "Limbaugh was not making a racist statement about black quarterbacks. He was making a racist statement about me.

Actually, about me and my colleagues. But I feel like he was talking to me. I am not going to make this about any political view Limbaugh might hold about affirmative action—or about anything, really, except his exact words. And I can tell you that they are incredibly absurd."[27]

Calling someone absurd usually is not a great defense, but the sports writer's larger point is that Limbaugh was taking a swipe at the media, something he generally likes to do, but in this case, at sports journalists. Whether he was right or wrong, the opinion was hardly any different than his assertions about the liberal media.

Just on the heels of that came a far bigger problem.

News reports surfaced that his former housekeeper, a woman named Wilma Cline, ratted him out to authorities for having an addiction to Oxycontin. Law enforcement officials told reporters that Limbaugh's name came up as part of an investigation into "doctor shopping," or going from one doctor to the next to get more prescription pain reliever.[28] Reports hovered over him for almost two weeks, a time which he was commenting on major news items such as the California recall election. But at the end of the week, Friday October 11, 2003, he cleared the matter up as much as possible for his listeners, considering a legal proceeding was moving forward.

"You know I have always tried to be honest with you and open about my life. So I need to tell you today that part of what you have heard and read is correct. I am addicted to prescription pain medication," Limbaugh said, in what was one of his few deeply personal monologues, one with great humility, not a characteristic Rush is known for. "I first started taking prescription painkillers some years ago when my doctor prescribed them to treat post surgical pain following spinal surgery. Unfortunately, the surgery was unsuccessful and I continued to have severe pain in my lower back and also in my neck due to herniated discs. I am still experiencing that pain. Rather than opt for additional surgery for these conditions, I chose to treat the pain with prescribed medication. This medication turned out to be highly addictive."

The drug, Oxycontin, is highly addictive and became known as "hillbilly heroin" after it became widely abused in rural areas and a black market surfaced.

"Over the past several years I have tried to break my dependence on pain pills and, in fact, twice checked myself into medical facilities in an attempt to do so. I have recently agreed with my physician about the next steps," Limbaugh said. "Immediately following this broadcast, I am checking myself into a treatment center for the next 30 days to once and for all break the hold this highly addictive medication has on me. The show will continue during this time, of course, with an array of guest hosts you have come to know and respect."

Holding to conservative principals of personal accountability, Limbaugh said, "I am not making any excuses. You know, over the years athletes and celebrities have emerged from treatment centers to great fanfare and praise for conquering great demons. They are said to be great role models and examples for others. Well, I am no role model. I refuse to let anyone think I am doing something great here, when there are people you never hear about, who face long odds and never resort to such escapes. They are the role models. I am no victim and do not portray myself as such. I take full responsibility for my problem."

He then explained why he could not go much deeper into the matter than that. "At the present time, the authorities are conducting an investigation, and I have been asked to limit my public comments until this investigation is complete. So I will only say that the stories you have read and heard contain inaccuracies and distortions, which I will clear up when I am free to speak about them. I deeply appreciate all your support over this last tumultuous week. It has sustained me. I ask now for your prayers. I look forward to resuming our excursion into broadcast excellence together."[29]

It was during the three-year investigation over the prescription drugs when Limbaugh's third marriage ended. In a statement, they said it had nothing to do with the drug charge.[30]

The legal matter, widely viewed as politically motivated, was carried out by the Palm Beach County District Attorney's office. It dragged on until late April 2006. Limbaugh and prosecutors reached a deal in which he pleaded guilty to fraudulently concealing information to get prescription drugs. But the prosecutors would drop the charge after 18 months if Limbaugh remained in treatment for drug addiction. Limbaugh also had to pay $30,000 to the state of Florida to help cover the cost of the investigation. Prosecutors did not have the goods to bring him to trial for doctor shopping. His attorney Roy Black said Limbaugh intended on remaining in treatment anyway.[31]

The warrant in the deal alleges that sometime between February and August 2003, Limbaugh withheld information from a medical professionals whom he sought to obtain prescription for a controlled substance. He was never charged with doctor shopping.[32]

Limbaugh fought hard on the air for Republicans in the 2006 midterms, but it was not enough as Nancy Pelosi became the new Speaker of the House and Harry Reid became the new Senate Majority Leader after the November election. That would of course give Rush new material, particularly with Reid, whom he called "Dingy Harry."

Democrats looked for chances to attack.

In the fall of 2007, MoveOn.org ran a full-page ad in *The New York Times* calling General David Petraeus "Gen. Betray-Us." The ad alienated most independents, and gave Republican lawmakers the chance to demand an apology from the left-wing activist group.

Leftwing activists, Democrats in Congress and the media pounced on Limbaugh by (in some cases knowingly and other cases perhaps unknowingly) mischaracterized what Limbaugh said about an anti-war activist that lied about his military record.

Jesse MacBeth was a self-proclaimed Iraq war veteran whom the anti-war movement celebrated by the movement and in interviews—largely in alternative media. He was a cause célèbre after accusing his fellow veterans of committing war atrocities.[33]

In an interview on Peacefilms.org, MacBeth said superiors told him, "Our job over there is to strike fear in the hearts of the Iraqis … to be brutal and to not feel" and that "the Geneva Convention doesn't mean crap." He further claimed he participated in night raids where he would "pull people out, on their knees and zip-tied," and if someone did not answer question he "would shoot his youngest kid and keep going." He made the extraordinary claim, "By my hand alone... almost 200 people were taken out by me. That's just a rough estimate. A lot of them at close range... they would actually feel the hot muzzle of my rifle on their forehead.... We'd do stuff that would scare them first... beat 'em up or kick 'em or hit the wife.... slaughtering 30-40 people a night sometimes, women and children.... I was trained, you know, in all the Ranger school, 18 months of that crap.... I got disappointed in my country... but I didn't say anything because I would have been locked up."

In another particularly sensitive matter, he said, "Other things they told us to do, man, we were ordered to go into a mosque. This really hurts me a lot. My nightmares come mostly from this... we infiltrated the mosque... a couple hundred of people of all ages were praying.... We started slaughtering them, we started shooting them, started taking them out.... We would burn their bodies, hang the bodies from the rafters.... after a while, it's just sickening to think that I took part in that." He said, "Our job was just kill, kill, kill," and sorrowfully said, "I'm so disappointed in my country. I'm ashamed to have actually served in Iraq."[34]

By May 2006, the Army asserted there was no record of Jesse MacBeth ever serving in the Army Rangers or Special Forces, or even in the Army. Hot Air blog called attention to the Peace Films interview and raised questions on the matter. Military bloggers helped debunk a photo showing MacBeth in uniform (with his beret backward, incorrect flashes and tabs, and missing wings).[35] In reality, his discharge form showed he was kicked out of the Army after just six week at Fort Benning Ga., in 2003, because of "entry level performance and conduct."[36]

In May 2007, he was charged in U.S. District Court in Seattle with one count of using or possessing a forged or altered military discharge certificate, and one count of making false statements in seeking benefits from the Veterans Administration.[37]

On Rush's morning update, on the website, Rush talked about MacBeth as a "phony soldier" in September.

"Now, recently, Jesse MacBeth, poster boy for the anti-war left, had his day in court. And you know what? He was sentenced to five months in jail and three years probation for falsifying a Department of Veterans Affairs claim and his Army discharge record," Limbaugh said. "He was in the Army. Jesse MacBeth was in the Army, folks, briefly. Forty-four days before he washed out of boot camp. Jesse MacBeth isn't an Army Ranger, never was. He isn't a corporal, never was. He never won the Purple Heart, and he was never in combat to witness the horrors he claimed to have seen. You probably haven't even heard about this. And, if you have, you haven't heard much about it. This doesn't fit the narrative and the template in the Drive-By Media and the Democrat Party as to who is a genuine war hero. Don't look for any retractions, by the way. Not from the anti-war left, the anti-military Drive-By Media, or the Arabic websites that spread Jesse MacBeth's lies about our troops, because the truth for the left is fiction that serves their purpose. They have to lie about such atrocities because they can't find any that fit the template of the way they see the U.S. military. In other words, for the American anti-war left, the greatest inconvenience they face is the truth."[38]

Later that day, during his full three-hour program, a caller complained about the anti-war movement. Rush said, "It's not possible intellectually to follow these people." The caller concurred, "No, it's not. And what's really funny is they never talk to real soldiers. They like to pull these soldiers that come up out of the blue and spout to the media."

That's when Rush said, "The phony soldiers."

The caller followed, "The phony soldiers. If you talk to any real soldier and they're proud to serve, they want to be over in Iraq, they understand their sacrifice and they're willing to sacrifice for the country."

Rush said, "They joined to be in Iraq. It's frustrating and maddening, and why they must be kept in the minority. I want to thank you, Mike, for calling. I appreciate it very much."[39]

*Media Matters* was the first to pounce, claiming that Limbaugh believed any war veteran who did not support the Bush administration's war in Iraq was a "phony soldier." Bad, huh? At least as bad as

MovOn.org's ad about the general. That's what much of this was about, seeking some moral equivalence.

Senator John Kerry of Massachusetts chimed in to say Limbaugh's comments were "disgusting and an embarrassment." Democratic Senator James Webb of Virginia also reacted. "I really regret Mr. Limbaugh saying things like that. You know, we have, uh, political diversity inside the military just like we do in the country. … I really react strongly when people politicize the service of our military people," Webb said.

Limbaugh responded, "That comment, 'phony soldiers' was posted yesterday afternoon on the famous *Media Matters* website, which is where all leftists go to find out what I say. I have a website, and I have a radio program that reaches far more people than *Media Matters* could ever hope to, but the critics of this program never listen to this program. They never go to my website. All they do is read *Media Matters* and they get the lies and the out-of-context reports. They assume it's all true because they want it to be true, and then they start their campaigns. This has led to me being denounced on the floor of the House. Howard Dean has released a statement demanding I apologize; Jim Webb; John Kerry issued a statement, three Congress people went out on the floor of the House last night and said some things, and it's starting to blossom now in the Drive-By Media. So this is the anatomy of a smear, and this is how it starts."[40]

Even the White House was asked to respond. During a White House press briefing, a reporter asked, "Apparently this week Rush Limbaugh used the phrase phony soldiers to describe American troops who opposed the Iraq war. Given that the president has commented, uh, last week, uh, on the MoveOn ad, on General Petraeus, and called it 'disgusting,' is this something that the president would, you know, feel compelled to comment on?"

White House spokeswoman Dana Perino replied, "It's the first I've heard of that comment. Taking that it is accurate—I have not heard it myself—the president believes that if you are serving in the military, that you have the rights that every American has, which is that you're free to express yourself in any way that you want to, and there are some that oppose the war and that's okay."

The reporter followed, "The phrase "phony soldiers" to describe these—"

Perino answered, "It's not a phrase the president would have used."[41]

Then, putting a stamp of officialdom on the matter, Senate Majority Harry Reid of Nevada sent a letter to Clear Channel denouncing him for what they believed he said, saying he made a "characterization of troops who oppose the (Iraq) war as 'phony soldiers'."[42] The letter also included signatures from 40 fellow Democratic Senators, including Hillary Clinton, Ted Kennedy and Kerry.[43]

As usual, Rush not only survived the political attacks, but won his war with Democrats.

Limbaugh auctioned the much publicized letter from Reid on eBay, with the proceeds to go to charity for the children of fallen Marines, and the highest bid to be matched by Limbaugh. Betty Casey of the Eugene B. Casey Foundation bought the letter for $2.1 million to express her belief in free speech and support for Limbaugh. Limbaugh matched, for a total of $4.2 million for charity.[44]

Reid was now unable to attack, and fecklessly took to the Senate floor, where he had been lambasting Limbaugh. "I strongly believe when we can put our differences aside, even Harry Reid and Rush Limbaugh, we should do that and try to accomplish good things for the American people," Reid said.[45]

A Zogby poll of 3,472 adults released on November 20, 2008 actually said that that 12.5 percent of respondents identified Limbaugh as the most trusted news personality in America, taking the top spot over Fox News host Bill O'Reilly and former NBC anchor, then the interim host of Meet the Press, Tom Brokaw. The same poll found that 88 percent of conservatives believed the news was biased, while 58 percent of liberals believed the same.[46]

Barack Obama's election as president would be a huge bonus, as referred to in an earlier chapter, with a White House orchestrated strategy of calling Limbaugh the "leader of the Republican Party." It was an attack strategy that worked about as well as Reid's, in that it only helped Limbaugh and did nothing for Democrats.

In the anecdote that got perhaps the most attention from the 2010 biography "Rush Limbaugh: An Army of One" by Zev Chafets was a failed negotiated golf game between the president and Rush. The author recalls a conversation in which he asked Limbaugh, "You guys are both golfers," Chafets told Limbaugh. "Would you play a round with the president and show the country that there are no hard feelings?"

Limbaugh said, "He's the president of the United States. If any president asked me to meet him, or play golf with him, I'd do it. But I promise you that will never happen. His base on the left would have a shit-fit."

"How about letting me ask?" Chafets said. "Go ahead," Limbaugh said. "Nothing will come of it." Chafets asked, "What's your handicap just in case?"

Chafets wrote that he reached out to Obama political advisor David Axelrod, but did not get a return call. He then contacted "a very senior Democratic activist with whom I'm friendly." The senior activist touched base with the White House and had a response for the author in two days. The White House message to Limbaugh on golf was "Limbaugh can play with himself."[47]

Limbaugh did not always defeat the smear campaigns against him. A very successful smear by Al Sharpton's National Action Network, was launched to stop Limbaugh from joining a group of investors to buy the St. Louis Rams, an NFL franchise. NFL Commissioner Roger Goodell rejected Limbaugh's bid believing him to be too controversial.

But on balance, Limbaugh has had a remarkable record of telling it as he sees it and attracting an audience to hear it. No one can challenge his success as a matter of record. While liberals loathe him and even establishment Republicans find him irritating at times, he has become the standard by which other political radio show hosts are judged, if not also the standard that defines modern conservatism. What's more, he did both, became a big player in New York and Lancaster.

## CHAPTER EIGHT

# The Roaring '90s

The elimination of the Fairness Doctrine was the best thing that ever happened to talk radio, but the election of Bill Clinton as president in November 1992 might have been a close second.

Just ask G. Gordon Liddy, the convicted Watergate felon who built a successful radio program around the unscrupulous Clinton years. "If someone like Sam Nunn were president, I'd have vastly less to criticize," Liddy said.[1]

Though history will view talk radio as the mortal enemy of the Clinton administration, the two were quite friendly at one point, before talk radio became a domain for conservatives. As a candidate for president, Clinton "played talk radio like a piano" said Michael Harrison, editor of *Talkers Magazine*. The Arkansas governor was not as well financed or as well known as some of his opponents in the Democratic primaries, so while they took the conventional media route, he reached out to popular local and regional talk shows in the 1992 Democratic nominating contest and in the general election against President George H.W. Bush. Appearances on the Don Imus Show helped him win the New York primary.[2] Imus, not a conservative per se, later became one of Clinton's harshest critics.

As president, Clinton did 82 radio shows in his first year in office. First lady Hillary Clinton did 80.[3]

In April 1994, in a conversation with radio and television news correspondents, President Clinton expressed the utility of talk shows over dealing with reporters. "You know why I can stiff you on the press conferences?" he asked the broadcast reporters. "Because Larry King liberated me by giving me to the American people directly."[4]

Given the cozy relationship, what better medium to help sell the Clinton administration's universal health care initiative and other agenda items than on radio? Right?

### Talk Radio and the Clinton Agenda

One of the first Clinton era issues talk radio impacted was the new president's nomination of Zoe Baird to be the Attorney General. *The New York Times* reported that the corporate lawyer hired an illegal alien to be her baby sitter. Most TV pundits, even the conservative ones seemed to not care. But Limbaugh told his audience no one should be above the law, particularly someone who would run the Justice Department. "This is something the people out there just picked up on real fast." Other hosts picked up on the controversy as well, and even programs sympathetic to Clinton were overwhelmed with outraged callers. Two days after his inauguration, Clinton withdrew the Baird nomination.[5]

On September 21, 1993, more than 200 talk radio show hosts from across the country came to Washington for a briefing by White House staff on the health care proposal that came to be known as "Hillarycare" because of the first lady's involvement in crafting the plan. They were then given space on the lawn to broadcast their programs "direct from the White House."[6]

Hillary Clinton told the hosts she was a "talk show junkie," and appeared on several programs, as did White House aide Ira Magaziner, Secretary of Health and Human Services Donna Shalala, Clinton advisor David Gergen and Tipper Gore, wife of the vice president.[7]

The support the White House hoped for never materialized,

and many local and regional hosts turned against the proposal. Rush Limbaugh, not one of the invited guests, was already leading the charge against it on air.

Still, the Clinton's had reason to be confident, with much glowing coverage from the networks about the 1,300-page plan with a $784 billion price tag. After her testimony before six different committee on Capitol Hill in September 1993 about the proposal, ABC News named the first lady Person of the Week on September 24, 1993, as anchor Peter Jennings calling her "Hillary the problem solver" adding, "This particular individual had come a long way in the last year or so. And then we thought—no, maybe it's the country which has come a long way." A few days later, Bob Scheiffer, speaking of Hillary's testimony, said, "It was a buffo performance. Republicans were impressed. Democrats just loved it."[8]

In the summer of 1994, the Clintons scheduled a national bus tour to promote the plan. This was a golden opportunity for Limbaugh, who kept his listeners informed of the itinerary every stop of the bus. The tour was to start out west, in Portland, Oregon, then Seattle, Washington and work its way back to Washington, D.C.

At the Seattle stop, protesters turned out in big numbers and would not be quite to suit Ms. Clinton, prompting her to fire back.

"You know, there's an old saying," she said. "If you don't have the facts on your side, yell. And there is a lot of yelling going on in America and the yelling is starting to drown out the majority of Americans."[9]

Limbaugh recalled the summer of fun in an interview for the book "Whitewash" by L. Brent Bozell III and Tim Graham.

"We thoroughly disrupted it," Limbaugh said of the bus tour. "Everywhere they went they were greeted with more protestors and more heckling signs, so they had to schedule meetings at night and redo their itinerary. It was fun and we did it in a fun way."[10]

After the health care bill died, the Kaiser Foundation surveyed members of Congress and congressional staff to find that 46 percent said talk radio had been the most influential media source during the health debate. Just 15 percent cited *The New York Times*, 11 percent cited *The Wall Street Journal* and 9 percent cited TV. *The Washington*

*Times*, *The Washington Post* and the *Los Angeles Times* each got 4 percent.[11] Such results are quite mind blowing if you compare the influence of talk radio just a few years before. Is there any way they could have had such influence with the dark cloud of the fairness doctrine?

Talk radio assisted in a string of defeats for the Clinton administration and Democrats.

A bipartisan lobbying reform bill co-sponsored by Republican Senator William Cohen of Maine and Democrat Senator Carl Levin of Michigan passed the Senate in May 1994 by a vote of 95-2. A similar bill passed the House on September 9, 1994. It was promoted as legislation to prevent lobbyists from giving gifts, meals, trips and other things of values to members of Congress or congressional staffers. With such lopsided majorities in both houses, a conference committee vote seemed forgone conclusion.[12]

There was a problem. The legislation also increased disclosure requirements for lobbyists, with provisions that would affect people other than paid lobbyists. The bill required political and civic groups to disclose the names and addresses of all their volunteers, with fines of up to $200,000 for those who did not comply. Limbaugh called it "anti-American and unconstitutional," and read on air a letter from House Minority Whip Newt Gingrich to every Republican member.[13]

Limbaugh had Senator Levin as a guest. "Anybody who is just lobbying to express their own, personal view is not affected in any way. It's just if you're paid to lobby on behalf of another person," Levin said.

Limbaugh responded, "Well, this is awfully confusing and vague. There are a lot of people who are scared of this because the attitude is that members of Congress are sick and tired of hearing from constituents." Representative Earnest Istook, an Oklahoma Republican, came onto Limbaugh's show to insist the bill would affect volunteers.[14]

Pat Robertson, speaking on the 700 Club, a news program on his Christian Broadcast Network, also criticized the legislation. Thousands of phone calls and letters poured into the congressional offices opposing the measure. Thus, 44 senators switched the voted that October to join a filibuster killing the legislation when the conference bill came up for a vote.[15]

So it was with the Clinton's crime bill, an innocuous sounding piece of legislation since we're all against crime, until the details are exposed to the public. Gingrich came on to Limbaugh's show to chat about the $30 billion piece of legislation. "I briefed him on a provision of the crime bill that establishes quotas for murderers and quotas for the death penalty and he spent twenty minutes on the air describing it. What was at first fairly obscure for millions of Americans now became very real," Gingrich said. The Democratic House defeated the crime bill after getting feedback from constituents.[16]

*The Nation* magazine, one of the oldest liberal publications in the United States, blamed talk radio for Clinton being unable to do away with the ban on gays in the military, instead settling for a don't-ask-don't-tell policy. [17]

None of those matters hit Limbaugh and others quite as personal as the 1993 push by the Democratic Congress, now with a president of their party, to restore the Fairness Doctrine by codifying it in law.

Senator Earnest Fritz Hollings, a South Carolina Democrat, introduced a bill in the Senate to restore the Fairness Doctrine, while in the House Representative, Edward J. Markey, a Massachusetts Democrat and chairman of the subcommittee on telecommunications and finance for the Energy and Commerce Committee, held a hearing in July 1993 about bring back the doctrine.[18]

Rush was quick to fight back and dubbed it the "Hush Rush Bill."

"I am equal time," he would frequently say, referring to the left-leaning news media he felt obliged to balance. "Within a free market environment I have flourished," Limbaugh said speaking out against the legislation. "I am being blamed for the fact that far more American listeners, exercising their free market rights to choose their hosts and programs choose me."[19]

The Democratic proposal withered away.

### Revolution

An ABC News report on November 4, 1994—just days before the mid-term election—sounded almost alarmist. Peter Jennings introduced a segment by reporter Jim Wooten about "one of the most contentious politicians in the country." Wooten then went on to talk about "Republican congressman Newt Gingrich, whose slash-and-burn rhetoric against Democrats has made him the national poster boy for the politics of resentment and rage. And he's proud of it."[20]

Gingrich, in September, had laid out a 10-point plan that most Republican House members and candidates signed onto, known as the Contract with America.

The agenda items including a balanced budget amendment, term limits for members of Congress, welfare reform and tort reform.

It was rare at the time that congressional elections could be nationalized, and the Contract with America made it as close to a pure issues campaign as any in history. Nevertheless, similar to ABC, the GOP's effort to win Congress was frequently reported as a based on anger, fear and hate.

That's where talk radio came in. While offering its own over-the-top, lopsided characterizations of the campaign, much of the public preferred to know upfront where the host was coming from rather than a pretense of objectivity.

Two pre-election surveys spoke to the power of conservative talkers. A *Times Mirror* poll found 64 percent of those who regularly listened to talk radio thought about the coming elections while only 35 percent of the non-listeners had. Another *New York Times*/CBS News Poll found that 50 percent of Americans say they tune in at least occasionally to political call-in programs on radio and television.[21]

President Clinton seemed very aware of the potential impact, at least of Limbaugh. In May of 1994, as he was departing the CNN headquarters in Atlanta, a reporter asked, "Do you take a fairly relaxed attitude about the fact that some Members of the Georgia delegation, congressional delegation, would just as soon stay in Washington and not right now come down and be with you?"

Clinton answered, "Sure, I take a fairly relaxed attitude about whatever they want to do. But I think the—but I think the—you've got to understand, in the rural South where you've got Rush Limbaugh and all this right-wing extremist media just pouring venom at us every day and nothing to counter that, we need an election to get the facts out."[22]

*The New Republic*'s Fred Barnes declared in a piece, "America is experiencing its first talk radio election. ... The issues on the table this fall are practically all negative: the flaws of the Clintons, limiting congressional terms, the 1993 tax increase, 'pork' in the crime bill, the political culture of Washington. These are not issues Democrats (or even many Republicans) are eager to dwell on. In fact, they're issues Washington has trouble dealing with, period. But they're staples of talk radio."[23]

"Talk Radio is one reason Republicans expect to pick up House seats in Washington state, but not next door in Oregon. Washington is a big talk radio state. Oregon isn't," Barnes wrote.[24]

The power of talk radio was enough to be included in the pre-election ABC report, seemingly as evidence that Gingrich was fraternizing with those too far out of the mainstream.

"He has campaigned for conservatives who have signed his Contract with America—a Reaganesque platform," Wooten reported. "But he has also promoted himself and his dream of being speaker and always on the attack, as in this call to Watergate felon G. Gordon Liddy's radio broadcast."

"He is practiced and skilled at deliberate lying," Liddy said in the clip.

Gingrich replied, "There is no other way to explain how the President is campaigning this week than to say he is deliberately, systematically lying to the American people about our contract."[25]

A few days before the election, Limbaugh sought to rally the troops going into the midterm. He predicted "one of the most massive moves to the right" in a long time. "I told you that in the last two weeks you'd see the dominant media culture do what they can to rescue not just Clinton, but Democrats as well." He stressed that,

"This is not the time to be depressed. This is the time to remember the weapon that you have, and that is the vote."[26]

Limbaugh was aired on 659 radio stations with an audience of 20 million a week.

Limbaugh would start each show with a countdown: the number of days since the "Raw Deal" or the Clinton economic plan went into effect, "hostage crisis" or the days left in the Clinton Administration (as it turned out the days in the *first* term) and the days until the midterm elections.[27]

Gingrich came onto Limbaugh's show to declare "The odds are at least 2-1 we'll be the majority."[28]

Limbaugh would analyze Democratic talking points and Democratic ads during his TV and radio programs, citing that the Democrats seemed to have honed in on three phrases: A return to "Reaganomics," the "Star Wars" missile defense system and "trickle down economics," based on a focus group by Democratic pollster Stan Greenburg, that found nearly half the people had a negative reaction to those terms. Limbaugh further pointed out, "Nowhere do you hear them singing the praises of the Clinton economic plan—Clintonomics. You don't hear them singing the praises of health care or any of the legislative agenda or of any of their people. They're going back and attacking Ronald Reagan. I mean, it's been—1988 when he left office—'89 actually—it's been six years. It's over for these—but they think that's what they have to do." He was also refreshingly honest in his defense of the Contract with America, stating that much of it likely will not pass, but the goal is to force a vote, putting the onus on their rivals to block popular legislation. "All it does—it says these 10 things that we believe in we'll bring to the floor of the House for a vote and for debate. We know that if we don't pass them and sign them they're dead and if the Senate doesn't go along they're dead, and if the president doesn't sign them--they're not guaranteeing anything but than a debate will take place on these issues. And these Democrats are hysterical about this because they know this stuff works. It worked in the '80s and they were obviated in the '80s; they weren't needed. And they're afraid of that again."[29]

Before what would turn out to be a historic election, a *New York*

*Times* article said, "if Larry King's CNN program functioned as a nominating process for Ross Perot, Rush Limbaugh may be a kind of national precinct captain for the Republican insurgency of 1994."[30]

Limbaugh somehow managed to both relish and downplay his influence. "I don't have any power in the Republican Party at all, don't want any. But I have just been suggesting as a commentator and an analyst and a public figure and a concerned citizen that you guys had better come up with a list of things you believe in, your principles, your vision for America, and stick to it."[31]

An election night poll by Fabrizio-McLaughlin of 1,000 people asked: "Who do you think has been more straightforward in discussing the issues of this election?" The survey found 34.3 percent said Rush Limbaugh and conservative talk radio hosts, while just 26.9 percent answered the mainstream media. Most others answered "I don't know."[32]

On November 8 Republicans took the House as Limbaugh expected, and took the Senate to boot. Congress was under new management. Gingrich was Speaker of the House of Representatives. Bob Dole was the new Senate Majority Leader.

Network exit polls of key races found that 71 percent of talk radio listeners voted for Fred Thompson in the Tennessee Senate special election, 69 percent of listeners voted for George W. Bush in the Texas governor's race, 66 percent of talk radio listeners voted for Bill Frist in the Tennessee Senate race, 66 percent voted for Jeb Bush in the Florida governor's race, 62 voted for Spencer Abraham in the Michigan Senate race, and 58 percent voted for Mitt Romney in the Massachusetts Senate race.[33]

The celebration commenced. Rush's show began with James Brown's "I Feel Good" on November 9.

He called it "one of the most massive shifts to the right in any country in any year since the history of civilization."

"This was a personal, political and ideological refutation and repudiation of the most amazing attempt to move this country to the left we've seen in 50 years," Limbaugh said. "It's going to be a lot of fun because now the liberals are out of power, and that's when they get kooky.[34]

In an appearance on the show days after the election, Gingrich told Limbaugh, "Without C-SPAN, without talk radio shows, without all the alternative media, I don't think we'd have won. The classic media elite would have distorted our message. Talk radio and C-SPAN have literally changed for millions of activists the way they get information."[35]

Liddy said Clinton was next.

"This marks the beginning of the end of the dreadful, disastrous, venal, corrupt, sleazy Clinton presidency," Liddy said. "The American people have rescued themselves." Since stock prices had soared after the GOP victory, Liddy said: "Even Wall Street is hailing the defeat of the Clinton socialists."[36]

Known for being a little on the militant side, Liddy said, "The way to get rid of Bill and Hillary Clinton is not to bomb and strafe the White House from Cessnas, or use semiautomatic weapons from Pennsylvania Avenue. The way to do it is at the ballot box. ... Send 'em back there to the chicken-guts, waste-fouled waters of the rivers of Arkansas."

Not surprisingly, President Clinton decried talk radio's role in society and politics.

"One of the things that's staggering to me is if you think about how we educate people, normally we educate children to go find information," Clinton said in December 1994. "First, we teach them to read. Then we teach them to go to the library and look it up in the encyclopedia. ... When they listen to three hours of, let's say, talk radio a day, and somebody's just screaming at them all the time, how do they know what is true and what is false? How do they know what is important and what is insignificant? How do they know whether a fact is presented in a fair context or not?"[37]

New Republicans in Congress were willing to show their gratitude. Shortly after the election, GOP freshmen held a networking event in Baltimore, and Limbaugh was the keynote speaker.

"We validate what's in people's hearts and minds. To think I came along and got people excited about these things is ludicrous," Rush told the freshmen.[38]

On the contrary, former Minnesota Representative Vin Weber

said, "Rush Limbaugh is really as responsible for what has happened as any individual in America. Talk radio, with you in the lead, is what really turned the tide."[39]

Limbaugh and Michael Reagan were made honorary members of the freshman class.[40]

Gingrich had invited talk radio show hosts to broadcast live from Capitol Hill during the first 100 days of the 104th session of Congress and more than 40 showed up.[41] The first 100 days is when members of the new Congress would be voting on all the issues of the Contract with America. The lead up caused a bit of a kerfuffle as it went against protocol. The Radio and Television Correspondents Association determines who can broadcast live from the Capitol. The RTCA, largely controlled by networks ruled that these hosts could not broadcast because they were not reporters, thus could not have access to press rooms.[42]

"When I became Speaker, we decided to sidestep a fight with the established media by simply giving the talk shows another space in the Capitol," Gingrich wrote in his 1995 book, "To Renew America." "Little did any of us realize what an outpouring of national and local shows would soon arrive."[43]

During that opening day at the Capitol, Hartford host Judy Jarvis began her program "Welcome to the revolution." John Carlson, who has a talk show in Seattle proclaimed, "I haven't felt this much excitement about genuine change since I arrived here just out of college in '81 in the heyday of the Reagan revolution." "I wanted to see it close up. I wanted to see the old guard packing their bags and the new guard taking office."[44] Meanwhile Bill Cunningham of Cincinnati said from the Capitol, "God bless America! Normal people are back in charge!"[45]

San Diego host Roger Hedgecock brought a plane load of people with him that were sent to go around the Capital grounds promoting the Contract with America while he hosted his program from the Capitol basement. In the final week of voting on the contract, space was so scarce that radio shows were broadcasting from the balcony outside Gingrich's window, he recalled.[46]

"The elite media still controlled the news gallery, but it seemed that the radio talk-show hosts had taken over the rest of the building," Gingrich wrote. "I would not want to live in an America where the only source of information was talk radio. But as long as the elite media remains so cynical and so out of touch with average Americans, I sure am glad we have Rush Limbaugh and his friends to keep us company, keep us informed and keep us on the offense."[47]

### Hate Radio?

Up to that point, April 19, 1995, the bombing of the Alfred P. Murrah Federal Building in downtown Oklahoma City was the worst terrorist attack on America soil in history. The blast killed 168 people, 19 of them were children. A daycare center was located in the building. Almost as shocking as the attack was that the culprit was an American, an anti-government extremist who committed the act on the two year anniversary of the botched Waco operation.

Timothy McVeigh, who would be convicted in 1997 and executed in 2001 was a friend of Terry Nichols, who was also convicted of being a co-conspirator in the crime. Nichols attended meetings of the Michigan Militia, an anti-government group. The affiliation drew much attention to the general cynicism toward government that helped sweep Republicans into office the previous November.

President Clinton, already sore at talk radio, seized on the opportunity. He used a national crisis that could have made him seem very presidential to take a partisan cheap shot. Just days after the terrorist attack, he delivered remarks to the American Association of Community Colleges in Minneapolis.

"We hear so many loud and angry voices in America today whose sole goal seems to be to try to keep some people as paranoid as possible and the rest of us all torn up and upset with each other," Clinton said. "They spread hate. They leave the impression that, by their very words, that violence is acceptable. You ought to see—I'm sure you are now seeing the reports of some things that are regularly said over the airwaves in America today."[48]

Clinton called for Americans to oppose what he considers purveyors of violence. "It is time we all stood up and spoke against that kind of reckless speech and behavior," the president said. "When they talk of hatred, we must stand against them. When they talk of violence, we must stand against them. When they say things that are irresponsible, that may have egregious consequences, we must call them on it."[49]

Clinton did not specifically mention talk radio, though it was clear what he meant when talking about the "airwaves." Further, he did not use the phrase "hate radio," even though he was paraphrased as saying this by both supporters and opponents after his Minneapolis speech.

Talk show hosts did not have to hear their names to take the president to task for the comment. "If he's going to point the finger, he should say who he's talking about. He should not paint everyone with the same broad brush," Michael Reagan said.[50]

Rush Limbaugh was clear about what he saw as a strategy. "Liberals intend to use this tragedy for their own gain," he said. "The insinuations being made are irresponsible and are going to have a chilling effect on legitimate discussion."[51]

"I will not be chilled," Limbaugh continued in response to Clinton and said "a national hysteria is breeding and brewing" to blame conservatives for the bombing. A caller accused Limbaugh of contributing to the atmosphere that led to the attack and called him the "poster boy." Limbaugh responded that McVeigh was "an anarchist, lunatic nut case," and said militia groups were "weekend Bubbas going out with their guns to play soldier." He further said, "You cannot draw one area of similarity between me and these groups." And that "nobody on the radio today has been more outspoken about seeing that every American gets a shot at the American dream."[52]

Clinton's denunciation became a story in itself and the Clinton White House sought to backtrack and say they were not talking about all conservative radio. Liberal commentators came out swinging, proclaiming the president was right to go after talk radio. And their rhetoric was working, as a Washington Post poll found that 58 percent agreed that some talk show hosts "spread hateful ideas and give the impression that violence is acceptable."[53]

"They can call the president 'Coward in Chief' and imply he killed Vincent Foster, but if he mildly criticizes them, it's censorship. Sorry. It would be censorship if the government tried to revoke their licenses or seize their studios," Newsweek liberal columnist Jonathon Alter wrote. "Clinton was talking about responsibility. That doesn't mean that hate purveyors are responsible for wackos' blowing up buildings, but that they—and everyone else—are responsible for trying to prevent such violence. Responsibility is when people in positions of authority (including movie, TV, radio and recording executives) assess the possible social consequences of what they disseminate. This should be elemental and obvious, but it isn't."[54]

Liberal syndicated columnist Molly Ivins made a less reasoned argument, implying that criticizing someone's political opinions equaled ethnic smears.

"We are currently engaged in a silly argument about whether hate radio fosters hate. Yes. It does. And do we liberals dare to suggest that Rush Limbaugh belongs in this category? This liberal certainly does," Ivins wrote. "Tell you what—try a little experiment. Tune in or get on tape one of Limbaugh's rants, preferably when he's in high gear and going good. Then try substituting the words 'Jew' or 'Jewish' every time Limbaugh uses the word 'liberal.' I guarantee it'll take you back more than 50 years."[55]

Though denying he was speaking out against conservative talk radio in general, President Clinton did name G. Gordon Liddy during a May interview with the *Detroit Free Press*.[56]

"Some speech is wrong," Clinton said before traveling to East Lansing, Mich., for a commencement address at Michigan State University, a state where the militia movement was found to have very loose ties to McVeigh. "I cannot defend some of the things that Gordon Liddy has said. I cannot defend some of the things some of these more extreme talk show hosts have said."[57]

Liddy shot back that he had "never heard hate radio," and added, "I don't feel that I am fueling the lunatic fringe."[58]

This came after Clinton's first blaming talk radio when Liddy, in typical Liddy fashion, talked about the absurdity of it all. "I've got all sort of faxes and calls saying, 'You're responsible,'" the G-Man said. "That's Bravo Sierra—military phonetics for BS."[59]

### Radio's Road to Impeachment

President Clinton, perhaps forgetting he had the most powerful platform in the world, became irate during one radio interview with KMOX in St. Louis in May 1994. "I have determined that I'm going to be aggressive about it. After I get off the radio today with you, Rush Limbaugh will have three hours to say whatever he wants, and I won't have any opportunity to respond, and there is no truth detector. You won't get on afterward and say what was true and what wasn't."[60]

Clinton's remark launched one of Rush's enduring catchphrases. After the interview, Limbaugh said, "I am the truth detector." Limbaugh has since referred to himself as "America's Truth Detector," among his many informal titles.[61]

Clinton, and all the baggage he brought with him from Arkansas, was a true gift to talk radio. Whitewater, Filegate, Travelgate, Chinagate, Monicagate and various other matters would plague the Clinton presidency for eight years.

The news media certainly had its moments. It was the New York Times, a bible of the left that broke the story on the failed Whitewater land deal. But it was talk radio, with the help of the Wall Street Journal's editorial page that put the scandal on the national agenda.

The controversy traced back to 1978 with a real estate investment by the Clintons along with Jim and Susan McDougal into the Whitewater Development Corp. The partnership began when Bill Clinton was the Arkansan attorney general and continued through his time as governor. Hillary Clinton was a member of the Rose law firm, which handled legal business for the McDougals. David Hale, a former municipal court judge facing legal scrutiny for his own business dealings, alleged that Governor Clinton pressured him to provide an illegal $300,000 loan to the McDougals. The questions followed the Clintons to the White House in part because Hillary's Rose law partners Vince Foster and Webster Hubbell each got administration posts.

Attorney General Janet Reno named Robert B. Fiske, Jr. as the special prosecutor to look into the matter in January 1994. But after the independent counsel law was reauthorized in June, a three-judge panel appointed Kenneth Starr to probe the matter starting in August of that year. Robert Ray eventually took over for Starr in 1999.

After the Whitewater scandal saw the departure of White House counsel Bernie Nussbaum and Associate Attorney General Webster Hubbell, a feature in the Wall Street Journal asked people who were involved in the Watergate scandal if there were parallels with that and the Whitewater scandal. While other figures took a stodgy, scholarly approach, Liddy had fun, playing on his Watergate past.

"Despite our political differences, Bernie, I offer this letter of encouragement and urge you to do the right thing. What is important is that you remain loyal, keep your mouth shut and don't give up Hillary!" Liddy wrote. "The feds will be angry when you refuse to turn rat. They will threaten you with a long prison term. They sentenced me to 21 1/2 years. Don't let that scare you. Hell, I did only five. They'll let you out shortly after the Clintons are run out of town. Be strong, Bernie."[62]

Out of the Whitewater investigation came the questions about Vince Foster's death.

Contrary to what's often said about that era, Limbaugh did not directly allege murder. Rather he was among the first to bring reports to a mass audience that the body might have been moved. Rather than kill himself in a Virginia park in the summer of 1993, Limbaugh suggested Foster died in a hideaway used by White House officials and other Arkansans in Washington, and that the body was transported to Fort Mercy Park after his death. The stock market even reacted negatively to the report. Rush's source was the consulting firm Johnson Smick International. The rumor got coverage the next day in mainstream media outlets as a way of explaining the dip in the Dow Jones Industrial Average.[63]

Limbaugh gave a disclaimer when reading it on the air.

"Brace yourselves. This fax contains information that I have just been told will appear in a newsletter to Morgan Stanley sales personnel this afternoon. ... that claims that Vince Foster was murdered in an apartment and the body was taken to Fort Mercy Park." Later in the program, Limbaugh clarified "that Vince Foster committed suicide in an apartment in Washington and owned jointly or rented jointly by a number of Arkansas people who came to Washington to serve in the administration and the body was then moved to Fort Mercy Park. ... The original rumor was that Foster was murdered in this apartment and then moved." He added that a New York Post reporter he talked to did not believe the report, "so there are those who disbelieve the Johnson Smick report. But that's the big news today."[64]

Meanwhile, it was Liddy who produced someone who claimed to have seen Foster's body somewhere other than the park.[65] The mystery witness eventually did garner some mainstream media coverage, first by widely read conservative columnist Robert Novak in 1994, then in a story by Scripps Howard, the *Arkansas Democrat Gazette* in Little Rock and a few scattered places.[66]

Liddy said the "Mystery Witness" was the "man in the white van," who reported to U.S. Park Service maintenance worker who in turn notified the park police about the body. It was a matter of public record—not a theory—that a maintenance worker said an unidentified man in a white van told him about the body. But that worker changed his story, claiming to have lied because he spotted the body while looking for a quite spot to take a drink on the job. The "Mystery Witness" told Liddy when he found the body, there was not a gun in Foster's hand. Liddy did not say this meant Foster was murdered. Liddy theorized that Foster died in the secret apartment leased by White House aides and his body was discovered and moved to the park by friends who forgot the gun used for the suicide, and sometime after the "Mystery Witness" discovered the body, Foster's "friends" were able to place the gun in his hand at the park.[67]

"I have no idea whether he committed suicide or whether somebody helped him," Liddy said. "I am certain that whatever happened to him did not happen to him where his body was found."[68]

One survey found that 49 percent of talk radio listeners were familiar with Foster's death, compared to just 22 percent of the general public.[69]

Whitewater Independent Counsel Kenneth Starr had FBI officers comb through Fort Mercy Park in search of the bullet that killed Foster. The New York Daily News quoted one anonymous person close to the investigation as saying, "Starr has been under attack from the G. Gordon Liddys and the Rush Limbaughs. They hold the hoop a little higher, so he jumps a little higher. That's all this is."[70]

Three investigations—one by the park police, another by Fiske and another by Starr all concluded that Foster's death was a suicide. Starr's 1997 report found that body was not moved. "And I'm proud of that report," Starr said. "And I do not apologize at all for taking the time, the effort, the energy and the expense to say to the American people: We can tell you conclusively, if you're a person of good will and you'll listen to the facts, that Mr. Foster died by suicide, his own hand, and his body was not moved from anyplace. I think that's a very good thing in terms of promoting public confidence and also just assuring well-meaning people that there was not some terrible act that had been committed by one or more persons."[71]

After Whitewater came the Paula Jones allegation of sexual harassment. This case led to the president answering questions about Monica Lewinsky under oath, a subsequent cover-up and the first impeachment of a president in 130 years. The 27-year-old former Arkansas state employee claimed a bodyguard for then Governor Clinton invited her to a Little Rock hotel room on May 8, 1991 where the governor kissed her and exposed himself to her, asking for oral sex. She was 24 at the time. She said she refused and fled the room.

"I felt raped, whether he touched me or not," she said on the 700 Club with Pat Robertson, among the few media outlets to give her attention, and they played that point up.

The segment was introduced as a story with "the potential to bring down the Clinton presidency, but the media won't cover it." Ironically in the Jones case—perhaps because it pertained to sex—was driven onto talk radio by the mainstream media when the

Washington Post covered the fact that Clinton hired Washington super lawyer Robert Bennett. The presence of Bennett seemed evidence to many observers that the president was concerned about some type of information coming out, and it gave Jones credibility she did not have before.[72]

Throughout 1996, Rush Limbaugh, G. Gordon Liddy, Michael Reagan, Oliver North and others piled on Clinton. So did radio host Alan Keyes, who jumped into the 1996 GOP president primary as did California Representative Robert Dornan, a frequent guest host for Rush.[73]

That summer was a highly publicized convictions in the Whitewater case, where a federal jury in U.S. District Court in Little Rock believed the testimony of Hale over that of President Clinton. Ultimately, 15 people were convicted in the scandal, including Hubbell, Clinton's successor Governor Jim Guy Tucker and Jim and Susan McDougal. Hale was also convicted.

Also that summer of 1996 was the FBI files flap, in which it appeared the Clinton White House was gathering a Nixonian-style enemies list. That was followed by the campaign finance scandal that erupted just before the election provided immense fodder for the talk show hosts.

Most hosts learned to love the insufficiently conservative Bob Dole, though not everyone.

"I predict confidently that Bob Dole will be the next president of the United States," Liddy said on the air.

Neal Boortz said, "Sorry, folks, but I just don't see how Bob Dole can be elected."

Meanwhile, Michael Reagan said the Republicans would have done better with a "cardboard cutout" of his father.

Limbaugh, on the other hand, said, "Bob Dole is the next president of the United States. It's a fait accompli."

But with a strong economy at his back, and a hapless Dole candidacy, Clinton easily triumphed over the conservative talkers, winning 31 states, though still failing to win a majority, with just 49 percent of the popular vote. Liddy said, "You sometimes have to wonder about the intelligence of the American people."[74]

Limbaugh had an unusual—if not a somewhat prophetic given the coming events—spin.

"The people said, let's not have him get away with this," Limbaugh said. "We sent Bill Clinton back so you Republicans can continue to investigate and find out exactly what has gone on in these last four years."[75]

Most of 1997 would slog along. The hosts talked endlessly about the campaign finance scandal that involved money from China pouring into the Democratic National Committee in 1996. This scandal had its moments of drama and intrigue, as Buddhist monks testified before a Senate committee about Al Gore's appearance there just before the election, other witnesses fled the country, numerous others invoked their Fifth Amendment rights, and the news was filled with tales of wealthy donors getting a night in the Lincoln bedroom in the White House. It was easier to grasp than the convoluted Whitewater scandal, even if it lacked the colorful cast of characters. But at the end of the day, it was a campaign finance scandal, which makes John Q. Listener's eyes glaze over and change the dial.

In lieu of an election year and an easy scandal, talk radio took a hit. In September, numbers were trending downward from 14.8 percent in 1996 to 13.7 percent in 1997 according to American Demographics, Inc. Even Limbaugh lost 1 million listeners.[76]

One Clinton scandal received a big boost that June when the U.S. Supreme Court ruled 9-0 that the Jones sexual harassment case can proceed against Clinton while he is still president. The Jones legal team had already planned to subpoena past romantic interests of Clinton from his time in Arkansas and the White House. Few knew this would drop a bomb on Washington that was perfect not just for the media in general but conservative talk radio in particular.

Clinton would give his testimony in the Jones case in January 1998, where he denied a sexual relationship with Monica Lewinsky, a White House intern. Lewinsky gave the same testimony. The story leaked that Starr had expanded the scope of his inquiry into whether the president had lied under oath in a federal lawsuit.

The Lewinsky impeachment scandal could not have come at a better time for talk radio.

"I cannot tell you how much Rush appreciates Monica Lewinsky," said Jacor Communications Chief Executive Randy Michaels. "Although we don't have the ratings yet for 'Zippergate,' the number of people calling and saying, 'Hey, what's 'ditto' mean?' tells you how much new audience we've got on that show."

Meanwhile, hosts such as Liddy and Janet Parshall proudly—and mockingly—claimed to be part of the "vast right wing conspiracy" that Hillary Clinton told NBC News was behind the Lewinsky allegation.[77]

Talk radio ratings were back to 14.8 percent in total listening audience in 1998, with a smaller than normal drop-off from the winter months, according to Arbitron. Listening usually goes down during the winter. In the final quarter of 1998, talk radio drew 15.3 rating, up marginally from 15.2 in the final quarter of 1997.[78]

Limbaugh, who in 1997 had fallen to the number three slot in radio behind Dr. Laura Schlessinger, a personal advice program and Howard Stern, a morning shock jock, reemerged as number one during 1998, according to magazine ratings.[79]

On the day the Lewinsky scandal broke, Liddy's program opened with a singing of "Oh, What a Beautiful Morning."[80] With impeachment in the air, Liddy proposed a question of the week to his callers. "Will President Gore pardon Bill Clinton?" Liddy's answer was no. He believed President Gore would learn from Gerald Ford and improve his chances for 2000. But he solicited caller input to see what his audience anticipated.[81]

In an interview with *The New York Times*, Liddy said he expected Democrats would eventually call on Clinton to resign similar to how Republicans called for his old boss to resign in the 1970s. "There is one other parallel," Liddy said. "What brought down Richard Nixon was not the burglary I was running but the cover-up. They never learn."[82]

When the Lewinsky scandal first broke, most Republican lawmakers barely made a peep, content to let the news media cover it non-stop. Rush said the liberal media coverage was equivalent to "white cells finally starting to fight a virus." Rush made no pretense of his glee. "We're going to have fun with this," he said. Limbaugh played the song by Garry Puckett and the Union Gap "Young girl, get out of my life, " the Mac Davis song lyrics, "Baby, baby, don't get hooked on me," and said "That's what Bill Clinton should have told Monica Lewinsky. How about that, Monica? Kind of true, huh?"[83]

Having once started his program—right after Clinton took office as Day [X] of American Held Hostage," Rush at this point switched to starting the show, "Day [X] of Tailgate."[84]

Neal Boortz asked his listeners to come up with a name for the scandal. "Tailgate" was the most popular, following the Rush lead. But "Fornigate" was also popular.

The Starr investigation dragged on throughout the summer, until the Clinton DNA-stained blue dress eventually forced the president to admit the truth. After his testimony to the federal grand jury, Clinton delivered an address to the nation that evening, August 17, 1998.[85]

"As you know, in a deposition in January, I was asked questions about my relationship with Monica Lewinsky," the president said. "While my answers were legally accurate, I did not volunteer information. Indeed, I did have a relationship with Ms. Lewinsky that was not appropriate. In fact, it was wrong. It constituted a critical lapse in judgment and a personal failure on my part for which I am solely and completely responsible."

The next day Rush conducted a mock interview with the president, asking him several questions such as why did he lie about Republicans cutting Medicare or why did he raise taxes. After each question, was the audio, "It constituted a critical lapse in judgment and a personal failure on my part for which I am solely and completely responsible."

Clinton eventually began showing more contrition, as the finger-pointing tone of the speech that mostly focused on the Starr investigation and the "politics of personal destruction," lacked the contrition he might need to survive impeachment. Clinton even shed tears at a prayer breakfast, surrounded by clergy, in which he confessed to being a sinner seeking redemption.

"Contrition is now defined as a strategy," Limbaugh said, shifting to a Clinton impression, "I'm very sorry, I'm very sorry." Limbaugh stated mockingly. "It's all phony, ladies and gentleman, plastic banana, phony baloney, good-times-rock-and-roll." With regards to the Democrats defense that the entire matter was about sex, he said, "The Democratic Party is now the party of lying about sex, now the party of perjury, now the party of adultery? Fine, you Democrats want it—you own it."[86]

Remarkably, Clinton's approval rating seemed to increase as the impeachment scandal dragged on. As the public grew sick of the matter, they seemed to support leaving Clinton in office. Clinton's personal charisma, a strong economy, and perceived overreaching by Republicans, allowed Democrats to actually gain seats in the 1998 midterm elections when the conventional wisdom was that Democrats would take a beating.

An impeachment was still a strong likelihood, as Republicans maintained control of House, but even talk radio was almost resigned to the fact that getting two-thirds vote in the Senate would not be possible. The issue had become a matter of principle, of making clear for the record that a president of the United States cannot commit perjury and obstruct justice. Just before Christmas, the House voted almost along party lines—only five Democrats voted in favor, four Republicans voted against—to send two articles of impeachment to the Senate, putting Clinton alongside fellow southern Democrat Andrew Johnson as the only two impeached presidents in U.S. history. This came with a cost, as House Speaker Gingrich and his designated successor Representative Bob Livingston of Louisiana both resigned from the House. Gingrich, as a result of the GOP's poor showing in the election and Livingston after his own past infidelities came to light.

Both articles of impeachment failed to even get a majority vote in the Senate. Only the obstruction of justice charge got 50-50 vote, while 10 Republicans bolted to vote against the perjury charge, making it a 45-55 vote.

It seemingly did not bode well for conservatives, but Rush took it in stride.

"I really view the approval numbers for the president more a statement from the people, 'Look, don't mess with anything here because, really what matters to me is my family and my back pocket and my future. I don't see this scandal affecting me in any economic way,' and I don't think people had a sense of—of what was at jeopardy here," Limbaugh said. "I don't think that people really understood that the rule of law here was being shattered, and we were establishing two sets of laws, one for the privileged and one for the not."[87]

### On the Air with the G-Man

Beyond Watergate, G. Gordon Liddy will likely be remembered most for his general advice should federal agents from the Bureau of Alcohol, Tobacco, Firearms and Explosives storm your home with guns blazing. He did not, as was frequently reported, give instruction on how to kill federal agents.

The comment was frequently used to attack Liddy by leftwing commentators and even by the president of the United States, though it was rarely presented in context. On August 26, 1994, Liddy said on his show: "Now, if the Bureau of Alcohol, Tobacco and Firearms comes to disarm you and they are bearing arms, resist them with arms. Go for a head shot; they're going to be wearing bulletproof vests." He went on to say, "They've got a big target on there, ATF. Don't shoot at that, because they've got a vest on underneath that. Head shots, headshots. Kill the sons of bitches."[88]

Even in context it may be inappropriate to encourage resisting arrest under duly sworn officers. But the ATF was different in the view of Liddy and others in the wake of mishaps such as Ruby Ridge and Waco. Liddy called the ATF "a pack of nitwits out to make war on those Americans who take seriously the Second Amendment." This was indeed more than a gaffe as he repeated the advice, explained and defended it

As over-the-top, and reckless as it might have been, once Liddy explained further, his statement actually seemed a little rationale, but only if one accepts the premise that federal agents would knowingly set out to invade a home and kill someone. "You are not in any way justified in shooting a BATF agent unless and until that BATF agent is attempting to kill you," Liddy said. "If they come at you with lethal force, shooting, as in Waco ... what are you going to do, let them kill you?"[89]

Another clarification was hardly what his diehard critics were looking for. He explained shooting for the head was bad advice because the head is difficult to hit. "So you shoot twice to the body, center of mass, and if that does not work, then shoot to the groin area," he said. "They cannot move their hips fast enough and you'll probably get a femoral artery and you'll knock them down at any rate." This prompted a station in San Bernardino, Calif. to immediately drop from the air.[90]

Liddy had been one of the key critics of the botched ATF operation in Waco, Texas at the Branch Dividian compound. He got much backlash for the comment, and essentially handed the proverbial sword to his critics to stab him. It was not the only time. He admitted to also drawing two stick figures for target shooting on July 4 and naming the figures Bill and Hillary. "Thought it might improve my aim, It didn't. My aim is good anyway."[91]

Though Liddy has often been considered on the fringe even for talk radio, he has an adoring fan base, is easily one of the most colorful hosts and is even a personal friend of comedian turned liberal talk show host turned Democratic U.S. Senator Al Franken. During the 1990s, he was a distant second to Limbaugh among political talkers with three million listeners. Syndicated nationally through Westwood One, his program airs from 10 a.m. to 2 p.m., allowing devoted Limbaugh listeners to at least get the first two hours of the program. The show has been broadcast out of Fairfax, Va., near Washington, and is nicknamed "Radio Free D.C." He called it the "jamming signal of the liberal establishment."[92]

Well before he came to be nationally known for masterminding the Watergate burglary, Liddy tried radio as a student working for Fordham College's radio station. It was not until 44 years later that he returned to the airwaves as a guest host for Bob Grant on WABC in 1992, 20 years after Watergate. Infinity chief Mel Karmazin liked what he heard and recommended him to WJFK-FM in Washington, D.C. The general manager Ken Stevens had a midday slot available

187

for the FM talk station. Liddy started doing a once a week before he was hired to do a daily program that almost instantly became syndicated. And, in 1995 amid all the controversy, the National Association of Radio Talk Show Hosts presented him with the Freedom of Speech Award.[93]

"We mean to throw the gauntlet in this historic battle. Let those who limit any person's speech pick it up," said NARTSH president Gene Burns. The board voted 21-4 to give Liddy the award.[94]

It was just in time for the president and first lady who were such a bonanza of material to help his show become a success.

Listening to Liddy, one will never find him inciting violence. Generally, it has been one of the funnier, irreverent conservative talk radio shows from a guy known by his tough guy reputation. Nearly every account of Liddy's life, after Watergate and his radio career, mentions the famous anecdote of Liddy putting his hand inside an open flame, to display how he can withstand pain.

"He brings with him the intrigue of his past—the Watergate connection, his careers as FBI agent, prosecutor, Treasury official and more—but his willingness to criticize Republicans when necessary sets him apart from many of his contemporaries," Talker's Magazine said of Liddy. "Far from being a conservative apologist, he demands an intellectual approach to his program from both himself and his listeners, which make his show more of an exercise in thinking than a sermon from the right-wing political establishment."[95]

The radio show frequently pitched him as "virile, vigorous and potent" even in his 60s during the 1990s boom. Female listeners often called him sexy. Female callers described the host as "sexy." On the lighter side of the Branch Davidians, a female caller talked about research she had done on doomsday cults and about a "mad messiah" who will "suddenly announce everybody is his wife." Liddy responded, "I'm just fascinated by having everybody be my wife. I'm just fixated on that … I'm a hell of a lot more interesting than David Koresh. I'm a lot more heavily armed." The female caller giggled.[96]

He frequently talked about "Washington's premier newspaper, *The Washington Times*," and would read articles on the air. When the tortured need arose to reference *The Washington Post*, the bleep signal was used, "The Washington BLEEP," as if it was an FCC violation.

While Liddy's critics suggest his felon status impedes his credibility, the former general counsel for the Committee to Re-Elect the President during Watergate, argues its one part of his broader life experience as a former FBI special agent, a Treasury Department official, an Army artillery officer, a prosecutor, a defense attorney, trained in martial arts, actor and prisoner who knows virtually everything about guns. So the man with numerous life experiences was carried by almost 200 stations a year after its summer 1993 launch.[97]

Liddy was not repentant about Watergate, asserting he did not believe it was a crime against the constitution. "It depends on what you include under the rubric Watergate. If you limit it to the break-in at the Watergate Hotel and subsequent cover-up, that had nothing to do with (subverting) the Constitution. I was not an officer of the government at that time; nor was I bound by an oath to defend the Constitution. This was a political intelligence-gathering operation," Liddy said. But he added, "I can see an argument if one includes the break-in of Dr. Fielding's office (Daniel Ellsberg's therapist) out in Beverly Hills because then I was a government agent. However, I would point out to you that it was a matter of national security. Here was a man (Ellsberg) who had access to the entire top-secret holdings of the Rand Corp. He said himself that he took them, including the so-called Pentagon Papers, which were highly classified. We did not know whether he was operating with the KGB. "I did not consider that to be a violation of the Constitution any more than I considered it a violation of the Constitution (to spy) against the East Bloc countries. I was serving my country."[98]

He always maintained the Clinton was a bigger crook than Nixon. "He's corrupt and venal. There's a hell of a lot more dirt to be found in the background of Bill Clinton than there ever was in Richard Nixon's."[99]

Speaking of Bill, he said, "When his country called, he was a coward. Character? What character?" He called Hillary "A committed, hard-left ideologue." With regards to her lucky commodity trades, he said, "She was in there to receive a bribe. Geez. Let's wake up and smell the coffee, people." And speaking about a new law banning semi-automatic weapons, "It's as phony as Bill Clinton's wedding vows."[100]

Liddy never shied from conspiracy theories, and generally questioned the death of White House aide Vince Foster. During the Obama administration, he was one of the few talk radio personalities to question the president's birthplace.

After reports that three Marines in Haiti had committed suicide, Liddy said, "There's a terrible amount of suicide going on, as you know, in the Clinton administration—it's apparently an Arkansas disease. We did have the alleged suicide of Vincent Foster, deputy counsel to the president, and now three of our troops in Haiti are alleged to have committed suicide. And the response is to send in a squad of psychiatrists, we understand, to Haiti. Now if they would send the psychiatrists into the White House, maybe they'd find out what the hell we're doing in Haiti in the first place ... The coward-in-chief can hardly be expected to give a damn about the troops down there."[101]

### Michael Reagan: The Great Radio Communicator

It is more than a little bit ironic. Ronald Reagan is the president conservatives most revere, almost universally, while they had at best mixed feelings regarding George H.W. Bush. Both presidents had sons with rowdy youths, with issues that could have presented liabilities in a political campaign. Yet it was the son of the moderate Bush rather than the son of the conservative Reagan that followed in the footsteps of his presidential father.

Reagan's other children, Ron and Pattie, were liberals known for embarrassing their political parents on occasion. The adopted Michael Reagan, who like George W. Bush turned his life around in his 40s, but never sought public office. Instead, Reagan followed his father's footsteps in other ways by becoming a radio announcer. In fact, the 40th president once dreamed of becoming little more than a radio sports announcer.

For Michael, given his last name, politics would have to be part of his on-air persona, as he became part of the 90s boom. Months after his father had revealed to the nation that he had Alzheimer's, the younger Reagan did not hold the matter out of bounds for discussion.

"Maybe we should have elected Ronald Reagan for a third and a fourth and a fifth and a sixth term, because no matter what his problems are with Alzheimer's disease, he would still be a better President than what we have," the son said during 1995 broadcast.[102] He did not limit his ridicule to Clinton alone, targeting White House advisor George Stephonoplos as "George Step-on-All-of-Us."[103]

It was after 1987 his life began to change for the better. Michael confessed to his parents, the President and actress mother Jane Wyman, that at age seven he was sexually abused by a camp counselor as a child.[104] He kept the experience hidden for his entire life. In 1988, his autobiography "On the Outside Looking In," he wrote about the divorce of his Hollywood parents, the shock of discovering he was adopted, and the abuse incident. The book was self critical, but also described his parents as neglectful. Though he explained that he told his father before the publication it was not a sensational tell-all "Mommie Dearest" book. Rather, he said, "If anything, my book is a Michael Dearest." He described that he once became so angry with his mother and destroyed his car with a sledgehammer, his debt problems, his fighting with his parents, and his temporary estrangement from Ronald and Nancy Reagan when the Secret Service accused him of being a kleptomaniac, a charge he said was false. During this time he had to call White House staff to reach his father.[105]

The college dropout did not live the typical privileged life of a politician or movie star's son. He loaded freight, raced and sold boats, and promoted chainsaws. However, he did move toward the entertainment arena becoming a game show host, a soap opera actor and hit the public speaking circuit. Of some embarrassment to the White House, he was investigated and cleared in a stock fraud case, and was criticized for using his father's name to help sell aerospace equipment.[106]

191

"I was so angry and hurt inside that I didn't know who I was until I was 43," Michael said. "I didn't want to succeed. I wanted my dad to succeed and pull me along with him. I didn't do anything for myself. Everything I did was to get my parents' approval."[107]

He got a modest start in radio when he was waiting to meet his wife at the studios of KABC in 1983. There, a station manager George Green asked him whether he had ever thought about getting into talk radio, he then began filling in for Michael Jackson, the talk show host not the musician.[108]

The memoir, he said, helped him reconcile with his parents, put much of his past behind him and gain the confidence for a talk radio program in 1989, a year when the country was just beginning to miss President Reagan.

There were rumors and requests for Michael Reagan to jump into the electoral arena to challenge California Democratic Congressman Bill Lowery in 1992. But a year ahead of the election, he said there would not be another Reagan on the California ballot. "I'm going to spend some more time doing talk radio before I run for Congress," he said, adding he would keep raising money for Republican candidates.[109]

Had he pursued a career in Congress, his radio show might not have taken off as it did. The program originally aired on a San Diego station. It began humbly, as he would be on the air for four hours sometimes barely getting any calls. He was nationally syndicated through Premiere Radio Networks on 200 stations and eventually reached 5 million listeners.[110] It was the number one night time talk show in the country.[111]

He believes talk radio makes up for his dropping out of college, as he said he would read eight newspapers per day. Talk radio "is like going to school every day and I think it is God's way of getting back at me for dropping out of college."[112]

Michael also wrote two other bestsellers, "Making Waves" and "The City on the Hill." He published *The Monthly Monitor* newsletter, and wrote a column for *Newsmax* magazine.[113]

For Michael Reagan, the 1994 Republican revolution was a touching moment, as he broadcast from the opening day of

Congress in January 1995. "More Reagan Republicans were elected on November 8 than when my father was elected in 1980," he said. "It's an exciting moment for me."[114]

He was not always in line with his father. He opposed the Brady Bill gun control law, named for President Reagan's former press secretary James Brady who took a life altering bullet the same time Reagan was shot. He also supported Oliver North's bid for the Virginia Republican Senate nomination in 1994, even though his step mother Nancy Reagan supported Reagan's former budget director James Miller.[115] He further broke ranks with the GOP and supported incumbent Senator Dianne Feinstein against Republican Michael Huffington. "I also think there are stupid Republicans. I think Michael Huffington is an embarrassment to the Republican Party. He should find another state to live in. I will take on people that others wouldn't think I'd take on. That's given me credibility.[116]

In 1996, when much of the talk radio community was solidly aligned against Pat Buchanan capturing the Republican presidential nomination, Michael Reagan said "Pat Buchanan has earned the right to carry the banner of conservatism," no doubt remembering his service at the Reagan White House communications director.[117] He even squared off with Limbaugh on the matter.

"Rush Limbaugh may run around with a letter from my dad, but Pat Buchanan's running around with delegates for a convention, which is a heck of a lot more important at this point," Regan said in a February 25, 1996 broadcast after Buchanan had won contests New Hampshire, Louisiana and Alaska.[118]

In March 1997, he announced he was taking a "leave of absence" from the Republican Party, registering as an independent. He believed the party had abandoned his father's legacy. He ripped into party leaders such as House Speaker Newt Gingrich and 1996 presidential candidate Bob Dole in "The City on the Hill," published the following fall. He did not even hold his fire on President George H.W. Bush, whose presidency he called a "footnote." He questioned why the Republican Party swept into victory on a promise to shrink government gave up on eliminating the National Endowment for the Arts and the Department of Education.[119]

"Every day I open the newspaper, hoping for some sign that the Republicans have grown a backbone—and every day I find that the Republican majority has caved on yet another issue," Reagan wrote. "Haven't Republicans learned why the Rockefeller Republicans, the moderate-to-liberal Republicans like George Bush and Bob Dole— keep losing elections? George Bush watched grass-roots Republicanism in action for eight years and learned precisely nothing from it. As soon as he was in office, he purged all the Reaganites ... He brought in the East Coast establishment Republicans and promptly began dismantling the Reagan legacy." He later adds, "Today's Republican Party, is rudderless, leaderless, and in full retreat from the conservative values and vision of Ronald Reagan."[120]

Despite his jabs at Bush the father in his 1997 book, he supported Texas Governor George W. Bush in the 2000 primary against Arizona Senator John McCain. Like other hosts, he was not happy when McCain secured the nomination in 2008.

He was also very tough on the Republican majority in Congress. Like many others, he had a tough time mustering support for the party during 2006. After the congressional page scandal involving Representative Mark Foley of Florida erupted, Reagan also tore into Republicans. "Any member of Congress who was aware of the sexual emails and protected the congressman should also resign effective immediately."[121]

Similar to Liddy, his prominence waned over the next decade as more hosts burst on the national scene. He stayed on the air until 2010. He's still heard on the public speaking circuit and as an occasional TV pundit.

### Michael Medved's Thumbs Up Media Career

Michael Medved grew up a California kid (though born in Philadelphia) who went to Yale, where he graduated with honors after protesting the Vietnam War. He went on to Yale Law School, among his classmates there were Bill Clinton and Hillary Rodham.[122] That's not the best resume for a future conservative pundit. And there's more.

He joined Bobby Kennedy's presidential campaign team in 1968 and was in Los Angeles when Kennedy lost his life. "It was as if Kennedy's death had put a holy seal on my commitment. Over the next three years, liberal politics became my whole life," he told *The Seattle Times*.[123]

And it did for a while. He quit Yale law school and took jobs writing speeches for Democratic candidates. But he began to become more theologically conservatives, observing the Jewish Sabbath, the plight of Israel and saw virtue in military power. He also saw the product of what he spent so much time protesting for, giving up in Vietnam. Ultimately, there were what he called the three Ps, Paychecks, Parenthood and Prayer.

"I became a parent for the first time in 1986 when, then 38. That was after hoping for children for a while. My wife and I suffered a miscarriage, which moved me strongly to the pro-life direction," Medved recalled in an interview for this book. "Then the paychecks aspects; I had scholarships in college and law school. Right after law school, I was working in campaigns, when you get paid in political campaigns, particularly for liberal Democrats, [pay] came in cash, some of it actually literally cash in brown paper bags. When I started getting checks and regular paychecks, I started noticing, wait a minute, where did all this money go?"

The most decisive event in his conversion to conservatism was the aftermath of the Vietnam War.

"One of the best arguments was whether or not an American withdrawal from Vietnam would result in a bloodbath. That term was used a lot by the administration. I even was on TV as a political activist and wrote speeches saying the whole bloodbath charge was absurd," Medved recalled. "The stories that I became obsessed with in Vietnam were occurring at a time when America was either indifferent or celebratory about communist butchery. That, it seemed to me, was the height of hypocrisy and demonstrated that the liberal platitudes that I had formerly enthusiastically embraced were toxic."[124]

His first foray into social criticism came when he and Palisade High School pal David Wallechinsky interviewed attendees to the 10-year-reunion of "Class of '65," turning it into a book, *What Really Happened to the Class of '65?* criticizing the boomer generation and painting the counterculture as a fraud. The book became the basis for a weekly TV series on NBC, which helped catapult Medved into some opportunities as a Hollywood screenwriter, and later a movie critic.[125]

After writing reviews for newspapers, he became a film critic for CNN and later was the co-host of "Sneak Previews," a TV show on Public Broadcasting Service about upcoming films.[126]

After immersion in Hollywood, in 1992, he came out with the book that would move him into the conservative movement. *Hollywood vs. America*, was among the first books from a film industry insider to indict the industry for its attacks on traditional American values.

"On Sneak Previews every month we used to do a trend show. And our trend shows were all outrageously conservative and people started to notice," Medved said. "We did a show called Hollywood vs. Religion. We did a show called Kids Know Best. We did a show called Does Hollywood Bash Big Business? So a lot of that material sort of fed into *Hollywood vs. America* in 1992."[127]

The book became a bestseller.

"Hollywood no longer reflects or even respects the values of most American families. On many of the important issues in contemporary life, popular entertainment seems to go out of its way to challenge conventional notions of decency," the book says.[128]

*The Guardian*, the leading liberal broadsheet in Britain said of Medved's book, "Just occasionally, a book changes the way the world thinks. Michael Medved's *Hollywood vs. America* is such a book."[129]

Then Rush Limbaugh interviewed Medved about the book for the Limbaugh Letter. It gained a huge response, and Limbaugh asked Medved to guest host his program. which Medved did about 30 times before getting his own program in 1996.[130]

As cultural trends were mixing more and more with politics, Medved got a talk radio program in Seattle's KVI-AM, from Noon-the 3 p.m. west coast time in 1996, which happened to be an election year.[131] That same year, he also became the chief film critic for the *New York Post* in 1996.[132] So movies and politics were a big part of his radio job and continue to be.

Medved's 2004 book *Right Turns*, talked about 35 "unconventional lessons" from his transition from "punk liberal activist" to "lovable conservative curmudgeon."

One example of his moderation: He has said, "There is a strain of conservatives that has over-reacted to environmental extremists. It drives me crazy that many conservatives fail to understand that saving old-growth forests is a profoundly conservative idea." At the same time, of global warming, he said, "It's a complete scam."[133]

Among the most measured programs, he took advice from the king of the medium on what not to do.

"One of the things that Rush actually told me: Don't try to pretend to be somebody you're not," Medved recalled. "The shows that I dislike on talk radio are shows where I think it's extraordinarily obvious to everybody that the host is just playing a part and is not the person he pretends to be. I like the fact that when people meet me and get to know me after the show, they get it. Yeah, I really am that guy. I don't make an effort to pretend to be anything that I'm not. In that regard, I'm not an angry person. I'm a grateful person. I've really had a wonderful life and I've had wonderful opportunities. I've been extraordinarily fortunate and blessed with my family. I don't, for the purpose of generating energy, pretend to be furious, enraged, or desperate or any of those things."[134]

While holding great reverence and appreciation to Rush, he said many hosts are inclined to never disagree with Rush.

"There is a tremendous tendency for everybody to follow the leader. Particularly because Rush is very close to Sean and Sean is very close to Mark Levin, there is a great sense of sort of the Limbaugh line," Medved said. "And also because so many people are grateful to Rush for getting their start—Sean is, I am—it was hard for me initially, but Rush takes this extremely destructive and I think wrongheaded point about Obama: That it's on purpose, Obama is deliberately trying to wreck the country. He has been doing that a little bit less thank God. But I think that makes conservatives look stupid. It's not a re-election strategy to wreck the country. I think that Obama is wrecking the country. But I think it's because he embraces a mistaken ideology and he's incompetent."[135]

197

He is also a multi-media star, as a columnist for Townhall.com, for USA Today and a regular pundit on various cable news shows.

He is a solid pro-Israel voice on the air, and since 2006, annually takes about 100 of his listeners there each year for an eight-day trip. "The basic idea is, again, to give people a more rounded picture, because the one thing you perpetually hear in the States is, how do they [Israelis] live there, how can people live there knowing that they could be blown up at any moment? The truth is, we emphasize that even with the terrorism statistics, Israel remains one of the safer countries in the Western world; your chances of being victimized by violence in Jerusalem, Tel Aviv or Haifa are significantly less than in most American cities. Basically we try to look at the positive and life-affirming aspects of Israel instead of focusing on it as a center of conflict."[136]

Despite being Jewish, he strongly embraces conservative Christians and their support of the Jewish state. "You have to ask yourself, if you're stuck in a foxhole with someone and you're defending your life, would you rather have someone standing next to you because he decided this is a good thing politically, or someone standing next to you because God told them to?"[137]

With a national syndication through the Salem Radio Network, he is carried on 200 stations drawing about 3.5 million listeners per week, Medved still mixes pop culture with politics.[138]

"Talk radio shows are often very repetitive. It's the same damn thing every day and it's very predictable," Medved said. "I try to be less predictable, not with positions that I take but with topics I will cover. I think, your daily dose of debate, which is one of our tag lines, privileging disagreeing phone calls, is one of the ways we keep the show a little more fresh and predictable. Very typically, you will hear more disagreeing phone calls in a single three hour broadcast in one day than you will hear in a month on most talk radio shows."[139]

### Dennis Prager: Speaking Objective Truth to Moral Relativism

The often time professorial Dennis Prager is a devout Jew who found common cause with politically active evangelical Christian in making morality a central focus. He has been a thought provoking and thoughtful broadcaster going back to 1982 on KABC in Los Angeles.

In the belly of the beast of moral relativism, he said country's "moral compass is broken" because of several factors. One has been the entertainment industry and public education, but also from progressive leaning churches and synagogues.[140]

"Moral relativism means that murder, for example, is not objectively wrong; you may feel it's wrong, but it is no more objectively wrong than your feeling that some music is awful renders that music objectively awful," Prager wrote. "It's all a matter of personal feeling. That is why in secular society people are far more prone to regard moral judgments as merely feelings. Children are increasingly raised to ask the question, 'How do you feel about it?' rather than, 'Is it right or wrong? ... In secular society, where there is no God-based morality, there is no moral truth to pursue. The consequences may be easily seen by observing that the most morally confused institution in America, the university—where good and evil are often either denied or inverted—is also its most secular.'"[141]

Like many other prominent conservative media figures, Prager used to be a Democrat. He deserted the party during the sad Jimmy Carter presidency, and referred to the "late great Democratic Party" that he thought moved too far left.[142]

He never held a formal government post, but during the 1980s, President Reagan appointed him to a U.S. delegation to the Vienna Review Conference on Helsinki Accords. He has even been known to conduct a classic orchestra.[143]

His radio show went national in 1999.[144] The next year, he left KABC to go to the rival station KIEV to continue his conservative message in the upcoming Bush administration, where his show continued to be carried.[145] His program runs 9 a.m. to Noon in the West coast, which is Noon to 3 p.m. in the East. That puts him head to head against Rush Limbaugh, never an enviable place to be. He nevertheless continues on the air.

He is the author of four books, two of them on Judaism and the culture, and has conducted interfaith dialogue forums with

Christians, Muslims, Hindus and Budhists, and teaches the Bible verse by verse at the University of Judaism.[146]

The Southern California broadcasting icon resisted calls in 2004 to challenge Democratic Senator Barbara Boxer, and chose to stay put behind the microphone and writing books. Some major GOP money men leaned on him to get into the race, believing that Boxer's ultra liberalism could be too much even for California. Jerry Parsky, who ran the presidential campaign of George W. Bush in California, White House Hollywood liason Lionel Chetwynd, an Emmy winning writer and director and even White House advisor Karl Rove all thought he represented the party's best hope.[147] Ultimately though, Prager did not share that enthusiasm and has continued his radio career.

### Mike Gallagher: In the Republican Trenches

Mike stands out in the Gallagher family, not simply for his on air personality. He grew up in Dayton, Ohio, the only son of a Democratic father and Democratic mother, with a Democratic sister. It was only natural that he married a Democrat.[148]

"We avoid politics whenever possible. And if we do talk about it, it doesn't go well," he said of his wife Denise, in a *Dallas Morning News* interview in 2005. "She's the best thing that ever happened to me. And I always have to remind myself of that even though she has a maddening respect and admiration for people like Bill and Hillary Clinton. She is the kindest, sweetest, most big-hearted woman I know. In my world, I like to believe she's wrong politically. And so we just focus on what we have in common."[149]

Listeners to the show also got to hear about the emotional struggles he faced when Denise battled with cancer, a battle she ultimately lost the day before her 52nd birthday. He has talked about how he held her when she died, surrounded by family.

Mike Gallagher was a Democrat just like his parents at one point. As happened with so many, Ronald Reagan won him over.

"I remember really liking Ronald Reagan. He didn't strike me as the Darth Vader my mother thought he was," he said. "The truth is, my mom and I were very close. I saw what a great man Ronald Reagan was. But, hey, don't get me wrong—Republicans get mad at

200

me, too. I don't agree with George W. Bush on immigration, for one. I think he's wrong on this amnesty approach of looking the other way."[150]

His other heroes growing up were actually liberals—Walter Cronkite and Larry King. But Gallagher admired them not for their politics, but because he wanted to emulate their success in broadcasting.[151]

He was just 17, a junior in high school, when he got his first radio job at Dayton's WAVI screening guests for talk shows. By the next year, the 18-year-old had his own show.[152]

By the mid-1980s, he was on local TV, WDTN Channel 2, but said, "The program director just didn't like me. He wanted me to lose weight, he didn't like my style, etc., etc."[153]

So, he ended up back in talk radio at WFBC (now WORD) in Greenville, South Carolina, where he became station manager. Then he went to the WGY in Albany, New York. From there he went to New York City to the kingdom of talk radio, WABC, where he worked two years as the morning drive host. In 1996, after Bob Grant was fired, Gallagher briefly got his coveted drive time show. But WABC had a hard time replacing Grant, particularly since he was beating them on rival WOR, which almost immediately hired him. Sean Hannity eventually got the spot.[154]

But it turned out OK, as Gallagher became nationally syndicated in 1998, carried on 12 stations at first. Carried on the Salem Radio Network, he has built an audience of 3.75 million listeners from about 200 different stations.[155]

He gained a huge following in March 2003 when he staged a counter-concert to the Dixie Chicks in Greenville, South Carolina, the country band that vocally opposed the war in Iraq and President Bush. The protest show was headlined by the Marshall Tucker Band. It drew only 3,200 fans, while the Dixie Chicks got a crowd of 15,000. Nevertheless, Gallagher was able to raise $105,000 for the families of American troops through the highly publicized South Carolina showdown.[156]

He weekly brings on Fox News Sunday anchor Chris Wallace to talk headlines and preview the weekend program.

Unusual for the typical talk show host, he has done on the scene coverage of major events, such as the post-9/11 attacks in New York in 2001; the Columbine high school shooting from Colorado; and the Virginia Tech shooting on site in Blacksburg, Virginia. Not so unusually, he generally attends every Democratic and Republican national convention.

Gallgher warmly embraced the tea party movement, and expressed his strong belief that talk radio would play a role in the 2010 mid-term election.

"Talk radio is quintessential. It is a grassroots medium. The tea party movement's mindset is grassroots. So there is perfect synergy between talk radio and the tea parties," Gallagher said before the Republicans took over the House in 2010. "I've been doing this since 1978. I've seen a lot of peaks and valleys. Now talk radio has the opportunity to make a true, real difference in the direction of the country. Most of us are taking that very serious. I know I am."

CHAPTER NINE

# The Bush Years

'The White House knew they were in trouble in 2006, with no sign—at least as far as the public was concerned—that the war in Iraq would turn the corner. Corruption had run amok among Republican House members such as Representatives Duke Cunningham of California, Bob Ney of Ohio, Mark Foley of Florida and even Majority Leader Tom DeLay of Texas all resigning. On top of that, the Bush-DeLay big government Republicanism disenchanted many traditional conservatives of the Reagan school of thought. The base was demoralized, and seemed unlikely to show up for voting. Republican strategists know no one spoke to the conservative base like talk radio.

So in late October 2006, the White House invited 42 mostly conservative hosts to broadcast from the White House lawn. Top administration officials such as Presidential advisors Dean Bartlett and Karl Rove, Press Secretary Tony Snow and even cabinet members such as Secretary of Defense Donald Rumsfeld, Secretary of State Condoleezza Rice and Homeland Security Secretary Michael Chertoff made their rounds giving interviews to the hosts.

The problem is that the hosts weren't that enthusiastic. They showed up, but expressed skepticism about the adrift Republican

Party as being only a better alternative to Speaker of the House Nancy Pelosi of California. "National security trumps everything," Atlanta host Martha Zoller said from the White House. "I don't think it does any good to say we're going to punish these guys by putting the other party in power, because it could be 10 to 15 years before we get conservatives back in power."[1]

Milwaukee conservative host Charlie Sykes told Bartlett on the air, "If the Republicans lose control of the House, they won't have anybody but themselves to blame." And Steve Gill of Nashville said, "The Republicans certainly deserve to get spanked. The problem is, if you turn the Senate over to Hillary [Rodham Clinton] and Ted Kennedy, and Nancy Pelosi in the House, it's America that gets spanked."[2]

It was a gloomy time for conservatives, with little to be excited about. Their party had control of the executive and legislative branch, and behaved like the ghost of Lyndon B. Johnson.

But the only thing talk radio had to be gloomy about was the direction of their conservatism. Talk radio was doing just fine.

The question was frequently asked in the 1990s: Can talk radio survive if the hosts don't have Bill Clinton to kick around anymore? The resounding answer was yes.

Throughout the first decade of the 21st Century, Limbaugh maintained his dominance, but a new crop of hosts snatched the top tier spots. Shows by Sean Hannity, Laura Ingraham, Mark Levin and Michael Savage soared past G. Gordon Liddy and Michael Regan in ratings and markets.

Talk radio was lucrative enough for folks in show business to enter.

Jerry Doyle, who made it big on Wall Street before becoming an actor, most noted for his role as Michael Garibaldi on the science fiction series Babylon 5, won the Republican nomination to run for the U.S. House in California's 24th District in 2000. After losing his race, he eventually found his way into radio. Though conservative, he frequently shows an independent, libertarian streak. His program is syndicated through the Talk Radio Network.

Another showbiz transition was Dennis Miller, the famed comedian whose most famous political commentary had been found on Saturday Night Live's Weekend Update. Though it seemed he was no fan of President Reagan in those days, he clearly became a conservative pundit after 9/11. His show was launched in 2007 and syndicated by Westwood One, reportedly reaching 1.7 million listeners per week and focus on public policy matters, while Miller still demonstrates his comedic wit.

Meanwhile, there was room for regional icons to reach national audiences. Oregon radio personality Lars Larson was now in national syndication on about 100 stations. After almost 25 years on the New York airwaves, Steve Malzberg went national through WOR Radio Network in 2007, reaching 75 cities across the United States. Rusty Humphries emerged from being the most popular host on KOH in Reno to gaining a national audience of about 3 million listeners.

Clinton was getting little attention in his final year in office, 2000, as most of the attention was focused on the presidential race. Hosts weighed in heavily to the Republican primary, which had become a two man race between Texas Governor George W. Bush and Arizona Senator John McCain by the end of 1999.

Rush Limbaugh threw all his support in the 2000 primary to Bush.

It is always impossible to know how much impact talk radio had on primary voters, but it is certainly reasonable to view talk radio having greater influence on a primary, when the choir seeks guidance in making a choice, than in a general election when the choir already knows what notes to sing and listens to the preacher for reaffirmation. So it would be with Limbaugh's near daily lambasting of McCain, even more than he built up Bush.

"The way the primary system is set up today, talk radio has more of an influence in encouraging primary voters to vote than general election voters because talk radio has a higher audience of people who are more in the extremes of both the left and the right," said Michael Harrison, editor of *Talkers Magazine*. "And statistics do indicate that the turnout for primaries are more o the zealots than the average person in the middle. Any radio show that specifically targets the extremes is likely to galvanize voters. I would think that talk radio has a bigger influence in primaries today than it does in the general election."[3]

McCain had a mostly conservative record, but his support of campaign finance reform was untenable to many conservatives, as was his eagerness to "reach across the aisle" and work with Democrats. Most Republicans liked him in spite of, not because of, the McCain-Feingold bill. Still, because of his biography as a war hero, a significant numbers of voters were enamored by him. The mainstream media especially loved him, because he kept things interesting, but also for the campaign finance reform proposal.

When McCain trounced Bush in the New Hampshire primary by a surprising margin, it posed the question whether the inevitability of Bush's nomination would happen.

Limbaugh warned that even though the media is "orgasmic" over McCain now, they are "love 'em and leave 'em liberals" if he is the Republican nominee (a prediction given credence by the 2008 election).[4]

One of Limbaugh's parodies featured a McCain supporter singing, "He's the candidate I adore. He can keep my tax cut and I'll be poor. And I'll send him more."[5]

The National Annenberg Election Study found that post New Hampshire primary listening to Limbaugh negatively affected the voters feelings about McCain. This is significant since Limbaugh's focus on McCain really began after the senator's victory in New Hampshire. The Annenberg study also found that the impression Republican voters in Super Tuesday states had of McCain took a negative turn after listening to Limbaugh. So there is evidence to show that talk radio can impact the outcome of a primary election.[6]

Vice President Al Gore had an easier road to the Democratic nomination, easily beating former New Jersey Senator Bill Bradley. Limbaugh and others rallied voters to get behind Bush, calling out Gore for various flip flops, scandals and lies/exaggerations, and never let anyone forget whose vice president he was even while Gore sought distance from Clinton. Further, the hosts cited Bush's successful record as a governor in Texas.

On Election Day 2000, Limbaugh expressed confidence that Bush would win by a comfortable margin, which is what a number of polls were reflecting. The next day, he portrayed Gore as a sore loser, unwilling to admit defeat. This was day two of the 36-day election of recounts and legal battles in Florida.

Conservative listeners to talk radio saw Gore as a continuation of Clinton believed they had ousted the corrupt regime. Now it seemed that might not have been the case. Worse, with Clinton having dodged removal from office, a Gore victory (along with a Hillary Clinton Senate victory in New York) would mean zero consequences for eight shameful years. Now it appeared that Gore wanted to steal the election.

"The anger about Gore is pretty intense," Liddy, told the *Baltimore Sun*, adding that 90 percent of his calls were about the election. "Gore is looked upon as a junior Clinton. One of my listeners said, 'Gore is a mouse trying to grow up to be a rat.' Another listener said, 'We're going to fight. We're going to fight.' They're just really angry. I tell them they are absolutely correct, that this is a well-orchestrated plan and campaign to take the election away from George Bush."

Liddy said that if Gore wins, it would drive Republicans to seek overwhelming majorities in both houses of Congress in 2002 to block his agenda. "If he gets up in the morning and says 'Good morning,' they'll veto it," Liddy said.

Meanwhile, Limbaugh urged listeners and readers of his website to support Florida Secretary of State Katherine Harris, who was going to certify Bush the winner of Florida's electoral votes.[7]

After the 36 day election, and a U.S. Supreme Court ruling, Gore finally bowed out, and Bush was inaugurated as president on January 20, 2001.

### Backing the War President

The first eight months of the Bush administration provided some fodder: The new Senate Majority Leader Tom Daschle of South Dakota was the most prominent Democrat in America but a less enticing target than Bill Clinton. A few important issues were debated. Chief among those was the Bush tax cut that passed Congress, the debate over the use of federal dollars on embryonic stem cell research and California Democratic Representative Gary Condit's alleged fling with a dead Capitol Hill intern.

Then America changed. Needless to say, the Bush presidency changed. On September 11, 2001, two planes flew into the World Trade Center, bringing both towers down. Another plane crashed into the Pentagon, and yet another Washington-bound passenger jet crashed a in crashed in a Pennsylvania field.

Talk radio became more popular as Bush became a war president with a 90 percent approval rating, astonishing for a candidate who lost the popular vote. However, the country was united in such a way that conservative hosts lacked the edge they might have otherwise had. Democrats joined Republicans in Congress to authorize the military action to overthrow the Taliban regime in Afghanistan that was providing refuge to Osama bin Laden and al Qaeda. The Taliban was defeated in fairly short order, thus, the U.S. was left to help establish a democracy in the country, which turned into a much longer war.

Hannity, who had just gone into national syndication earlier that year, was on a public speaking tour raising his already national profile. The topic was usually terrorism.

"We have no choice," Hannity said at the Grand Rapids Michigan Right to Life annual dinner in October. "It is a race. ... There must be complete eradication of those involved in this effort. It's like a cancer. It must be removed totally."[8]

Still, there was a logical amount of introspection about how a comparably rag tag organization like al Qaeda could breach the most sophisticated national security system in the world and murder thousands. After the harmony, Democrats and Republicans began to do what comes natural and blame one another. No doubt 9/11 happened on Bush's watch. But numerous reports surfaced that the Clinton administration had bin Laden in their crosshairs and failed to kill or capture him several times.

"If we're serious about avoiding past mistakes and improving national security, we can't duck some serious questions about Mr. Clinton's presidency," Limbaugh said.[9]

On the air, and in his first book, Hannity laid out the case against Clinton for failing to bring bin Laden to justice.

"Well, I'm very clear to say, I don't blame the left. I don't blame President Clinton for the attacks. You can't blame him," Hannity said in an interview with ABC News. "I blame the people that hijacked those airplanes and dive bombed them into those buildings because they have no respect for human life. But, there were four opportunities when Sudan offered Osama Bin Laden, on a silver platter, to America and we turned it down."[10]

The war on terror was not the only issue going into the 2002 mid-term elections. In fact, there were times when Limbaugh became irate with Bush. Bush needed the help of Democrats to pass his No Child Left Behind education reform bill, which many conservatives felt was too much federal encroachment on local school districts. Limbaugh accused Bush of "letting Ted Kennedy write the education bill." Further, Bush also signed into law the McCain-Feingold campaign finance law, which put limits on political speech, such as prohibiting independent advertising for or against a candidate 60 days before a general election and 30 days before a primary—when most voters are paying attention. "I was one of Bush's biggest critics the first two years because he was siding with the Democrats on every important domestic issue. Campaign finance reform—I flipped a wig. There was no reason [for] that. That's an assault on the First Amendment," Rush said.[11]

But it was the war on terror and the debate over the Iraq war that garnered most interest going into the midterm. Democrats, including Daschle, soon-to-be presidential nominee Senator John Kerry of Massachusetts, along with House Minority Leader Richard Gephardt and other Democrats voted for the congressional resolution to use military force in Iraq. Nevertheless, 2002 was largely about which party made Americans feel safe. Republicans won big that year, retaking the Senate and increasing their numbers in the House, giving the GOP control of the White House and both houses of Congress for the first time since Dwight D. Eisenhower.

Daschle, now the minority leader, blamed talk radio for his

plight. In a November 13, 2002 press conference, he decided to bring back the charge that Limbaugh was inciting violence.

"What happens when Rush Limbaugh attacks those of us in public life is that people aren't satisfied just to listen," Daschle said. "They want to act because they get emotionally invested. And so, you know, the threats to those of us in public life go up dramatically and—on our families and on us in a way that's very disconcerting."

He continued, "If entertainment becomes so much a part of politics, and if that entertainment drives an emotional movement in this country among some people who don't know the difference between entertainment and politics and who are then so energized to go out and hurt somebody, that troubles me about where politics in America is going."[12]

On his program following the Daschle attack, Limbaugh said his listeners should take note. "It's not just against me, but it's against you folks, the entire audience. You all now are being characterized as unsophisticated barbarians. You don't know the difference between politics and entertainment," Limbaugh said.[13]

Adding to Daschle's griping was former Vice President Gore who created his own view of the vast right wing conspiracy. "Fox News network, *The Washington Times*, Rush Limbaugh—there's a bunch of them, and some of them are financed by wealthy ultraconservative billionaires who make political deals with Republican administrations and the rest of the media," Gore told The New York Observer. "They'll create a little echo chamber, and pretty soon they'll start baiting the mainstream media for allegedly ignoring the story they've pushed into the zeitgeist. Pretty soon the mainstream media goes out and disingenuously takes a so-called objective sampling, and lo and behold, these RNC talking points are woven into the fabric of the zeitgeist."[14]

Limbaugh lumped the Gore and Daschle criticisms together. "Maybe these guys are just trying to rally their base," Mr. Limbaugh said on his top-rated radio program yesterday. "They know the base hates me, the base hates Fox News Channel, base hates conservative anything. And that's where you start if you're rebuilding. You've got to get your base."[15]

210

The next move that divided the country, giving Limbaugh, Hannity, Savage and others an important voice was going to war with Iraq. It was not necessarily something that united all conservatives. Commentators such as Pat Buchanan and Robert Novak never supported the action. George Will was lukewarm. But these individuals did not speak for the conservative movement of the day they way radio did.

Democrats argued that going to war to depose Saddam Hussein would put American in a bad light with the rest of the world.

"I don't give a darn about what the French think and I don't care what the Germans think," Hannity said, referring to the two nations most vocally opposed to the war in Iraq.[16]

With Vic Kamber, a Democratic political consultant on his show, Hannity debated the case for going to war. Kamber asked why shouldn't the United States go after North Korean tyrant Kim Jong Il. Hannity replied, "one at a time."[17]

Leftwing columnist Ellen Goodman quipped, "Talk radio has become the Bush National Radio Network, a support system for the pro-war movement."[18]

The morning after the Shock and Awe, Rush began his program with a spoof of the Beach Boys "Barbara Ann," song with "Bomb-bomb-bomb-bomb-bomb Iraq."[19]

Glenn Beck staged pro-war rallies in various cities, and promoted them on his show, which reportedly made his employer Clear Channel Communications a little uncomfortable.[20] Further, Limbaugh, Liddy and Hannity joined a rally on the Mall that April that included numerous other conservatives, sponsored by the Young America's Foundation, as a counter rally to the anti-war demonstrators protesting that same day.[21]

The country would have gone to war in Iraq without talk radio's help. There was at the time a stern bipartisan view that Iraq had weapons of mass destruction. Further, many liberals think the mainstream media had war fever. That's a bit of a stretch. *The New York Times* editorial page was vehemently opposed going to war. *The Washington Post* was stridently in favor of regime change. *The Wall Street Journal* editorial board supported the mission as liberating

Iraq, while *USA Today* editorially opposed war. There was only meek opposition from Democrats in Congress to the war. But as years wore on, every misstep in Iraq was magnified by the mainstream media.

After the Saddam regime was out of power, and the insurgency began to make things really ugly for Americans, much of the public that was previously for the war had turned against it. Most major hosts would stick with Bush—with the exception of Savage.

Who can say whether Bush needed talk radio in 2004? We do know that the media had a distinctly anti-Bush narrative throughout 2004, and an opposing narrative could only help the Republican keep the White House. The Swift Boat Veterans for Truth might have been ignored by the mainstream media had it not been for talk radio. The various Kerry flip-flops might also have been ignored. Talk radio, though lacking the penetration of network news, presented an equally devastating narrative of Kerry as indecisive and unprincipled at a time when the country needed a steady hand. Bush was reelected in November, with 51 percent of the vote, being the first president to win an actual majority since his father in 1988.

With all the talk about talk radio's survival in a post-Clinton era, Hannity saw advantages to a Bush reelection victory, in that it would mean plenty of angry guests for him to debate on radio and TV. [22]

In her post-election *Wall Street Journal* column, Peggy Noonan paid special homage to the talkers for their work in the 2004 election. "Oh, another last note. Tuesday I heard three radio talkers who refused to believe it was over when the ludicrous, and who knows but possibly quite mischievous, exit polls virtually declared a Kerry landslide yesterday afternoon. They are Rush Limbaugh, Sean Hannity and Laura Ingraham. The last sent me an e-mail that dismissed the numbers as elitist nonsense and propaganda. She is one tough girl and they are two tough men."[23]

## Supreme Problems

In the fall of 2005, after navigating the successful confirmation of John G. Roberts to be chief justice of the United States, Bush still had another spot to fill. He originally nominated Roberts to fill the spot of retiring Associated Justice Saundra Day O'Connor. But after the unexpected death of Chief Justice William Rehnquist—and seeing that Roberts was on a easy glide toward confirmation, he bumped his nomination to fill the chief justice vacancy, winning over a bipartisan 72 votes in the Senate.

To the shock of many conservatives, the president tapped the unknown White House Counsel Harriett Miers, a long time friend and former president of the Texas Bar Association, but someone who had never been a judge. "In selecting a nominee, I've sought to find an American of grace, judgment, and unwavering devotion to the Constitution and laws of our country," Bush said. "Harriet Miers is just such a person."

Almost immediately the conservative commentariat was miffed. Bill Kristol, George Will and Charles Krauthammer immediately questioned the decision. Rush and Hannity were if anything squishy.

The administration sought to plug the hole of conservative support, sending Vice President Dick Cheney on to Rush's program, where he faced some skeptical questions. "You'll be proud of Harriet's record, Rush," Cheney said. "Trust me."[24]

Conservative pundits did not.

A Supreme Court nominee is a lasting legacy of any president. This nomination was replacing the swing vote on the Supreme Court, so the stakes were even higher. Yet, Miers was a blank slate in the eyes of conservatives. Party loyalty was asking too much.

In a Fox News interview with Sean Hannity, Limbaugh said, "But, Sean, I mean, she may be fine. Harriet Miers could be one of the best justices on the court. The problem here is, we don't know. We're being asked again to roll the dice."[25]

Limbaugh said the choice of Miers was a "pity" that "needn't have happened."

"They think it's a single-issue group of people based on abortion. And I think they thought that, if they just get a candidate out there that people can be persuaded to believe is going to do the right thing on Roe vs. Wade, that they would have the base in their back pocket and they could move on," Limbaugh said. "And I just—I think they misunderstand that, because the conservative movement's not monolithic. It's not made up of single-issue people. Some of them are, but there are a lot more people who have far more interest than just one issue."

Also speaking with much authority on the matter was Laura Ingraham, who clerked for Associate Justice Clarence Thomas. An hour after Bush announced the nomination on September 29, Ingraham criticized the move on air. She continued the criticism as did others.[26]

"Well, I think, when it comes to the swing vote on the Supreme Court, I think—the conservatives that I've spoken to—and it's a lot—and people who have been immersed in this struggle of trying to transform the court, pretty much over the last 25 years, they understand that, when you get up on that court, on that Supreme Court, not only do you have to be just a good person with good legal credentials, you actually have to be someone who has had a very firm and solid judicial philosophy to take with you to that court to be able to withstand the pressures, and they're very elite pressures, to be able to move on this or that issue," Ingraham said.

A justice's legacy—not just a vote—is highly important. "But writing a decision that will then be looked upon 30, 40, and 50 years from now with law students and young judges saying, 'Wow, that opinion really changed the way I looked at the law.' That's the point."[27]

Ingraham's credentials prompted writer Richard Miniter to suggest she was qualified to be on the U.S. Supreme Court—or at least more qualified than Miers. Miniter pointed out that Ingraham went to an Ivy League college, a top-10 law school, litigated for an A-list law firm and clerked for a Supreme Court Justice. Miers did none of these. "Miers does not have much a paper trail, or at least one that the public will be able to see. By contrast, Ingraham has written two books, including one bestseller, as well as many bylined articles in national newspapers and magazines. ...The point is not that Laura Ingraham should have been nominated instead of Harriet Miers, but only that Miers is a perfectly competent but ordinary lawyer and that there are many more accomplished women with resumes better suited for the U.S. Supreme Court."[28]

By the end of the month, Bush withdrew the nomination. The White House cited the Senate's demand for White House memos that Miers believed would violate the principle of attorney-client privilege. But *Washington Post* media reporter Howard Kurtz suspected other powers at work.

"This time, no one can blame the liberal media. And what made the right's revolt all the more remarkable was that its opinion-mongering wing didn't simply stand in polite opposition to Miers. Its troops hit the trenches, attacked Miers as unqualified, ripped President Bush for cronyism and in some cases raised money to defeat the nomination," Kurtz wrote.

The article quoted Ingraham saying, "I received phone calls and e-mails saying I was being disloyal to the president and we were Borking Miers," said Ingraham, referring to the attacks on Reagan Supreme Court nominee Robert Bork who was not confirmed after a sustained character attack campaign that spawned the verb borking in the political lexicon for future judicial nominations. "I was standing up for what I believe are conservative judicial principles, and no one was going to dissuade me from that. ... Without alternative media, the talking points on Miers would have carried the day."[29]

### Sounding the Amnesty Alarm

When Senate Republicans sent out their talking points to friendly media sources on the bipartisan comprehensive immigration reform proposal Hugh Hewitt read them on the air before calling them "four pages of crap."[30]

It was the beginning of a near united front by talk radio show hosts that led to one of the most famous triumphs and prompting a Republican—not some RINO, but the former conservative Senate Majority Leader Trent Lott of Mississippi—to gripe "talk radio is running America."

Limbaugh, Hannity, Beck, Savage, Levin and others kept the drumbeat up against the immigration legislation supported by Republican President George W. Bush, the eventual Republican presidential nominee Senator John McCain and the Democrat- controlled Congress to wipeout the legislation. Calling the measure amnesty, a characterization supporters called untrue, the hosts encouraged their listeners to melt the Senate phone lines. Listeners obliged.

It would be the second time the measure would go down. The last time, in late 2005, a Republican controlled Senate voted for the measure to grant a pathway to citizenship for the estimated 12 million illegal immigrants in the United States. The McCain-Kennedy pathway would allow those who entered the country illegally to pay a fine, and go to the back of the line to go through a procedure for legalization. The Republican-controlled House passed a tougher enforcement-first measure. A conference committee never reconciled the two approaches.

In 2007, it was different. Democrats controlled both houses of Congress, and Republicans—so it seemed—would have to be willing to accept compromise. The bill mostly resembled the 2005 pathway-to-citizenship legislation, with a few tougher enforcement restrictions. This time the bill was sponsored by Ted Kennedy and Jon Kyl, the Arizona Republican who opposed the previous bill. Bush was also on board, one answering the critics, "I'll see you at the bill signing."[31]

But Limbaugh warned the legislation that could potentially add millions of new Democratic voters should be called "Destroy the Republican Party Act." He said the passage of the legislation would lead to Democrats "getting a brand new electorate, reshaping it and being able to win election after election after election."[32]

This irked Republican National Committee Chairman Senator Mel Martinez of Florida, who said Limbaugh "has emotion on his side, but I think I have logic on mine. Hispanics make up about 13 percent of our country and by 2020 will be closer to 20%. It is a demographic trend that one cannot overlook."[33]

Hannity interviewed McCain, then one of many GOP contenders, on his show, telling the Arizonan about the "groundswell of opposition" to this legislation among Republican voters. McCain, quipped, "So I am supposed to gauge my behavior on whether I am booed or not? Please, Sean."[34]

However fewer and fewer Republicans seemed willing to accept

216

the proposal. Senate Majority Leader Harry Reid of Nevada sought first to use procedural rules to cut off debate and move to a vote. When that didn't work, he sought to use a procedure sometimes nicknamed "clay pigeon," or splitting a bill into several pieces. It was typically a procedure for stalling legislation, this time Democrats sought to salvage at least some of the bill.[35]

But the tide, thanks largely to talk radio, was too strong for Reid to salvage anything. The public was making itself clear and the bill died. The blowback against talk radio was tremendous, as much of establishment Washington viewed the hosts as demagogues and the senators who shrunk from a fight as cowards.

Regardless of whether one agrees with the policy, the "coward" senators were simply responding to their constituents who were using their First Amendment right to petition government, after being encouraged to do so by host using their freedom of the (electronic) press. Most Washington opinion leaders, even the centrist Roll Call editor Morton Kondracke lashed out at talk radio.

"The measure guaranteed extra money for building fencing between the United States and Canada, a requirement (onerous, in my mind) that guest workers return home for a year after two-year stints in the United States, plus fines and fees for illegal immigrants to be used to help communities bear the costs of the federal government's past failure to make the border secure," Kondracke wrote. "These and other gains were not enough, however, for radio and TV shouters such as Sean Hannity, Rush Limbaugh, Laura Ingraham, Pat Buchanan and Lou Dobbs, who convinced masses of citizens that the Kyl-Kennedy bill still amounted to 'amnesty' for 12 million illegal immigrants."[36]

One very prominent host that did not follow the amnesty line on talk radio was Michael Medved, who thought the move was potentially destructive.

"I think talk radio played a crucial role in defeating immigration reform in 2007," Medved said in an interview. "Had that immigration reform been passed in some moderated form, some adjusted form, we would be a better country today and I think it's very possible John McCain would have won the [2008 presidential] election.

217

John McCain won white votes by 12 points, almost identical to what Bush won in 2004. However, among Latinos, McCain—who had always gotten Latino votes as a candidate in Arizona—Bush got 44 percent of the Latino vote in 2004. McCain got 30 percent in 2008."[37]

Trent Lott—among the GOP senators who refused to bow to public pressure on the bill—was irate, and was quoted as saying, "Talk radio is running America. We have to deal with that problem."

"Deal with that problem" sounded an awful lot like he wanted a legislative fix. The return of the Fairness Doctrine was already a concern since Democrats recaptured Congress. Was Lott joining the cause? He was quick to say no.

"I'm not trying to resurrect the law called the Fairness Doctrine. I've done hundreds of talk radio programs, from local stations in Mississippi to the big ones, like Hannity. Hardly a week goes by when I'm not doing some talk radio program talking about an issue," Lott said. "But, I don't think the Senate should just react to talk radio or any other form of media. The Senate needs to be much more proactive, to lead the discussion and lead the nation. That's what Senators are supposed to do—take on issues, no matter how hard, and produce legislation. We're not doing that to the extent we should."[38]

Despite concerns about the Fairness Doctrine, most hosts loved the assertion by Lott, even if they really snickered at the absurdity. The cover of the Limbaugh Letter featured a picture of Rush with the words "I Run America."

Michael Savage took it serious enough.

"We have more power than the U.S. Senate and they know it and they're fuming," Savage said on his show. "We're going to have government snitches listening to shows. And what are they going to do, push a button and then wheel someone into the studio and give their viewpoint?"[39]

Almost immediately after the defeat of the immigration, many Democrats began talking of the need for a return to the dark ages of talk.

218

Sounded like a good idea to Representative Maurice Hinchey, a New York Democrat. He introduced legislation to bring back the Fairness Doctrine—this time codified in law—along with a package addressing media ownership rules. "It's important that the American people make decisions for themselves based upon the ability to garner all the information, not just on what somebody wants to give them," Hinchey said.[40]

Nothing of course came of this. While big shot Democrats such as Senators John Kerry, Richard Durbin and Dianne Feinstein all said they wanted to see the rule restored, the House sent a clear bipartisan message against bringing back the doctrine. Representative Mike Pence of Indiana, a former talk radio host himself, introduced a bill to block the dark ages from returning. The legislation, that passed the Democratic House 309 to 115, blocked funds from the Federal Communications Commission to impose the Fairness Doctrine.[41] While the legislation did not become law, it sent a strong enough message that making it into law would not work. Still, the abrupt push to restore the rule demonstrates the perceived power talk radio had over the immigration debate.

Part-time radio host Dean Barnett, who would fill in for Hugh Hewitt occasionally, wrote in a January 2008 piece in *The Weekly Standard*, that it is actually America that runs talk radio.

"We're factors in the conversation, but we don't lead it. The interests and concerns of the people lead the conversation. It's truly a bottom-up phenomenon," Barnett wrote. "Conservatives didn't need talk radio hosts to discover their antipathy towards the McCain/Kennedy reform. I pinch-hit for Hewitt several times while that debate raged. Whenever I tried to steer the discussion to anything other than the immigration dispute (merely to disrupt the monotony of talking about the same issue for three hours a day for days on end), the phone lines would die. Most of the listeners who called in would hang up; those who decided to dial in anyway did so to discuss immigration, even though I had changed the subject. I'm pretty sure all conservative talk show hosts found the same thing. The month of June 2007 was all-immigration-all-the-time on the air. The listeners had made up their minds on the merits of McCain/Kennedy before a single talk show host had said a word."[42]

### Sean Hannity 'Born to Argue'

Though he sort of came up on it by accident, Sean Hannity managed to make a good living from what he's just naturally done his whole life. "I was born to argue," he once said. "I don't know why. I mean, from arguing with my teachers and, on occasions, my parents. I think I've mastered the art of argument at a fairly young age."[43] He has used that gift to soar to the number two spot on both talk radio and cable news, and has done what both Limbaugh and Beck could not do, maintain a huge following on radio along with a longstanding TV presence.

The Iran Contra affair may have been the low point for the otherwise successful Reagan presidency, but it gave Hannity the opportunity to do what he loved with an audience to listen.

When allegations that the Reagan administration had sold arms to Iran in exchange for hostages, and used proceeds from the sales to illegally fund the Contras in Latin America, the Senate—controlled by Democrats after the 1986 midterms—leapt to investigate the matter. The main witness prompting the must-see TV moment at the time was Lt. Col. Oliver North. Hannity heard the senators haranguing North, and routinely called into conservative talk shows to give his two cents.

Hannity was never a fan of handouts. In the late 1980s, he was a contractor, painting houses, because he did not want to rely on his parents to pay for his tuition at New York University. He dropped out and headed west to California, continuing to work in construction to save enough money.

"I was a contractor. I was working my way in and out of college. Didn't want my parents to help pay for college. So, I'm, I'm running out of money all the time. So, that's how I was making my living and, I'd be 40 feet up in the air on radios, calling into talk shows," Hannity, who grew up on Long Island and continues to live there today, recalled in an ABC News interview.[44]

"The things I had to say began attracting more feedback,

spurring more people to call, until sometimes I was getting bigger response than the host," Hannity wrote. "Before long it dawned on me that I ought to be on the other side of a microphone as a host rather than a caller."[45]

"People say, 'I want to talk to that guy that just says what he just said, because I loved what Ollie was doing'" Hannity recalled.[46]

His course in life was set.

"I'd grown up listening to Bob Grant, Barry Gray, John Gambling and Barry Farber," Hannity wrote. "That experience taught me early on that a passionate argument, well made, could make a difference, even if the person was speaking as a private citizen.[47]

He volunteered his commentary at radio station in *KCSB-FM*, the station for the University of California- Santa Barbara. It was not a good fit, as the station did not like his politics after he expressed opposition to homosexuality at a liberal university. Reportedly, a lesbian caller to his program said she had a baby after being artificially inseminated and Hannity responded he felt sorry for her child. The university fired him, or at least banned him from volunteering, for supposedly "discriminating against gays and lesbians." Interestingly enough, the ACLU Foundation of Southern California came to Hannity's defense. The university backed down and told Hannity he can have his airtime, but at this juncture, he didn't want it.[48]

"I was too conservative, the higher ups said, and they didn't like the comments one guest made on the show. So much for free speech on a college campus!" Hannity wrote. "The station was dominated by leftwing public affairs programs, including a gay and lesbian perspective show, a Planned Parenthood show, and multiple shows that accused Reagan and Bush of being drug runners and drug pushers. The leftwing management had a zero tolerance policy for conservative points of view and I was promptly fired."[49]

The northeasterner left the West Coast to go south. A talk radio show opened up at *WVNN* Huntsville, Alabama in 1989 for $19,000 per year that he took, "because they gave me a microphone."[50] He occasionally did a local TV debate show with liberal David Pearson, whom Hannity described as a "fierce defender of the left."[51]

"When I got there, the first thing I discovered was that my New York accent—which I never even noticed—didn't go down easy in the south." But he said, "I tried to connect with callers. I read everything that I could get my hands on, scouring newspapers and magazines."[52]

The program took off and was a spring board to Atlanta's WGST-AM, a top 10 market. Hannity moved to WGST in 1992—as talk radio was on the verge of becoming a powerful political force —to replace the legendary Neil Boortz, who had jumped to WSB-AM. However, because of a no compete clause in Boortz's contract, Boortz could not go on the air for several months on WSB. Hannity used this time to build an audience. And it worked due in part to Boortz's hiatus.[53]

Hannity became the top rated show in Atlanta, and often interviewed Georgia Congressman Newt Gingrich, the House Minority Whip. Then, the ultimate opportunity came when he got to be the guest host for the Rush Limbaugh Show on a few occasion, giving him his first national exposure. After that, he was brought on as a conservative pundit for CNN's Talk Back Live. Roger Ailes, then head of CNBC, liked him so much he brought him on for a few shows on that network.[54] He also got other TV appearances on popular 90s talk shows hosted by Phil Donohue, Sally Jesse Raphael and Geraldo Rivera.

When Ailes took the job running the new Fox News Chanel in 1996, he hired Hannity in September of that year to do a debate show with New York liberal radio show host Alan Colmes. It was to be the Fox version of Cross Fire, the long time Left-Right debate show on CNN.[55]

Asked if he would jump ship if CNN offered him millions, Hannity answered. "Nope. Wouldn't do it. Where was CNN in 1996? They weren't knocking on my door. No, I love being here. I love working for Roger and I love being here."[56]

Even though Fox News was a fledgling operation at the time, Hannity had attained enough prominence to get called to the biggest station in the biggest market of them all, WABC in New York, where he had been doing a few programs as a substitute host since moving to New York. At first, his show aired from 11 p.m. to 2 a.m. The night time show doubled in ratings after Hannity took over, so WABC moved him to the 3 p.m. to 6 p.m. drive time slot, once occupied by his hero Bob Grant.[57]

He was a huge drive time star in the New York market, and Hannity & Colmes—with its 1.5 million viewers—surpassed Larry King to become the top rated cable news show in the 9 p.m. hour, and number two in cable news overall behind The O'Reilly Factor. He continued filling in for Rush Limbaugh on occasion.

Then, he became nationally syndicated. His first national show was—oddly enough—September 10, 2001, a day before the worst terror attack in history. He became a staunch supporter of President Bush's prosecution of the war on terror. When *Time* magazine asked him, "Whose a bigger threat, terrorists or liberals?" Hannity answered, "Obviously terrorists. But there is an internal, bloodless war that has to be won first."[58]

His first best seller "Let Freedom Ring: Winning the War of Liberty over Liberalism" was released the following year. It was on *The New York Times* Best Seller List for 17 weeks.[59] He called his first book tour the "Hannitization of America" tour. He traveled the country for various speaking engagements.

Though he likes to paint liberals into a corner whenever possible, some of his popularity could be owed to the fact that underneath the arguments he just seems like a nice guy from Long Island. "One of the things I think works for me is, I am passionate about my belief system but I try never to forget the human side of the debate. I don't take it personally, and I don't make it personal. You can play golf with liberals, be neighbors with them, go out to dinner. I just don't want them in power," Hannity said.

The Sean Hannity Show has grown to more than 500 radio stations with 13.5 million listeners. Along the way, Hannity won two Marconi Awards for the National Syndicate Host of the Year from the National Association of Broadcasters and a three time winner of the Radio & Records National Talk Show Host of the Year Award in 2003, 2004 and 2005.[60]

He does not buy into the view that too much political debate, or

223

division between parties, is a bad thing. "I don't think that's necessarily true. I think it's a healthy thing to have passionate debate. Our founders had it at their convention in 1787. If it's good for them, it's pretty good for us in the battle against terrorism."[61]

His election year book in 2004, "Deliver Us from Evil: Defeating Terrorism, Despotism, and Liberalism," debut in the top spot on *The New York Times* best-seller list, remaining on the list for five consecutive weeks. "Conservative Victory," is book released in 2010 also debut at number one for paperbacks.[62]

A vocal supporter of going to war in Iraq, Hannity was not content to simply sit on the sidelines waving the flag. He organized "Freedom Concerts" in 2003, which have taken place year since. The concerts raise money and awareness for The Freedom Alliance, a charity group that provides college scholarships for children of U.S. soldiers killed in the line of duty. The concerts have featured top country artists such as Hank Williams Jr., Sara Evans, Lee Greenwood, Montgomery Gentry and many others have performed at the concerts. The event drew top country music stars each year and was such a success that by 2007 it extended beyond one venue to five concerts—Atlanta, San Diego, Dallas, Cincinnati and New Jersey.[63] The concert series has continued to be held at multiple venues since.

Newsday's media writer Verne Gay called Hannity the third most significant player in influencing coverage of the 2004 presidential race, because "observers say Hannity is considered more influential than FOX News' Bill O'Reilly, who's somewhat suspect in the eyes of the Right, or even Limbaugh, who has no TV berth."[64]

Hannity had long described himself as an independent conservative, someone who does not drink Republican Kool-aid.

"If my party is wrong, or the people in our party are wrong. I'm open enough that I'm going to criticize them. You know, right now we're engaged in a war on terror," Hannity said. "The President has laid out a plan for moral clarity to defeat terrorists wherever they are. And go after those that aid, abet, support and harbor. But if he veers away from it, I'll be the first one to criticize him."[65]

He stood firmly with Bush on almost everything, but did criticize the president on too much spending and for the $700 billion bank bailout that came at the end of the Bush presidency. Further, Hannity was so unhappy with the GOP nomination of John McCain for president—whom he had high personal regard for—that he changed his party registration from Republican to the Conservative Party of New York state. He fully support McCain in the presidential race, and had fewer negative things to say about the Arizona senator than most hosts.

Liberal critics accused Colmes of being too weak to challenge the strong willed Hannity, but Hannity didn't see it that way. *Time* magazine asked Hannity, "What about the critics of your TV show who say [liberal co-host] Alan Colmes is a patsy?"

He responded, "I know Alan's good at what he does because I sit there getting aggravated every time he's speaking. We have a producer with a stopwatch who says he gets 3 1/2 minutes, I get 3 1/2 minutes," Hannity said.[66]

Though it was clear who carried the show. Hannity got his own Sunday night program called "Hannity's America," in late 2007. It would run through the 2008 election cycle as the top rated show of its kind in that time slot. It was also—as some suspected—a precursor to dumping Colmes.

After Barack Obama was elected president, Colmes left the show. He has remained with Fox in a much diminished role, appearing as an analyst on several shows. Thus Hannity & Colmes became just Hannity on January 12, 2009—a few days before Obama was inaugurated. The name change was simple enough. The format changed as well, with Hannity conducting interviews, and bringing in the Great American Panel—that has at least one liberal—toward the end of the show that has 2.8 million viewers each night, a bump in viewership.[67]

We don't know the "real story" to how this happened, but it appears to have been an amiable parting, not something that Hannity necessarily pushed to have the program all to himself, but rather a corporate decision based on the belief that the franchise player would better hold an audience as a solo host. The two, who were friendly during the show together, never had a cross word after the split. Though it is unlikely that Colmes would publicly express any pent up resentment, given that he is still working for the network. And with Crossfire ancient history, it made little since to hold back one of the network's franchise players.

### Hugh Hewitt Mastering New Media

Hugh Hewitt rarely slows down. Perhaps he learned to multitask as a former White House staffer for two presidents. In addition to his radio show, that has aired since July 2000 now reaching an audience of about 2 million on 75 stations, he's blogger, columnist and has been a visionary of conservative new media. He also teaches constitutional law at Chapman University.

Beyond just the conservative world, he has proven his bona fides as a broadcaster, winning two Emmys for his work on PBS as co-host of "Life & Times," program, a news and public affairs show that aired in Los Angeles from 1992 to 2007, and for the 1996 series "Searching for God in America."[68]

After graduating from Harvard, Hewitt worked as an assistant in the Richard Nixon White House briefly. He left to attend law school at the University of Michigan. After law school he returned to Washington to work for President Ronald Reagan, as an assistant counsel in the White House and as a special assistant to the U.S. Attorney General.[69]

After Reagan was out of office in 1989, Hewitt headed to Orange County, California to work for the Nixon Library and practice law. He took the faculty position at Chapman in 1995. He also hosted a local Los Angeles radio program during the early 1990s. After a hiatus, he returned to radio in 2000 with national syndication. An evangelical Christian, his program is not Christian focused, but he frequently interviews authors of Christian books. It can be a very high brow show as he brings on perhaps more establishment media journalists from *The Washington Post*, *Politico*, ABC News and elsewhere than most hosts and frequently puts them on the spot about media bias.

When Salem bought Townhall.com in 2006, it put Hewitt in charge of breaking the barrier between reporting and activism, Hewitt encouraged readers to report, blog and participate.

Townhall, under Hewitt, was among the earlier sites to offer talk radio and columnists on the same site, with podcasts and other features available.

"Both spoken words and written words are powerful," he said. "Acting in harmony, the effect is exponential."[70]

Nicholas Lehman, dean of the Columbia University Graduate School of Journalism, wrote that conservatives, were "devising their own version of what journalism ought to look like: faster, more opinionated, more multimedia, and less hung up on distancing itself from the practice of politics than the newspapers and the network news. Hewitt is at the center of this effort."[71]

Hewitt, for his part, predicted the coming end of the old media order.

"What's the rule? That the elite media are hopelessly biased to the left and so blind to their own deficiencies, or so in denial, that they cannot save themselves from irrelevance. They're like the cheater in the clubhouse, whose every mention of a great round of golf is met with rolling eyes and knowing nods," Hewitt wrote. "There is too much expertise, all of it almost instantly available now, for the traditional idea of journalism to last much longer. In the past, almost every bit of information was difficult and expensive to acquire and was therefore mediated by journalists whom readers and viewers were usually in no position to second-guess. Authority has drained from journalism for a reason. Too many of its practitioners have been easily exposed as poseurs."[72]

Hewitt had an active blog, and one of his books "Blog: Understanding the Information Reformation That is Changing Your World," strongly encouraged all conservatives to blog as well. When left-wing sites like the Daily Kos were gaining a big following, Hewitt did not want conservatives to lose ground on the Web the way liberals lost ground on the radio. Another book that sold well was "A Mormon in the White House?" a flattering book about former Massachusetts Governor Mitt Romney, published in 2007, when Romney was seeking the 2008 GOP presidential nomination. Hewitt has continued to be an ardent Romney supporter, among the few conservative pundits that doesn't rip into him.

### First Lady of Conservative Radio

The most listened to woman on talk radio scoffs at the idea of simply doing politics, frequently talking about entertainment, the culture and "pornification" of America, her dog, her adopted children and family in general. Of course all of these things have some connection to politics, or at least to conservative philosophy. She also has one of the funniest programs on air, plays pop music leading into commercial breaks, goes off on irreverent chats with her staff in the studio, making fun of them, and they her. She is heard on more than 350 stations nationwide with 5.5 million listeners per week. She interviews occasional celebrities as well as politicians, and carries segments such as "Lie of the Day."[73]

"I would shrivel up and die if my show was entirely focused on politics," she said in 2003 after the publication of her second book "Shut Up and Sing" an indictment of the entertainment industry. "I think you win hearts and minds with facts, passion and humor. And you win young minds by knowing the culture, not just by trashing it. I'm a huge [Bruce] Springsteen, Coldplay and Ryan Adams fan ... and they are all hopelessly left-wing. Hence the title, 'Shut Up and Sing.'"[74]

She led a successful on-air campaign in 2007 that prompted Verizon, the telecom giant, to drop its sponsorship of rap artist Akon, over his obscene on-stage performances. She also lets the pop culture have it, such as critiquing the absurdity on display at the MTV Video Music Awards.[75]

"You have this spectacle of narcissism, materialism, lack of talent and sheer stupidity all coalescing on one stage in one hideous Las Vegas venue and not one of these freak shows mentioned the military." Ingraham said. "None of these talentless bubble brains mentioned the sacrifice of these men and women or referenced 9/11. You contrast the image of Britney [Spears] with the lieutenant from Newark with 80 pounds on his back with 120 degree heat walking the desert and that tells you how much we are disconnected from that notion of sacrificial consequences."

The notoriety has launched her to the top of *The New York Times* best-seller list numerous times. Her earliest book was in 2000, "The Hillary Trap." That was followed by "Shut Up & Sing,"; "Power to the People," a mixture of a call to grassroots action, memoir and commentary; "The Obama Diaries," a spoof of what Obama would say from Ingraham's perspective in his diary. Most recently she wrote, "Of Thee I Zing: America's Cultural Decline form Muffin Tops to Body Shots."[76]

A native of Glastonbury, Connecticut, Ingraham attended Dartmouth College, where she became editor of the *Dartmouth Review*, the campus's conservative newspaper, and interviewed notables such as Education Secretary William Bennett, conservative commentator Pat Buchanan and American Spectator publisher R. Emmett Tyrell.

"The *Review* took over my life," Ingraham said. "Here you had all these '60s liberals—who used to be storming administration buildings themselves—in power at Dartmouth, and they didn't know what to do with this conservative independent paper. I was sued a couple of times for libel by professors. We ended up on '60 Minutes.' It was a real catalyst for political involvement—and made doing 'Crossfire' look like nothing."

From there, she went to Washington to work for the Department of Education, the Department of Transportation and as a speechwriter for the White House in the last days of the Reagan administration. From there, she headed to the University of Virginia School of Law.[77]

She returned to Washington to clerk for U.S. Supreme Court Associate Justice Clarence Thomas. Then, she went to work for the Washington firm Skadden, Arps, Slate, Meagher & Flom working with Bob Bennett, President Clinton's attorney in the Paula Jones suit and brother of Bill Bennett, where she stayed from 1993 through 1996.[78]

While working for Bennett's firm, she was a co-founder of the Independent Women's Forum, meant to be a conservative counterpart to the liberal National Organization for Women. That was largely because she and others felt the press coverage during the Thomas confirmation hearing regarding the Anita Hill allegations, NOW was presented in the media as the consensus voice of women. "I don't think there is a 'woman's view.' Women are people. They have different views on a whole range of subjects. But if you watched television, every time someone said, 'From the women's point of view,' it was always a liberal. It was the National Organization for Women. It was just ridiculous."[79]

She said defending white collar criminals did not fit her populist "power to the people" view. "Why do you think I got out of it? It was folly," she told the *Philadelphia Daily News*.[80]

From there it was on to punditry, first on TV. She appared as a news analyst on CBS, where she was paired with former New Jersey Senator Bill Bradley, a Democrat, in a short crossfire-style segment. By 1999, she had her own MSNBC show called "Watch It." Not enough people did and it was off the air.

She gained a nationally syndicated radio program in 2002 with the Talk Radio Network.

"When I was on TV, MSNBC, it was 'Oh, she's on television because she's a blonde.' But now that I'm on radio, where do they go with that?" Ingraham said in a *Boston Globe* interview in 2003. "It's so tedious—expressions like 'pundette.' It show how lazy journalists are recycling the same phrases."[81]

Her chief target, whether on radio, TV or books, has been elites. Conservative populism she explains is not targeted at incomes. "When I say 'elite,' I mean a state of mind. I don't think George Bush is an elite. He came from a prestigious family. And he's wealthy, but when I say 'elite' I mean a state of mind that believes that America's traditional values are kind of passé. They want us to get away from that red, white and blue, mom and pop, traditional family thing, there are all sorts of different lifestyles and they all work."[82]

During the Bush administration, she regularly had high ranking guests such as Bush's two Secretaries of State Colin Powell and Condolezza Rice, Defense Secretary Donald Rumsfeld and others.[83]

Ingraham was a big Bush booster in the 2004 reelection campaign, ridiculing John Kerry as "very left-wing," and running mate John Edwards as "Silky Pony." She would also tear into the "the media machine helping John Kerry." She also gave plenty of airtime to the Swift Boat Veterans for Truth, a group who cast doubt on the authenticity of Kerry's war hero status.[84]

In spring of 2005, Ingraham told her fans that she had been diagnosed with breast cancer. "People have gone through much worse, and I know I'll obliterate this," Ingraham said on her Web site. She added, "within a few days, we'll know more about the future. I am hopeful for a bright future and a 'normal' life—well, scratch the 'normal' part."[85]

She was OK after surgery. "It couldn't have gone better," Dr. Katherine Alley said on Ingraham's Web site. She added that initial testing showed no signs the cancer had spread to the lymph nodes. The operation took place at a hospital in Bethesda, Md.[86]

By 2008, contract renegotiations with Talk Radio Network took her off the air for more than two weeks, but the two parties finally came to an agreement, as TRN did not want to lose one of its starts. She also got a temporary tryout for a 5 p.m. program on the Fox News Channel. That did not pan out, but she has become the primary guest host on the O'Reilly Factor, whenever Bill O'Reilly takes time off.[87]

She adopted a three-year-old from Guatemala that year.[88] The next year, she adopted a 13-month old from Russia, where she had spent a college semester. She remarked, "The only question now: Are we having borscht or rice and beans for dinner?"[89]

Ingraham helped rally support against President Barack Obama's agenda and how he handled international affairs.

"It's no wonder fewer countries are taking us seriously," she said, referencing that Saudi Arabia planned to form ties with China and Russia. "When America ceases to lead, the world starts falling into chaos."[90]

She also took comical shots at other Democrats too. "There's nothing more terrifying to me—no Stephen King movie, no Jason-Freddy Krueger combo—nothing is more terrifying than the fact Nancy Pelosi is third in line to be president," she said.[91]

She helped lead an eleventh hour rally at the Capitol in December 2009, telling listeners they must do all humanly possible to stop the Democratic health care overhaul from passing.

"The American people must take this political system back from those who have hijacked it in one of the most abhorrent power grabs that we the voters have ever seen," Ingraham said on her website on December 9, 2009.

It was to plug a rally scheduled for Decebmer 15. "It's the holiday season so the Democrats are counting on you to be otherwise occupied and too busy to stand against their massive expansion of government. Let them underestimate us again just as they did last summer," Ingraham said. "Let these unrepresentative politicians proceed with their legislative chicanery and self-righteous grandstanding. We can expose them and confront them in the classic American spirit—a public gathering on their doorstep."

After the death of Senator Ted Kennedy, the liberal lion from Massachusetts, it was presumed that the torch would be passed to Democratic state Attorney General Martha Coakley. The only Republican to step up for the impossible task of winning the Kennedy seat was state Senator Scott Brown. The race received little national attention, until Brown was a guest on the Laura Ingraham Show.

It made the race a national phenomenon, as former Decatur, Illinois city councilman Dan Caulkins went Massachusetts work for Brown. "I was tuned into the Laura Ingraham show, and she was talking about this guy running for Senate, and had him on, and so I went online and looked him up and sent him a bit of money and started following what he was doing," Caulkins said. "It started to turn around. I thought 'This guy's got a chance.'"[92]

While Republicans had won victories in Virginia and New Jersey, this was—come on—Massachusetts. Yet, Brown came to represent a possible 4st vote in the filibuster proof Democratic majority. After the appearance on Ingraham's show, money began pouring into his campaign and the nation focused on Massachusetts where a tea party candidate won the Kennedy seat in the most liberal state in the union.

### Savage Radio

Michael Savage angrily barked back at a caller one evening who supported the president declaring, "He is the worst leader in the history of our country. He's inarticulate and he's incompetent. ... The man has shown he is incompetent as commander-in-chief." On other occasions, Savage repeatedly called the president a "fiscal socialist."

That would not seem unusual for a conservative radio show except the president he was talking about was not Barack Obama but George W. Bush.

While Rush Limbaugh, Sean Hannity, Mark Levin, Laura Ingraham and especially Glenn Beck have all found times to critique Bush, no conservative talk show host has made it as personal as Savage, the former herbalist living in the liberal bastion of San Francisco.

Further ranting against Bush's policy in Iraq, Savage implied it was run by his political advisors.

"What is he talking about? The same strategy of letting them get shot before they can shoot? Uh oh. Incoming. Now you can fire back. George said it's OK. He just called from the fundraiser. He asked Karl Rove," Savage said. "I don't want to see another body bag coming back. Every death didn't have to happen. Every one of them. Every injury didn't have to happen. I never heard of this in my lifetime. We have the most powerful weaponry in the world and we rarely use it. Instead we send boys into hand-to-hand combat. Why? Why? Why? You don't know the answer? You can't figure it out? No bid contracts."[93]

To be sure, Savage let Obama have it even worse, but during the Obama administration, he never let up on the legacy of Bush. He also regularly lambasts other conservative talk radio hosts for defending Bush.

"He's nothing but a checked pants, country club, Rockefeller Republican, a compromiser and a phony through and through," an irate Savage said to one caller trying to defend Bush. "The man expanded the government more so than his previous four presidents. Are you aware of any of that or have you taken the Kool-Aid for so long from Rush Limbaugh and Sean Hannity you don't know what the hell you're talking about?"[94]

After the 2008 bank bailout, he even called for impeachment—which only the most fringe left activist had called for and Democratic leaders in Congress had rejected.

"If you love your country, why do you let George Bush get away with this? I'm going to tell you something, and I'll say it right now, I would welcome an impeachment investigation of George W. Bush," Savage said. "You can put me on record for that. I would welcome an impeachment investigation of George W. Bush and Hank Paulson."[95]

Michael Savage does not want to be part of any clique, and has been as much an annoyance to many conservatives as a scourge to many liberals.

Michael Weiner, his non-radio name, grew up in New York, living in Manhattan, the Bronx and in Queens. His grandfather Sam Weiner was a Russian Jewish immigrant that came to the United States during World War I, bringing his wife and children, including Savage's father. His father was an antiques dealer.[96]

After earning a bachelor's at Queens College, Michael Weiner worked as a school teacher and social worker before going to the University of Hawaii, where he earned two master's degrees, one in one in medical botany and one in medical anthropology in 1972.[97]

By 1978, he earned a doctorate at University of California Berkeley in Epidemiology and Nutritional Ethno-Medicine in 1978. He said he sought professorships "but I received 'drop dead' letters from universities because I was not black, or Hispanic, or a woman."[98]

Still, he wrote 18 books on homeopathic medicine and folk-remedy books, in his field.[99] After promoting his books on many radio shows, he launched his own show. His radio career began on KSFO in 1994 as a local Bay Area host, and he went from being known as Dr. Michael Weiner to Michael Savage. He went into national syndication in 2000 through Talk Radio Network.[100]

His family has kept up the previous career with a family business in Southern California called Rockstar, an herbal energy soft drink firm.[101]

To make a point, Savage applied to be the dean of UC Berkeley's

Graduate School of Journalism, after taking on his radio position. When the school gave the job to Orville Schell, an author and journalist, Savage sued. But he later dropped the case.[102]

He was not always so dour on Bush.

He was a major cheerleader for going to war in Iraq in 2002 and 2003. He once said, "If it's all about the oil, and seizing the oil for America, then so what?" he said. "If we permit those Arab cutthroat murderers to keep all the oil, we'll be down on all fours in 20 years."[103]

Savage claimed to love his adopted hometown, but rarely missed a chance to denounce its leftism and political correctness, in his book "The Savage Nation," he wrote, "San Francisco is filled with human plague like this because of the ultraliberalism that is killing the city. I'm convinced it's the only city left in America that permits eels like this to crawl around. It's the city of, well, not tolerance, but of hatred. Hatred for anything normal. Hatred for law and order. Hatred for decency. Hatred for mama and apple pie and the roses in your hand."[104]

Before MSNBC became the San Francisco of cable news channels, it hired him to do a one-hour show. The Gay and Lesbian Alliance Against Defamation (GLAAD), the National Organization for Women and other liberal groups immediately opposed the network giving him the show. Savage explained they should not be opposed. "On a sexual level I'm a libertarian," he said, and added, as a way to show he does not discriminate, he said he hired "a nice big strapping lesbian" as his personal security guard.[105] That hardly defused GLAD's protest, but then again, that was probably never the intent.

"Michael Savage is brash, passionate and smart," MSNBC President Erik Sorenson said at the time. "His conservative point of view adds to the kaleidoscope of perspectives already heard on MSNBC—a place where a range of voices have their say, without any one dominating the channel itself."[106]

Savage said MSNBC called him out of the blue, and he told them he would not tone down his routine for TV. "I said, 'Look, I can't change gears for television and do sort of a meek version of myself. I'm going to do what I do,'" Savage said he told MSNBC. Savage said the MSNBC executive told him, "As long as you don't say f--, you can do whatever you want.'"[107]

He didn't say the F word, but what he would say was almost as bad in the eyes of the network.

A 39-year-old prankster named Bob Foster, a Sacramento computer technician, had called CNN 25 times, including three times to Larry King's show, and would always find a clever way to plug his favorite radio program "Don and Mike," broadcast out of the Washington, D.C. area. Foster called Savage's show in July 2003 and said "'Don and Mike' should take over your show so you can go to a dentist appointment, because your teeth are really bad."

Savage chose to take it personally. So he asked Foster if he was a "sodomite." Foster said yes. Then Savage said, "Oh, you're one of the sodomites! You should only get AIDS and die, you pig! How's that? Why don't you see if you can sue me, you pig? You got nothing better than to put me down, you piece of garbage? You got nothing to do today? Go eat a sausage and choke on it. Get trichinosis. OK, got another nice caller here who's busy because he didn't have a nice night in the bathhouse and is angry at me today?"[108]

MSNBC fired Savage after the comment was aired.

For his part, Foster said that was not his intent. "My intention was not for him to get fired. My intention was to drop the 'Don and Mike' name.'" Foster said.[109]

Savage said he didn't know the cameras were rolling and that the show had gone to commercial break. "I'm sitting in front of the camera. I have no control over that," Savage said. "In radio, I have total control. ... He got really vile with me ... I meant to insult him personally, not all people with AIDS." Of MSNBC, he said, "They put the leper bells around me. I'm dead in the water on television."[110]

He continued to be alive and well on radio. He left KSFO for a lucrative deal with rival KNEW.

On the radio program, he said, "I slept quite well. I slept like a baby. I snoozed like a lamb. Because I believe in freedom of speech. The American people understand what went on. I am the underdog.

I am Daniel in the lions' den. I am a victim. They know very well that the left are like jackals in this country. They do not believe in freedom of speech, they only believe in freedom of their speech."[772]

He had far more listeners on radio—8 million—than MSNBC has viewers, spreading to more than 400 stations nationally. He won the Freedom of Speech Award in 2007.[112]

After writing 18 books on plants and nutrition, he wrote subsequent political books that made it onto *The New York Times* bestseller list: "The Savage Nation" (2002), "The Enemy Within: Saving America from the Liberal Assault on our Schools, Faith, and Military" (2003), "Liberalism Is a Mental Disorder" (2005), "The Political Zoo" (2006), and "Psychological Nudity (2008) and "Banned in Britain: Beating the Liberal Blacklist" (2009).[113] In 2011 he published his first work of fiction, "Abuse of Power," a fictionalized account of being banned in Britain.[114]

As the war in Iraq dragged, he became increasingly hostile toward Bush.

"Everybody does not have to back him. A leader could do this without being backed. A leader sells his position to the people. A leader says, although I have been unfairly attacked by the media, I am going to pursue this war for the following five reasons, and you're going to follow me, you're going to listen to this, because you are in danger, 1,2,3,4,5, and you've got to make a decision, do you want to live or do you want to die. If you want to live, here's why we've gone to war in Iraq. He won't do that," Savage said. "And I am angry because it's the young boys he is sending over there and the men in their 50s that he keeps recalling to the national guard. They're being used like cannon fodder my friend. I'm not going to support George Bush just because you think I should. I won't do it."[115]

Enraging gays and feminist was one thing. But in 2008, he enraged parents of children with autism.

"I'll tell you what autism is. In 99 percent of the cases it's a brat who hasn't been told to cut the that out," Savage said on July 16, 2008.[116]

*Talk Radio Network* said in a statement, it was "satisfied that he did not mean any disrespect to autistic children or their families but was instead reiterating his longstanding concerns on public health issues." The company added that it was "not appropriate to censor the opinions of its hosts on legitimate issues."[117]

A crowd of 60 people, many of them parents of autistic children, gathered outside Savage's studio to protest the decision by TRN and KNEW to keep him on the air.[118]

On May 5, 2009, Savage used a boneheaded move by the British government to become a free speech martyr. The British Home Office released a list of 16 undesirable people on the "name and shame" list that were not allowed to enter Britain. The list includes a neo-Nazi, Hamas cleric, and Savage. British Home Secretary Jacqui Smith stood by the decision on all the choices.

"Coming to this country is a privilege and that we won't allow people into this country who are going to propagate the sort of views, and more than that, that fundamentally go against our values," Smith said. "You know, I believe—we discussed free speech before. I believe in free speech. I want to defend that. But I don't think free speech should be a license for people to preach or to promote hatred or to exhort other people actually to carry out criminal acts."[119]

The blacklist from Britain included Stephen "Don" Black, founder of a Florida-based white supremacist Web site and a former Ku Klux Klan leader; the Rev. Fred Phelps Sr., an anti-gay preacher who leads a church/cult in Topeka, Kansas that carries out protests at funerals; Yunis al-Astal, clergy and Hamas lawmaker in Gaza that foments terrorist acts; Samir Kantar, a Hezbollah militant who served 30 years in prison for his role in killing four Israeli soldiers and a 4-year-old girl; Safwat Hijazi, an Egyptian cleric who promoted terrorism; Artur Ryno and Pavel Skachevsky, leaders of a Russian skinhead gang imprisoned for 10 years in Russia in 2008 for 19 racially-motivated killings; Erich Gliebe, an American neo-Nazi leader; and Abdullah Qadri al Ahdal, a Muslim cleric who foments terrorism.[120]

"This lunatic is linking me up with Nazi skinheads who are killing people in Russia, she's putting me in a league with Hamas murderers who kill Jews on buses," Savage said. "My views may be inflammatory, but they're not violent in any way. So who else will be banned—all the people who listen to my show, 10 million people? Should they also not go to Britain?"[121]

Savage sued in British courts, citing international laws. Article 10 of the European Convention on Human Rights protects the right to "freedom of expression," and states "this right shall include the freedom to hold opinions ... and ideas without interference by public authority and regardless of frontiers." Further, Article 19 of the International Covenant on Civil and Political Rights, signed by both the United States and Britain, "protects the right to freedom of expression."[122]

The British Home Office released a statement in response saying, "Any legal proceedings would be robustly defended; we stand by our decision to exclude this individual. Coming to the UK is a privilege that we refuse to extend to those who abuse our standards and values to undermine our way of life."[123]

As the legal action drags on, the new government of Conservative Prime Minister David Cameron announced it would keep Savage on the list.

"I had hopes but did not expect this 'new' UK government to restore sanity to Britain," Savage said. "They are still pandering to the Muslim masses. To continue to martyr me by including me on a list of known murderers and terrorists is bad enough but for the U.S. and Western media which considers itself 'progressive' to continue to ignore this outrage against freedom of speech is indicative that the media and governments are one and the same. This includes so-called conservatives. Has freedom of the press become greed-om of the press?"[124]

### Bill Bennett: Socrates on the Air

William J. Bennett's success in academia, in government and in the publishing world was based largely on his friendly demeanor, one who could talk about morality in America and never seem like he was moralizing. Normally good qualities; but would it work for talk radio, a medium that thrives on passion and boiling down the complex?

Bennett has been the most prominent morning host since his

began in April 2004, running 6 a.m. to 9 a.m., cleverly titled, "Morning in America," the slogan of President Ronald Reagan's 1984 reelection campaign. Bennett served in the Reagan administration, first as the chairman of the National Endowment of the Humanities in the first term from 1981 to 1985 and as the Secretary of Education in the second term from 1985 to 1988. Then he was the director of national drug policy, or drug czar, for President George H. W. Bush from 1989 to 1990.

He graduated Harvard Law, has written or edited 16 books, and went on to be the co-chairman for Partnership for a Drug Free America with former New York Democratic Governor Mario Cuomo, a former liberal talker. While Bennett took some criticism for his high gambling debts, in April 2005, *The New York Times* named him the "leading spokesman of the Traditional Values wing of the Republican Party."

"I often joke that I got my PhD in philosophy so I could be in talk radio," Bennett said. "I didn't intend for it to happen that way, but it did and it's worked. My experience in both government and academia has enriched by knowledge of culture, politics, and the human condition so that I can better engage in a daily conversation with the American people. For example, as the former Secretary of Education, I find that there is perhaps no topic more interesting to my listeners than the education. Once we start talking about education, the phone lines don't stop ringing. Many of the same conversations that I've had in classrooms around the country and in government, I can have with the American people."

From the outset of the program, Bennett said there would be a different tone. "When my program first started, our idea was to pitch the show higher. Many people said it couldn't be done and that talk radio could only be successful if you were riled up and over the top. It doesn't have to be," Bennett said in an interview for this book. "The American people are smart and will rise to the level of discourse. On my show we hold to the Socratic conditions of dialogue: candor, intelligence, and good will. So far, I think we have proven that civil, intelligent talk radio can be successful."[125]

Radio is his preferred media.

"I've done a lot of TV appearances as well as radio. Radio is much more cerebral," Bennett added. "When people hear you on the radio they are more inclined to talk about the content of what you said. On TV, your outward appearance can distract people from your message. Radio is a more cerebral medium and should be so if people stopped a lot of the yelling."

His show was syndicated by the Salem Radio Network, which seems to specialize in the more subdued brand of political thought.

Starting in 2004, Bennett and most of his guests favored the re-election of President George W. Bush. After just one year on the air, Bennett was heard in 116 markets and 18 of the top 20 in the United States.[126]

Bennett—with an unquestioned intellect and academic records—has said of his broadcast that he tries to "keep up" with his listeners and callers. Center right columnist Kathleen Parker, referencing Bennett's reserved radio style, wrote a column headlined, "When Bill Bennett Listens, People Talk."[127]

"Thus, stumbling across Bill Bennett on the radio is like bumping into Socrates at Starbucks," Parker wrote. "Not only is he coherent at 6 a.m. when his three-hour show begins, he's the anti-media man: no yelling, no dumbing down, no condescending."[128]

Bennett describes the show as a fast-paced morning conversation.

In some ways, Bennett seemed to be carving out a brand for himself as among the non-confrontational talk host.

That does not mean Bennett's show escaped controversy altogether. In fall 2005, liberal critics accused Bennett—who had been in the forefront of encouraging Republicans to reach out to minority communities—of racism.

A caller proposed using the pro-life cause as a means of saving Social Security. The caller's rationale is there would be more workers per retiree if abortions are banned. Bennett—who has unimpeachable pro-life credentials—said the proposal was "far-reaching, extensive extrapolations." He went on to say, "I do know that it's true that if you wanted to reduce crime, you could, if that were your sole purpose, you could abort every black baby in this country, and your crime rate would go down. That would be an impossible, ridiculous and morally reprehensible thing to do, but your crime rate would go down. So these far-out, these far-reaching, extensive extrapolations are, I think, tricky."[129]

Newly-minted Illinois Senator Barack Obama said, "Mr. Bennett should immediately apologize to the nation for making a statement that clearly crossed the line."[130]

Representative John Conyers, the ranking Democrat on the House Judiciary Committee, sent a letter to Salem President Greg Anderson calling for Bennett's immediate suspension. "It is difficult for us to understand how an individual granted a show on your network could utter such a statement in 21st century America," the Conyers letter on September 29, 2005 said. "While we all support First Amendment Rights, we simply cannot countenance statements and shows that are replete with racism, stereotyping, and profiling. Mr. Bennett's statement is insulting to all of us and has no place on the nation's public air waves. The fact that Mr. Bennett later acknowledged that such abortions would be 'morally reprehensible,' but added again that if it was done 'the crime rate would go down,' is equally outrageous. We ask that you immediately suspend this radio program."[131]

*Media Matters* and Democratic National Committee Chairman Howard Dean were among the many others to pile on. Even Republican National Committee Chairman Ken Mehlman was pressured into calling the comment "regrettable and inappropriate."[132]

Bennett came back to defend his comment. "A thought experiment about public policy, on national radio, should not have received the condemnations it has." He added, "Anyone paying attention to this debate should be offended by those who have selectively quoted me, distorted my meaning."[133]

African American economist Walter Williams, a professor at George Mason University, defended Bennett as making conditional statement with some basis in past evidence, similar to saying, "If a 100 square-mile meteor strikes the Earth, millions of people will be killed."[134]

"According to the Federal Bureau of Investigation (FBI) Uniform Crime Reports for 2003, blacks, who are 13 percent of the population, were 49 percent of murder arrests, 33 percent of arrests for rape, and 54 percent of arrests for robberies. That means Bennett's statement was true," Williams wrote in an op-ed. "One could make another conditional statement: If male babies were aborted, there would be an even larger reduction in crime. While males are slightly less than 50 percent of the population, according to FBI reports, they constitute 90 percent of the arrests for murder, 99 percent of the arrests for rape and 90 percent of the arrests for robberies. What the crime statistics unambiguously demonstrate is that males, as a group, and blacks, as a group, are disproportionately represented in criminal activity."

Williams went on to point out that economists Steven D. Levitt and Stephen J. Dubner make the argument Bennet made in their book best-selling book, "Freakonomics," which argued if aborted babies lived, they would have grown up poor and more likely to commit crimes. The difference is that Levitt and Dubner were serious, while Bennett made the statement as an example of over extrapolation. "Their [Levitt and Dubner] hypothesis has encountered criticism within the profession, but so far, no one has charged them with racism, sexism or making inappropriate comments."

The left's assault did not work. Bennett still remains on the air as of this writing because in part the attack did not fit. The comment may have been ill-considered, given that there was certainly room to be misinterpreted in a politically charged world. But Bennett is a difficult person to depict as an angry right winger. Further, he deserves credit for clarifying what he said without buckling and giving an insincere apology for the appeasement of the politically correct forces.

The attack was not what sticks with him. He views two memories—one patriotic and personal and another political—as his most memorable moments on the air.

"Several years ago I was hosting a special live Veterans Day show and we were talking to veterans about their service and sacrifice for the country and uniform," Bennet recalled. "A guy stopped his car on the side of the road somewhere in Texas and called in. He was sobbing and very moved by what he had heard. He called because he had once been a soldier and he wanted to apologize to all the veterans for abandoning the military and deserting. He had never gotten over the guilt and listening to the show that day made him want to publicly confess and cry out for forgiveness. We talked quite a while and I told him that every saint has a past and every sinner has a future and that he should seek a way to set it right. As is the norm on our show, his call was followed by many thoughtful and gracious people who were moved by him and offered their judgment and advice. It was the most moving and human moment I've ever had on radio."

On the political front, that happened when he confronted Newt Gingrich.

"On another level and on a different occasion there were two interviews with former Speaker Newt Gingrich, candidate for president in 2012, which were seminal moments in my radio career," Bennett said. "In the first interview, I took Newt to task for criticizing the bold budget plan of his fellow Republican Rep. Paul Ryan. I told Newt that he was undermining an important Republican leader at the worst time and that his campaign could be finished. Gingrich retracted his statements about Rep. Ryan and several months later, in another radio interview, he thanked me publicly on my show for calling him out. He said that my honest and direct confrontation had given him the opportunity to turn his campaign around. Many people think it was an influential and memorable moment in radio."[135]

CHAPTER TEN

# Liberal Failures

It would be wrong to say liberals have had no success on talk radio.

Alan Colmes had a local show in New York before getting a national name as a Fox News personality. Now he has a show nationally syndicated by Fox News Radio.

Dial Global has a whole stable of progressives. Two of their hosts, Ed Schultz—who also has an MSNBC TV show—and Thomas Hartman have about 3 million listeners each. Stephanie Miller has more than 2 million listeners, and briefly had a MSNBC gig. Bill Press, former co-host of CNN's Crossfire and onetime power player in the California Democratic party, has had a nationally syndicated show since 2005. Press wrote a book published in 2010 called "Toxic Talk: How the Radical Right has Poisoned America's Airwaves," lambasting conservative radio.

The left, for the purpose of playing victim in need of fairness regulation, may be prone to act shut out of the radio conversation. The right, on the other hand, might love to gloat. But having millions of listeners is hardly a sign of being locked out of the market.

Nevertheless, even the most successful liberal talk shows have a long way to go before catching up to conservatives. In the *Talkers Magazine* Heavy Hundred list, six of the top 10 are conservative political shows (Limbaugh, Hannity, Beck, Savage, Ingraham, and Levin). It would be seven if you want to count Dave Ramsey, who occasionally makes his political leanings known on his financial show.[1] Generally, conservative talkers reach an audience of about 87 million while liberals reach just 24.5 million, a number that includes National Public Radio.[2]

But since the early 1990s, the left has relentlessly tried to find their Rush Limbaugh. The ambition has led to a string of failures.

"One of the reasons that conservative radio works so well is that it targets people that consider themselves conservative and there's unanimity among them that make them a targetable audience per radio terms," said Michael Harrison, editor of *Talker's Magazine.*" "Whereas people who are liberal don't necessarily have as much in common, so it's more like conservatives and non-conservatives as opposed to conservative and liberal."[3]

That does not mean there is no future for liberal radio.

"I think progressives have had a hard time getting an audience similar to conservatives because progressives are making the huge mistake of targeting their programming to the same audience that conservatives have," Harrison continued. "They are not targeting their audience to people that vote liberal or Democrat. They are more anti-conservative than they are truly progressive. Progressives would do a lot better if they targeted their programs to serve the interests of poor people."[4]

### The Folly of Ex-Politicians

Putting an ex-politician behind the microphone seemed like an easy solution. It was someone who would know how to communicate with the public and someone who would have an instant following. But success in the political arena did not necessarily translate into success on the airwaves.

Though he did not invent progressive talk, Jim Hightower was really the first on air voice the left pinned their hopes on as being their version of Rush Limbaugh. Hightower probably was the only person folksy enough on the left to even come close to such a feat. He also came close to following Michael Harrison's advice of speaking to the concerns of poor people, as opposed to simply bashing Republicans. Nevertheless, his show did not come close to being on a par with Limbaugh.

"What happened is the progressive side forgot radio," Hightower said. "My generation looked to television and mass demonstrations and other ways of communicating, whereas conservatives—like Ronald Reagan and Paul Harvey—hung in there and continued to build an audience. Now it's just follow the leader. People look across the street and say 'if that sucker is doing well with a conservative, that's what I need to."[5]

Hightower was a longtime favorite of liberals; drawing national attention for the holding a statewide office that rarely gets much attention. After being a longtime activist and onetime editor of the liberal *Texas Observer*, he was elected Texas state Agricultural Commissioner in 1982. He ran on a platform of standing up for the family farmer and railing against agribusiness, promoting organics and championing wageworkers. He delivered one of the best lines of the 1988 Democratic National Convention in, saying Vice President George H. W. Bush was "born on third base and thinks he hit a triple."[6]

He was a fixture in Texas politics, outpolling all other statewide constitutional elected official in the 1986 election. But then his political star fell when his office became engulfed in corruption allegations. Hightower was accused of misusing federal funds for political purposes, and the FBI launched an investigation of his office that resulted in the conviction of three aides on charges of bribery and conspiracy. Hightower was never charged with anything, but the scandal was enough to tip the scale in favor of Republican Rick Perry who beat him in a closely fought race in 1990.[7]

After his public life, he began syndicating a two-minute commentary to radio stations around the country, picked up by 150 stations. By early 1994, he got a three hour program to air on Saturdays and Sundays on WABC in New York and syndicated nationally by ABC Radio. His program was broadcast from an Austin studio, syndicated nationally by ABC radio. The call in number was 1-800-AGITATE. He called the program "investigative radio" and asked listeners to "track power and follow money."[8] He told listeners he was standing up to the powers that be to advocate for "the powers that oughta be." He told *Texas Monthly*, "I'm in the tradition of the pamphleteer. It's not enough to be agitated. You have to agitate."[9]

*The Nation* magazine called him "the long awaited relief to Rush polluted airwaves."[10] His on air sound bites included, "Sure, Wall Street's whizzing. It's whizzing on you and me," and "NAFTA, do we hafta?" in reference to the North American Free Trade Agreement that President Clinton and many Democrats supported, much to Hightower's angst.[11]

His liberal populism was not partisan, as in the age of a Democratic president who proclaimed the era of big government over, Hightower had a lot to be upset about, and being upset drew listeners for a while. "The debate, the national discussion, is so narrow! It's an embarrassment," Hightower said. "It's between the wacko right and corporate centrism." He also said that "The political spectrum in this country is not right to left, but top to bottom," and called Clinton "corporate centrist," and Gingrich "just another political whore."[12]

Hightower made the mistake of attacking the people he works for, or at least the people he would be working for, at a time when Disney was in the process of buying Capital Cities ABC that at the time included WABC in New York. He pointed out on the air that Disney CEO Michael Eisner is paid $78,000 per hour, and then aired a skit with Mickey Mouse singing, "I'd love to own the world." After less than two years on the air, ABC fired Hightower, who proclaimed, almost proudly, "ABC didn't fire me. Mickey Mouse did."[13]

"The media conglomerates aren't necessarily conservative, or the people who run them aren't. They're liberals," Hightower said. "They take delight in talk about immigration, abortion, and welfare, but they don't want you to talk about Big Money. That's too close to home."

"I was rallying people to stand up against global greed-heads who are running away with our country and our money and our environment. Mickey didn't like that. What other reason could there be?"[14]

Blaming the evil, godless corporation is generally easy to do. But the ratings just were no longer very good, ABC said. "I take sole credit for the decision to fire Hightower," said Frank Raphael, then-vice president for programming at ABC Radio. "The reason was audiences were precipitously declining. We lost Los Angeles and Minneapolis." Raphael added, "He was not entertaining. He was dogmatic. His passion and humor, that I know to be present, didn't come over."[15] That's not to say that ABC would be honest if politics or corporate interests were the reason. In fact, it is difficult to think of when being too dogmatic was ever a reason to can a radio host.

A year later, Hightower was back on the air with the "Jim Hightower Chat & Chew Show," carried by 107 stations, this time syndicated by the United Broadcasting Network, whose owners included the United Auto Workers and airing for two hours five days per week for three hours. "I finally had ownership that liked my message," he said. The show was broadcast from Threadgill's, an Austin restaurant.[16]

"Chat & Chew" lasted through the 2000 campaign, when Hightower endorsed Green Party candidate Ralph Nader for president over Democrat Al Gore. But the show sputtered out after being carried on fewer and fewer stations. Hightower continued his two-minute commentaries financed by foundations.

Jerry Brown was one of the more successful in terms of longevity, if not market penetration. He was carried on 42 stations. Brown, a former Democratic governor of California who sought his party's presidential nomination in 1976 and 1992 was often called, Governor Moonbeam for his hippie persona. Of course, Brown went on to make one of the most remarkable political comebacks ever, getting reelected governor of the Golden State in 2010.

In 1994, Brown routinely lambasted his successor Governor Pete Wilson. He was all over Wilson for supporting Proposition 187, which would deny certain state benefits to illegal immigrants.

"How far will you go to win an election? How far are you willing to go out of fear, much of which is manipulated by the media? Yep, manipulated by this whole engine of what I would call radical rightism that is sweeping across many parts of America, in California, in the Southwest," the angry Brown said. "When it doesn't focus on the underclass, on the crime issue or on welfare, it likes to bash immigrants, even though the immigrants are brought into the country primarily by employers who are seeking to take advantage of the cheaper wages.... This is a direct consequence of the multinational corporate control of so much of the work force.... There is so much hypocrisy, so much dishonesty."[17]

His show was broadcast from an Oakland studio and was nationally syndicated through Talk America Radio Network.[18]

Brown railed against big companies, and other favorite liberal targets. "You throw a candy wrapper out of your car window and you get a $500 fine because every state in the union has an anti-litter law," he said on "We the People," the name of his radio call-in show. "But a chemical company can get an official permit to poison your neighborhood. ... Industry lobbyists say everything's OK, a little cancer is the price of progress, you have to take your risks in life. I don't think so. I don't think the government's doing enough to protect us. Not when a kid's lungs are being irreparably damaged, when breast and prostate cancers are increasing and when the sperm count is down, when the forests are dying, when frogs and birds are disappearing all over the world."[19]

The one thing he had in common with conservative talkers is that he routinely attacked the mainstream media. "I wanted to get into the media because I think the mainstream media is part of the problem," he said. "I just want to make the show work and shake up the system."[20] He referred to the media as "a latter day oligarchy." "There's a protective *The New York Times*, *The Washington Post* and the networks give to the status quo. I see a rather narrow class organizing the information for this society. Those Sunday shows, assuming somebody watches them, they're all talking to themselves. I want to provide an outlet for a perspective I believe is definitely excluded."[21]

In 1997, he stepped away from the microphone, ending his radio career to make a run for mayor of Oakland.[22] This would spring-board him to the state attorney general's office and later back to the governor's mansion.

Mario Cuomo, the eloquent New York governor who never pulled the trigger after years of being asked to run for president, had to find another means of using his speechifying and policy analysis having been voted out of office in 1994. So he took up radio, getting a one-hour Saturday and Sunday show on WABC that was syndicated nationally to 50 stations by SW Network.[23]

He touted The Mario Cuomo Show as "not talk talk but thought talk," an apparent dig at other talk shows he did not believe raised the dialogue. He would frequently start the show saying, "This is our weekend conversation, listening, learning, sharing, trying to think things through, trying to make them a little bit better." He stopped sometimes short of insulting conservatives, which some believed led the downfall of the show. While criticizing GOP presidential candidate Pat Buchanan, he added, "I think he's a good man. I think probably God will allow him into heaven."[24]

Being out of the governor's mansion and actually hearing from people admittedly shocked Cuomo. When a self-identified libertarian caller was on the show, Cuomo asked, "What if you have a plague? Floods? You'd just let everybody drown?" When the caller answered, "I wouldn't let my neighbor drown," Cuomo said, "Great, Tom, the law of the jungle."[25]

Cuomo overall thought he was vindicated by the "affirmation of the thesis that I started with, which is that there are a lot of people out there who want more than a slogan and want more than a shout and want more than some wisecrack and want more than somebody hanging up on them if they don't agree. So, yeah, I'm very pleased with it."[26]

But just one year of disappointing ratings, Cuomo announced he was quitting. He had political commitments, agreeing with the Democratic National Committee to hit trail for President Clinton and other Democratic candidates, while also making appearance as an analyst on CNN. Upon his departure, he said he was "pleasantly surprised" by "the number of people, Republican and Democrat, who were eager for a reasoned dialogue on issues about which we disagreed. You can make talk radio a pro wrestling match if you want to just raise your voice and start calling people 'dummies.' But I didn't find that was what people wanted."[27]

But he later had another assessment as to why his show did not take off. In an interview with Phil Donohue he said that conservatives "write their messages with crayons. We use fine-point quills."[28]

In 1996, former Connecticut Senator and Governor Lowell Weicker, a liberal Republican turned independent got a progressive radio show as well that did not endure for too long. The always gruff Weicker said the goal of his show would be to "respond to all the unanswered BS all over the country." Weicker's program lasted less than a year. Virginia Governor Doug Wilder met a similar fate with his radio show that only reached eight stations, and only lasted a short time on the air.[29]

Former Senator Gary Hart, whose pursuit of the Democratic presidential nomination was cut short in 1988 by his extramarital affair, managed to get a short-lived radio program as well. He also blamed the audience for its failure. "The reformer, the progressive, the liberal, whatever you want to call it doesn't see the world in blacks and whites but in plaids and grays. There never is a single simple answer."[30]

### Chaotic Rise and Horrendous Fall of Air America

Air America Radio was a chaotic mess from its launch, with changing ownership, a revolving door of management, and worse yet, a corruption charge.

With seed money from venture capitalist Sheldon Drobny and a few others, the idea for a liberal radio network was decided on. Sheldon and his wife Anita were upset that their favorite radio host Mike Malloy had recently been fired, so they looked for a way to get him syndicated nationally. They contacted Atlanta radio executive Jon Stinton about the prospect of a national liberal radio network.[31]

A fund-raising event in October 2002 was held at the California home of Arianna Huffington, publisher of the *Huffington Post*. The Drobnys brought in fellow venture capitalist Javier Saade for the project. Stinton managed to sway Daily Show co-creator Liz

Winstead into joining the team. He also brought CNN executive Shelly Lewis away from her job at American Morning, thus assembling an impressive team.[32]

In February 2003, the first news reports surfaced that a left-leaning radio network was about to rise up and challenge Limbaugh, Hannity and other on the right. The new CEO would be John Stinton, who said in a press release, "We believe this is a tremendous business opportunity. There are so many right-wing talk shows; we think it's created a hole in the market you could drive a truck through." The company initially claimed to have $10 million available. Stinton believed there would be plenty of money to draw more investments from. "Those who lean left have better connections to the entertainment world in Hollywood and New York."[33]

Drobny sold the fledgling company to Evan Montvel Cohen, an experienced advertising professional, and his partner Rex Sorensen, a Guam-based broadcaster. They named the venture Progress Media. They named Mark Welsh the company CEO. Cohen was chairman. Stinton remained as president. The company produced Air America Radio, which signed a lease with WLIB-AM 1190 in New York, the largest media market in the world, as its home base.[34]

The network also managed to get affiliates in Los Angeles, Chicago, San Bernardino, California and Portland, Oregon. In all, Stinton managed to get 100 radio stations in 18 of the top 20 affiliates.[35] In some cases, the network was leasing the time just to get the exposure. The executives then reached into Hollywood to sign Al Franken and Janeane Garofalo to host programs, and also tapped Robert F. Kennedy Jr., son of the former senator and attorney general, to host a program. Florida host Randi Rhodes also jumped at the chance to have national exposure.[36] Rachel Maddow would use the exposure to launch a MSNBC program.[37]

Franken's show went against Rush at noon to three. Rhodes challenged Hannity and the first hour of Levin/Savage, airing from 3 p.m. to 7 p.m. Garofalo aired from 8 p.m. to 11 p.m.

The network launched on March 31, 2004 with much media attention. Two weeks after the launch, Air America sued Multicultural Radio. Multicultural said Air America owed it about

$1 million from bounced checks, while Air America claimed Multicultural wasn't paid because it sold airtime in its Chicago and Los Angeles stations that were supposed to go to Air America. Air America sued Multicultural and lost, having to pay the firms attorney fees, as well as $250,000 in damages.[38]

Other money problems were discovered. Though the network touted having $30 million when it began, *The Wall Street Journal* estimated that at closer to $6 million. Sorensen, the vice chairman, said this was because a major investor had backed out. But it did not sit well with the remaining investors, who voted to force both Cohen and Sorensen out of their jobs.[39]

Scandal arrived next. The Gloria Wise Boys and Girls Club of Co-op City, a non-profit organization that provides assistance to children and the elderly in the Bronx, loaned $480,000 to the Air America parent company Progress Media. Further, there had been four separate financial transfers between October 2, 2003 and March 14, 2004. The four transfers were in the amount of $80,000; $87,000; $218,000; and $490,000, respectively. This totaled $875,000. When this was first reported, in a story broke by the *Bronx News*, no interest had been paid on these loans. *The New York Sun* reported that Cohen and Franken were among the co-signers.[40]

So why would a non-political organization steer its money to Progress Media? It could have been that Evan Cohen was the director of development for Gloria Wise Boys and Girls Club.[826] Both New York City and New York state authorities began an investigation.[42]

Danny Goldberg became the new CEO and Gary Krutz the new president in February 2005. Both bolted by mid-2006. That's about the same time Garofalo and evening host Mike Malloy (who was part of the reason for creating the network) left.

On October 13 of that year came the Chapter 11 bankruptcy filing that showed the network's assets were $4.3 million compared to liabilities of $20 million. Chapter 11 bankruptcy allows for the restructuring of a company. The network still owed Franken $360,750. Franken left the network the following February to prepare for his U.S. Senate run in Minnesota. The company lost $9.1

million in 2004, $19.6 million in 2005 and $13.1 million in 2006.

On January 29, 2007, New York real estate magnate Steven L. Green announced his interest to buy and salvage the network. Air America was sold the Green Family Media for $4.25 million in March 2007 after going through the bankruptcy. Bill Clinton appeared in the Air America re-launch video and Senator Hillary Clinton was interviewed on the air. The former president said, "You are really important. ... This is a big deal." Stephen Green was the new chairman, while his brother Mark Green, a one-time candidate for New York mayor, was the new president of the company.[43] [44] But the network lost another major name in the midst of the 2008 presidential campaign.

Rhodes was suspended by Air America Radio shortly calling Hillary Clinton a "[expletive] whore." It was during the Democratic primary and Rhodes supported Barack Obama. She quit after Air America suspended her, and said the main reason for the separation was long standing contractual disputes. She was shortly thereafter picked up by XM Radio.[45]

Air America plodded and struggled along for the last two years of the Bush administration, the 2008 campaign, and the first year of the Obama administration, without making much headway. After 10 consecutive quarters of losing money, on January 21, 2010, Air America announced it was shutting down because of financial pressures. It soon filed for Chapter 7 bankruptcy, which would liquidate the company. "The very difficult economic environment has had a significant impact on Air America's business. This past year has seen a 'perfect storm' in the media industry generally," Air America said in a statement on its website announcing its decision to close.[46]

The lasting legacy of Air America would be giving Franken a platform to launch his successful Senate bid and launching the career of Maddow, who has the highest rated show on MSNBC.

The problem with Air America and other liberal radio ventures that sought to be their movement's version of Rush Limbaugh was entirely a matter of messaging and marketing, as Harrison of *Talkers Magazine* described it.

"Whereas conservatives are preaching to the choir, advertising agencies want affluent, rich people—upper, middle class car buyers, people that buy stocks, people that spend money, people that are active, people that are voting, people that are educated, people who have a stake in the system—that's what has made conservative talk radio successful," Harrison said.

"When progressives go after that same audience, the only audience radio really understands, radio is an advertising based business subject to the commercial interests of corporations, when they go after the same thing, they are in fact preaching against the choir," Harrison added. "The conservatives are preaching to the choir. If they [the liberal hosts] had the courage to preach to a new choir, that is the folks outside the system, alienated, can't afford things, not making money, uneducated, they would have huge numbers. But they don't think that way. People will listen to radio if radio has things they want. If there isn't anything on the radio that people want, they won't listen to radio."[47]

## CHAPTER ELEVEN

# All Political Talk is Local

It was in the summer of 2001 that Tennessee legislators began to open their mail to what would become a staple of small government protests a decade later. In those envelopes were irate letters telling them to vote against adopting a state income tax or imposing other tax increases on the public. The envelopes also contained tea bags. Huge protests and rallies soon followed outside the state Capitol.

The tea bag idea, symbolic of the Boston Tea Party in which colonist threw barrels of tea into the Boston harbor to protest King George's taxation without representation, was promoted by Steve Gill and Phil Valentine. Gill did the morning drive 5 a.m. to 9 a.m. on WWTN Super Talk in Nashville. Valentime did the afternoon drive show on WLAC, the top rated show in Nashville at the time.

Gill was an attorney and two-time Republican nominee for the U.S. Congress. He came just 900 votes short of winning a U.S. House seat in 1994. Valentine is the son of a former Democratic congressman.[1]

The national Tea Party movement that began almost spontaneously in 2009 through talk shows and blogs was largely an organic

257

movement of citizens coming together after being fed up about their tax dollars paying for a Wall Street bailout and a stimulus program they did not believe would work. Many took credit for it. Chief among those were CNBC host Rick Santelli, talk radio host Glenn Beck, and GOP presidential candidate Representative Ron Paul.

Gill and Valentine were not even the inventors of the Tea Party. Still their actions were repeated by North Carolina radio host Jerry Agar on WPTF, who did an afternoon show. Agar worked with conservative advocacy groups in the state to organize a "Tar Heel Tea Party" outside the Capitol in Raleigh in hopes of preventing the legislature from adopting Democratic Governor Mike Easley's tax hike proposal.

It was an improvement from the Nashville protest, which was marred by some minor violence and a few broken windows. The worst thing to happen in Raleigh was a woman sitting in the House gallery dumping a box of tea bags on the House floor, and another man being escorted from the gallery for interrupting legislators who were speaking. Other than that, those gathered outside the North Carolina Capitol—between 700 and 1,000 depending on whose estimate you read—involved speeches, chants of "no new taxes," and honking horns by those driving past the rally to show support.

While Rush Limbaugh, Sean Hannity and Glenn Beck have accomplished great things for the conservative movement, local conservative radio hosts are unsung heroes. They lack the notoriety of the prominent national hosts. But, they can at times have more direct influence on matters.

Melanie Morgan, a longtime California radio host, believes radio activism increased even more after the successful recall effort against California Governor Gray Davis.

"I watched local hosts across the country take up the activism banner after California shocked the country, especially the MSM which refused to recognize the reality of the movement as it was happening, and delighted in the dramatic results," Morgan said. "Most people who love and admire Rush Limbaugh (and I am one of them) also understand that he doesn't give a call to action. His self-description is educating and entertaining, but he expects his audience to act on their own. Sean Hannity, who is another of my heroes, gives a platform for activists like myself. He supports those of us in the grassroots and at the local level of radio by giving us an amplified voice. It is because local radio show hosts blazed a trail to stop excessive regulations from the government, cancer causing mandated gasoline additives, fuel and car taxes and outrageous taxation that the Tea Party movement began."

She continued, "We have radios and we know how to use them. Al Gore gave us the Internet, and we used it to blog and link to the shows we were listening to. Radio listeners began meet-ups and corner protests, and then showed up by the hundreds of thousands across the country. A small movement became a bigger one, thanks to local talk radio, and the mega giant hosts like Rush, Sean and Glenn who reported and supported local radio hosts as well as our shared audience."

### Congressional Pay Hike and Radio

On December 14, 1988 Detroit radio show host Roy Fox got a call from an angry Tony of Roseville, Michigan. Tony was ticked off that the Democratic-controlled U.S. House of Representatives voted to increase their salaries by an astonishing 51 percent, from $89,500 to $135,000 annually. To protest the pay hike, Tony wanted to send tea bags to members of Congress, with a note attached to the string that says "No Pay Increase."[2]

Fox was a local host who networked with other local hosts, and even got the interest of consumer advocate Ralph Nader to protest the pay increase. Fox was not enthusiastic about the idea in the beginning, believing it to be "moronic," until he realized it was the anniversary of the Boston Tea Party. He and his producer, wife Mary Fox, built a network of talk show hosts, contacting Jerry Williams in (where else) Boston and Mike Siegel in Seattle. Also, deejays, who didn't have their own talk shows, were persuaded to join the cause, reaching audiences in Washington, Los Angeles, Cleveland, San Antonio, Des Moines and West Palm Bach, Florida.

The National Taxpayers Union, a conservative group, also joined in. Congressional Democrats held their annual retreat at the

Greenbriar hotel in West Virginia. Fox and other radio voices gave out the hotel's fax number over the air. Though people weren't marching in the streets as with modern tea party rallies, they were protesting with faxes, enough that the Greenbriar shut the machine down.[3]

A few weeks later protesters dumped 160,000 tea bags in front of the White House. Congress withdrew the pay hike vote. Representative Tony Coelho, the House Democratic Whip, was not happy that his compensation would not jump. "The talk show hosts and Ralph Nader won this round at the expense of the long-term interests of the country." Fox, for his part, was astounded at the success. "What really surprised me was how little it took to turn the tide," Fox said. "It just shows how little impact there is from the public."[4]

Talk radio, still a few years from coming of age with a multitude of national hosts, made its mark on national policy by drawing attention to an issue much of the public was not informed about but once informed was very easy to understand.

"There are things that talk radio helps catalyze. Again, its people making the argument on talk radio. It's not talk radio itself. If they hadn't done it with talk radio, they might have done it with facebook or they might have done it with telephone calls or they may have done it in newspapers. To give the credit to the medium is to miss the point," Michael Harrison of *Talkers Magazine* said. "There have been issues that have been decided on talk radio. Usually talk radio—and again you're writing about conservative talk radio—usually any kind of politically oriented, opinion oriented talk radio can have influence under two conditions. One, when it's a very, very tight situation and any vote, anybody, any small shift can make the margin of difference. Or, two, when there really is a crazy injustice out there that people know about and care about that the rest of the media is missing. Other than that, you cannot get people to do what they don't have a great disposition to do. You cannot in America get people to change their minds too easily or too readily."

### Tennessee Tax Revolt

In November 1999, the Tennessee state legislature adjourned without any changes in the state's tax system that Democratic leaders in the legislature and Republican Governor Don Sundquist told the public were needed to keep the state running. This occurred amid signs waiving, anti-tax chants and honking horns outside the Capitol for what proved to be just a warm up of voter anger that lawmakers would see in a couple of years. Of particular concern was how to fund TennCare, the state's public health insurance plan that was essentially an expanded version of Medicaid.

"Those problems remain unaddressed, willfully ignored by a majority of the people's representatives. They have failed in their duties and they have failed in their responsibility to our citizens," the governor quipped, saying the state needed another $382 million in revenue to keep funding existing programs in fiscal year 2000-2001.[5]

Tennessee was one of nine states that did not have a state income tax. The proposal backed by Democratic legislators and some in the Republican establishment would have imposed an income tax of 1.3 percent and 5 percent on adjusted income starting at $15,000 for singles and $30,000 for married people.[6] It further would have eliminated the state's 6 percent sales tax on food and reduced it to 3.75 percent on other items.[7]

Again in June 2000, legislators tried to pass an income tax to no avail. One talk radio program reportedly called Governor Sundquist "a liar" and Democratic House Speaker Jimmy Naifeh of Lebanese ancestry, the "Arab Boss Hog of West Tennessee." Even when lawmakers targeted only salaries of more than $100,000, they were met with demonstrators.[8] It would set a graduated rate from 3 percent to 6 percent.

It was during both 1999 and 2000 that Gill and Valentine whipped their listeners into frenzy, as most of the Tennessee media would portray it. The hosts urged listeners to send empty tea bags in the mail to their member of the state House and state Senate to express their opposition to an income tax.

Then in 2001, lawmakers assumed three times would be a charm. Tennessee went from a $200 million budget gap the first time it was tried to an $850 million gap in 2001.[9] An income tax proposal by state Representative Tommy Head and state Senator Bob Rochelle—both Democrats—was supposed to raise $800 million in revenue, taking between 3 percent and 6 percent of the workers' income and increasing the state sales tax to 7 percent with exemptions for food, clothing and non-prescription drugs.[10]

By contrast, Governor Sundquist backed a plan to broaden the state sales tax to cover all businesses and services that were currently exempt. This included prescription drugs, home energy, financial services and real estate agents. All would be subject to a 4 percent sales tax. That would be a lower rate but a broader base.[11]

Conservative Republicans believed that neither the Democratic nor the Sundquist plan addressed the growth of state government and spending, and put the entire focus on revenue.

Gill made the case why the budget gap was not a revenue problem but a spending problem.

"TennCare eats up 30 percent of the state budget, which has grown from $13 billion to $19 billion in the past seven years," Gill said. He further pointed out that the Tennessee state budget grew 20 percent over two years. "That's four or five times higher than the rate of inflation."[12]

Prominent Washington groups such as Americans for Tax Reform and Club for Growth weighed in.

In what was becoming a regular occurrence, another rally erupted on the Capitol in May. Phil Valentine set up his broadcast booth across the street from the Capitol, where protesters stood and shouted. Valentine yelled above the volume, "This is the way people are speaking." Inside the Capitol, members of the House and Senate had to run through a gantlet of protesters on the second floor of the Capitol to get to their respective chambers.[13]

On July 12, state senators briefly resurrected a state income tax proposal. Democrat and Republican leaders met in private at to work out a budget compromise they thought they could slip through. The idea was to push a flat-rate income tax of 3.5%, followed by a nonbinding referendum on the issue in 2003 and more exemptions from the sales tax.[14]

State Senator Marsha Blackburn sent an e-mail to Valentine warning what the lawmakers were up to. "Income tax vote should be around 5, TIME FOR TROOPS." Valentine did just that, telling his listeners, "They're trying to raise our taxes! Get to the Capitol! Quick!"[15]

Shortly before 5 p.m. about 2,000 protesters again ascended on the Capitol.[16] Frightened lawmakers called for a lockdown of the Capitol and four state law enforcement agencies were present to maintain control, dozens of state police wearing riot gear and some Nashville police on horseback. A window near Governor Sundquist's Capitol office was shattered and protesters shouted through the hole, "No New Taxes."[17]

The window near the governor's office cost $150 to replace. Two other windows were also broken at the Capitol. Police made no arrests, but issued four citations—two to drivers for violating the city's noise ordinance after refusing to cease honking their horns, one to a woman for disorderly conduct for shouting names at a police officer and one to a man who refused to detour around a police barricade.[18]

But the Tennessee legislature passed a budget with no new taxes. Gill triumphantly proclaimed, "We're the voice, But the people are the volume."[19]

The *Tennessean* newspaper reported that "a mob of tax protesters broke a window in Governor Don Sundquist's office, accosted lawmakers in the hallways, banged on locked doors and shouted so loud lawmakers could barely conduct business."[20] *The Knoxville Sun-Sentinel* reported that the demonstrators "shouted catcalls and chants in the hallway outside the Senate chamber while others roamed the state Capitol grounds and drove their cars and trucks on surrounding streets, honking horns."[21]

State legislators ridiculed the protesters for the demonstrations. But Gill and Valentine held firm, even basked in their victory.

"There was more violence on the part of the police" than protesters," Valentine told his listeners. Talking to a Nashville police spokesman on the air, Valentine said, "You can call a cop any names you want to. It's not against the law. He's got to take it." Gill meanwhile said "Don Sundquist's storm troopers" escalated frustration among protesters, making the situation worse than it needed to be.[22]

Gill called state legislators "cockroaches" and said Sundquist was "more corrupt than Ray Blanton," the former Democratic Tennessee governor convicted on corruption charges for selling pardons.[23]

The talk radio victory gained national attention, as the Los Angeles Times wrote, "The lesson isn't that a state income tax is unpopular; it's that Tennessee now has three political parties: There are Democrats. There are Republicans. And then there is talk radio. The protest this month was a coming of age for the state's conservative shock jocks and the high point of a long, well-organized battle against the effort to bring an income tax to Tennessee, one of the nine states that doesn't have one."[24]

### Tar Heel Tea Party

Just weeks after the Tennessee anti-tax rallies, the same occurred in North Carolina.

The state legislature sought to pass a $600 million tax hike by the Democratic legislature and Democratic Governor Mike Easley. The plan called for increasing income taxes on couples earning $200,000 or more, putting a 6 percent sales tax on liquor and allowing counties to raise their sales taxes by 0.5 cents. This proposal came on top of $260 million increase in state taxes already approved that year.

Jerry Agar of Raleigh's WPTF prompted the protests. Agar was distraught over the tax increases. Agar teamed up with John Hood, the president of the John Locke Foundation, a state-based free market think tank. They essentially arranged the event over a weekend. They started on a Friday spreading the word to other talk radio hosts and to the North Carolina chapter of Citizens for a Sound Economy. They also enlisted the help of the state's Republican Party and the state Libertarian Party, so one could theoretically call it a bipartisan movement.[25]

Governor Easley, perhaps seeking to steel headlines from the protest, announced 278 state employee layoffs as part of budget cuts recommended by the legislature. He called a press conference that day, with his entire cabinet present, and said he would do anything to ensure the state keeps its AAA bond rating. The practical effect of losing that would mean the state would face $15 million in higher debt payments, he said.[26]

Hood responded, "What kind of buffoon would raise taxes $600 million to save $15million? Apparently the kind of buffoon that sometimes gets elected to the North Carolina legislature."[27]

By 3 p.m. the following Tuesday, the four-hour "Tar Heel Tea Party" drew about 1,000 protesters to the Capitol in Raleigh. Some wore tea bags attached to their lapel pins.[28] Though rambunctious, it never approached violence as the earlier Tennessee event. There were no rocks thrown through windows, just a lot of tea bags.

The crowd cheered Agar as he began his program with the broadcast booth set up near the Capitol.[29]

Some of the signs in the crowd included one held by an eight-year-old Charlotte girl that said, "Tax my parents and I can't get a puppy."[30] Others read, "Backroom Tax Hikes Are Not the Answer," "No New Taxes, Do Your Job" and "God Please Save Us From the Democrats."[31]

It was also a bit of a costume ball, rare for July heat. One person was dressed at the Grim Reaper with the words "Taxes Kill" on his black robe. Another demonstrator was dressed as Santa Clause holding a sign that read "Santa Claus Should Be Fat. Not Government." An Uncle Sam and a Revolutionary War soldier were also in the crowd. The revolutionary outfits, as well as the "Don't Tread on Me" flag present at this rally would later become popular at Tea Party rallies across the country. The North Carolina crowd chanted "Axe the Tax" and "No New Taxes."[32]

The most disorderly moment came when a 67-year-old woman, Mary Copeland of Mebane, N.C., sitting in the House gallery tossed tea bags on the House floor. Protester Dick Carter, also sitting in the gallery, stood up and attempted to have a discussion with Speaker of the House Jim Black. Carter, of Wilmington, N.C., was removed from the gallery by security, which prompted others to begin chanting, "No new taxes." Carter said, "They will not listen to us. I think they must have blinders on." A few Republicans, including Representative George Holmes came to the gallery to ask the protesters to settle down claiming they were hurting the cause. "I'm on your side," he told the protester who grew angry with him.[33]

The House vote on the tax plan was cancelled after Speaker Black and Democratic leaders could not muster enough votes to pass it. To his credit, Black did not resort to rhetoric that Washington Democrats resorted to against Tea Parties, calling them terrorists and un-American. "I can appreciate people at least paying attention to what is going on," the House Speaker said.[34]

### California Recall

Perhaps the most astonishing achievement of talk radio's influence was galvanizing enough voters in a liberal state, a state larger than many countries, to forcefully remove a liberal Democratic governor from office less than a year into his second term, installing one of the biggest names in Hollywood in his place.

In November 2002, California Governor Gray Davis was reelected by a comfortable margin against Republican Bill Simon, bucking the national trend that favored the GOP that year. While the election was less about Davis's popularity, and more about the weak candidacy of Simon, the turnaround in the governor's standing in the largest state in the country was startling.

For context, a brief history of recall in California: During the progressive era of the early 20th Century, citizens demanded more accountability of their politicians. In 1911, California Governor Hiram Johnson signed the public official "lemon law," which allowed voters to recall an elected official so long as certain thresholds are met, such as the signatures from at least 10 percent of the state's voters to place the matter on a special election. "Lemon law," is derived from the old expression of calling a defective product that should be returned to the retailer a "lemon." Thus, Californians have a means of dealing with buyers' remorse from voters.[35]

There are compelling arguments against allowing recall, but it is law in California, and it is not something that is easy to achieve. Before 2003, there were 31 recall efforts, including one against

Governor Ronald Reagan, which like the others failed to gain the necessary number of signatures to force a referendum. Thus, the argument—from mostly Democrats but a few conservatives including George Will—that the Davis recall would set a horrible precedent, allowing wily nilly recall efforts, undermine representative democracy and lead to mob rule were not really valid.

That said the difficult threshold for a special election would have never been achieved without California talk radio personalities and help on the Internet. Like most successful movements, this one had more than one parent. In this case, it was Melanie Morgan and Eric Hogue. Because of the size and influence of California, the matter national talk radio shows, which weighed in heavily for ousting Davis.

When the author asked Morgan if the recall effort would have every happened without talk radio, she answered, "Without a doubt. Would it have been successful? I seriously doubt it."

"Californians were watching the rolling black-outs from San Jose to Santa Barbara, and people were literally dying as a result of a botched state government effort to intervene in the marketplace," Morgan said. "Governor Gray Davis deserved the blistering criticism that we leveled at him and his corrupt administration. Talk Radio used the intimacy and immediacy of the medium to rally individuals to action. It wasn't hyperbole; it is a daily recitation of facts. The facts won. Talk Radio funneled the outrage, but it would have been much more difficult without the medium in which we were operating."[36]

When Davis was elected to his first term in 1998, California had a $12 billion surplus. By the time he was up for re-election, the state's budget had a $38 billion gap after massive spending hikes. Also, beginning in 2000 Davis signed electricity generation contracts that sent energy prices skyrocketing. He also appointed a policy board that allowed a refinery to increase toxic discharges into San Francisco Bay shortly after the firm donated $70,500 to his political war chest.[37]

Still, despite the unpopularity, voters begrudgingly gave him a second term as Simon was a little too conservative for California.

Then came the post-election revelations that the state was in worse fiscal shape than it appeared. Republicans accused the governor of lying to the electorate.

The Davis re-election celebration had barely ended when on December 30, 2002 on San Francisco's KSFO, Morgan first mentioned the possibility of a recall. She was interviewing California Republican Party Chairman Shawn Steel and asked why the party did not launch a recall drive.

"I have been dubbed 'the Mother of the Recall' but I think Gray Davis thinks of me as just a real mother bleeper," Morgan joked. "Seriously, others were discussing the idea, specifically Ted Costa, a Sacramento tax reform crusader. But we kicked the idea around on *KSFO* radio during an interview with Shawn Steel. When Steel mentioned the possibility of recalling then-Governor Davis to my co-host Brian Sussman, I paused three seconds while the M-80's started firing off in my brain. Three seconds is a long time for dead air. By the time I began speaking again, I had the entire campaign mapped out in my head. Sometimes you just know when history and opportunity intersect. That was one of those moments."

Shortly after his interview on Morgan's show, Steel found himself getting phone calls from former California Assemblyman Howard Kaloogian, Republican strategist Sal Russo, who managed Simon's campaign, and Costa. Steel began to think it might be a real possibility, but was still uncertain.[38]

"I was thrilled by the response, because it was exactly what I envisioned would happen. But I did not expect other talk radio hosts to jump onboard so quickly," Morgan said. "Radio show hosts are feral animals, and they usually do not want to become involved with an idea or concept that another host was pushing. This time was different. And everyone could take a piece of the credit because it took a sustained political effort, a daily push, to get the buzz, build the anticipation for change, and demand action from the citizens of California. It had to happen in Los Angeles, Sacramento, the Central Valley and in the Bay Area. Every talk show host provided the wind for change."[39]

While the Republican Party establishment wanted to wait until everything was lined up. Costa the activist wanted to plunge in. He called the Eric Hogue Show, which aired on Sacramento's *KTKZ* at 6 a.m. on February 4, 2003. Hogue described himself as a "conservative Ohio Buckeye boy" who came to "the land of fruits and nuts," meaning California.[40]

During an on-air break he told Hogue all he needed to launch the effort was 60 to 100 signatures to file with the Secretary of State's office to get the drive moving. Back on the air, Costa and Hogue talked about the burgeoning recall petition, and Costa told the listeners to the program, "I'm here now at 3407 Arden Way. I just put on a fresh pot of coffee. Come on down."[41]

*The Los Angeles Times* described the location as "hard to find."[42]

Still, the reaction was almost immediate despite the early hour, Hogue recalled. "My phone lines lit up with callers asking, 'Where is it again? How do I get there?' I had a taxicab driver named Rick call in and say, 'I'm taking the rest of the day off.' He was going to go down there and sign himself, then pick up anyone who needed a ride and take them down for free. Businessmen already commuting to San Francisco called in and said: 'I'm going to be late for work because I'm turning around and coming back to sign.'" Costa had more than 100 signatures in less than two hours. Hogue called the signers, "The 100 Patriots of the Recall."[43]

Costa and Hogue organized "drive by signings," where state residents could sign a recall petition at orange-coned drive-up lanes that offered coffee and donuts. By 8:30 a.m. the first morning of the "drive-by signing" event 350 listeners showed up, some in their pajamas to sign the petition.[44]

Meanwhile, Kaloogian traveled the state appearing on conservative talk radio shows, directing listeners to www.RecallDavis.com. The site drew 85,000 visitors who downloaded a petition.[45]

The effort would still need more resources, which is where U.S. Representative Darrell Issa came in. The wealthy businessman who could tout his economic bona fides to revitalize a state in despair considered running for the office in 2006. But those involved in the recall effort talked to him about not only being the designated candidate to win the office but also the financier of the operation.

269

Convinced by the 120,000 signatures gathered, Issa poured $1.6 million into the effort.

In a move that appeared he wanted to be recalled, Governor Davis on June 21 issued an executive order to increase the state's vehicle license fee, even though the state's registration fee was the most expensive in the country.[46] Perhaps he did not believe the recall effort would actually go anywhere since none of the other 31 did. More and more outraged voters added their name to the petition.

On July 23, California Secretary of State Kevin Shelly certified that the recall effort collected 1,356,408 legitimate voter signatures—about 50 percent more than needed to qualify the first gubernatorial recall election in state's history. Under the law, a special election was to be held 80 days later, on October 7.[47]

Hogue began calling his show the "Home of the Recall."[48]

Hogue asked Issa if he was prepared defend himself against the "Davis slime machine," and asked if he had a "flak jacket" to take expected criticism. Other talkers consistently referred to Governor Davis as a "jerk," "incompetent" "dishonest" and "corrupt." On Burbank's KFI, hosts John Kobylt and Ken Chiampu called themselves "ward leaders."[49] They regularly called Governor Davis "Gumby" and skewered the major newspaper such as *The Los Angeles Times* and *San Francisco Chronicle* that editorialized against the recall as "media idiots."[50]

Kobylt and Chiampu, before getting the most listened to program in California, had a record of assisting in bringing down governors. They hosted a popular talk show out of 101.5 FM in Trenton, N.J. where they began the "Dump Florio" campaign in the early 1990s. They began attacking the governor early on in his administration, and in 1993 went the extra mile to promote Christie Whitman, who beat Florio. Along with Bob Grant, they gave the biggest assist to her slim victory.[51]

Most talkers seemed to feel personally invested in the matter, such as former San Diego Mayor Roger Hedgecock of KOGO. "I don't intend to lose. I was involved in this from Day One, and I'm going to see it out to the end," he said, sounding almost like a candidate himself.[52]

"My listening audience has been energized by this issue like no issue I've ever seen," said Hedgecock. "They actually see it as a solution, a way to focus their frustration and anger and make a specific move."

Then everyone was thrown for a loop when action movie star Arnold Schwarzenegger announced on the Tonight Show with Jay Leno that he would be a Republican candidate. Shortly thereafter, Issa dropped out of the race, and the muscle bound moderate became the leading Republican.

Eventually the race included Davis's Lt. Governor Cruz Bustamante, who had become a de facto Democratic nominee when it became apparent Davis was likely on the way out. State Senator Tom McClintock tried to run as the conservative alternative in the race. Eventually celebrities such as Gary Coleman entered, as did conservative-turned-liberal commentator Arianna Huffington. The race had more than 100 candidates, but was largely seen as a Davis vs. Schwarzenegger contest.

Schwarzenegger knew he had to appeal to conservative voters, and talk radio was the best way to do that.

"When you think about Gray Davis, you have to think at the same time Bustamante, because it's one team," Schwarzenegger said on Hedgecock's show. "I think one newspaper pointed out that Bustamante is Gray Davis with a receding hairline and a mustache."[53]

On Hugh Hewitt's syndicated program, broadcast out of California, Arnold said "Davis and Bustamante are into overspending, overtaxing and over-regulating ... I think the people have been punished enough."[54]

Speaking on Larry Elder's KABC Los Angeles show, Schwarzenegger conceded he supported gun control measures such as background checks, trigger locks, a ban on assault rifles, and efforts to restrict the sale of guns at gun shows. But added he believed the Second Amendment. Schwarzenegger went on the Sacramento KFBK Mark Williams and said he opposed school vouchers. None of the positions were popular to conservatives. But going on the national Sean Hannity show, he said, "I'm pretty conservative. You know, I don't believe in spending. The first thing I'm going to do is go into Sacramento and put a spending cap on the politicians, because they can't help themselves, because it's ridiculous to spend money that you don't have."[55]

Morgan said she voted to recall Davis then voted for McClintock for governor. It was still clearly a net win and she was very ecstatic on election night.

"I was glued to the returns at the Recall Gray Davis Headquarters in Sacramento, broadcasting back to San Francisco," Morgan said. "When the numbers showed that the Governor was officially finished, I quietly cried. I offered up a prayer for Gray Davis and his family. I did not expect to be so emotional, but it was the first time in my adult life where I witnessed citizen activism challenge and change the system. I now know that anything is really possible in this country, but there must be passion and commitment, plus great timing, to make it happen. Change is a powerful notion."[56]

Arnold won on election night, though his victory speech never gave credit to talk radio or for that matter Darrell Issa. Talk radio hosts were not humble in the triumph.

As the polls closed Tuesday night, Kobvlt of "The John & Ken Show" said "I want a bottle of champagne in here right now."[57]

Reflecting on his vote, Chiampou said "Aiming with that little stick, right into Gumby's heart, I punched my chad with glee."[58]

The elation was evident the next morning on the dial elsewhere in California.

"Folks, it's history," Hogue said on his program after the recall, with his guest Bill Simon on the air. "It's total recall."[59]

Former state GOP chairman Steel, who helped start the wildfire when he was on the Melanie Morgan show, noted that most major newspaper editorial boards opposed the recall. "Historians will look back on this election as the time that the combination of the Internet and talk radio overtook the power of daily newspapers."[60]

### Lars Larson and Citizen Gabriel

In 2007, Lars Larson got a call from a woman named Angela Brandt who told him him about their foster child.

"We're planning to adopt him and the state is going to take him away and send him to Mexico," she told Larson.

Larson did not believe every call he got. As a long time TV newsman he was skeptical about everything. But he did his due diligence and checked the matter out.

Angela Brandt was a stay-at-home mom and her husband Steve Brandt was a sheriff's deputy. They lived on a farm in Toledo, Oregon. They had then-two-year-old boy Gabriel Allred since he was four months old. The boy's biological parents had their rights terminated. The father was an illegal immigrant from Mexico, and a convicted sex offender. The mother, an American citizen was also convicted on drug charges. The fact that Gabriel's mother was an American citizen made him an American citizen. Nevertheless, Oregon Department of Human Services Children's Adults and Families Division had a strict policy about sending children back to the closest blood relative, and decided to send him back to his grandmother in Mexico, Cecilia Martinez.[61]

Larson found the policy extremely objectionable, since in some cases children could be put in danger by such a policy. In the case of Mexico, Larson believed they would be putting the boy in a much worse situation.

"It became one of the things I'm proudest of because I had to beat on that story on the air as a talk show host for two full weeks before anyone would get the story out," Larson said in an interview. "By the end of the story, all the major media were covering."[62]

Larson was an advocate for the family, but was far more than a commentator. He became very much a reporter again on this story. He dug more into the policy and found the state of Oregon had sent at least 17 children to foreign countries. He gave tough interviews to state officials on the radio, asking what type of monitoring goes on once the children are handed over. The answer: that was left to the individual country.

"To come to find out that we were taking American citizens and shipping them off to foreign countries—where in some cases they were murdered—that had to be one of the most stunning times," Larson said. "I mean for all the people, the big name politicians you interview, nothing is more surprising than that kind of development where you find out that real people's lives are being affected by what you do on the air."

Larson, who got his start in radio at age 16, was a TV news reporter and anchor man in Oregon with an Emmy and Peabody award to his name, along with awards from the Associated Press and the National Press Club. He got his own radio program in 2000 free to air his own opinions. The local show airs on 17 stations through the Northwest Radio Network; the flagship station is KXL-AM in Portland, Oregon. By 2003, the Larson got a separate national show now airing on more than 100 stations across the country through Westwood One.[63]

The transition from a straight news reporter to radio commentator was a natural progression, Larson said.

"As a reporter, you try to ask really good questions. At times, there are things about a story that you wished you could say, but they involve your opinion, they involve you ability to take the totality of all the circumstances and all the things you know about a story, all the things you know and all the things you've heard, all the things you're not hearing," Larson said. "Sometimes the most important data point is the dog that didn't bark; what you're not hearing and the question that is not being asked."[64]

Eventually, the state news media took notice of the Baby Gabriel saga. The Oregonian newspaper editorialized for the state to reverse its decision and allow the boy to stay with his foster family where he would have four brothers. Then it became a national story and more of the public became more enraged.[65]

Politicians were surprisingly slow to weigh in, Larson said, but eventually did. In November 2007, Oregon Governor Ted Kulongoski asked for a legal opinion to determine if he had the power to reverse the decision by the state agency.[66]

A few weeks before Christmas, and after a meeting between the grandmother and a foster family, the matter was settled on December 12, 2007. The state announced that the Brandts could move forward on adopting Gabriel and he would remain in the United States. But, the agreement required that the family provide him with Spanish-language lessons to allow him to remain in contact with his family in Mexico. "This agreement gives Gabriel the best of all worlds," boasted Dr. Bruce Goldberg, director of the Oregon Department of Human Services, the agency that made decision in the first place that caused such a public uproar.[67]

It was a galvanized public, along with negative media attention focused on the Oregon state government that forced the state to reconsider and eventually change course.

"I'm pretty confident that if we had not beat on that story hard, the little boy would have been sent to Mexico, he was not," Larson said in an interview for this book. "The other media would not have taken notice. They finally did and ran it front page. We called him baby Gabriel Brandt."[68]

He said this is a case where both reporting and commentary were needed to put the real story in perspective.

"That's where even conventional reporting wouldn't have done it, because you have to have some opinion in there of what should happen to this child not just what was happening to this child," Larson said. "If a conventional reporter got a hold of it, he might have said, well there's this child and he has blood relatives in Mexico and he's being sent back to Mexico."[69]

## Chapter Twelve

# Obama, Tea and Talk

Just four days before the inauguration, or as Rush Limbaugh jokingly called it, the "immaculation" of Barack Obama as the 44th President of the United States, Limbaugh talked on the air about a publication that sent him a letter asking for "400 words on your hope for the Obama presidency."

"So I'm thinking of replying to the guy, 'Okay, I'll send you a response, but I don't need 400 words, I need four: I hope he fails.'"[1]

The war was on.

Obama, speaking to Republican congressional leaders he had invited to the White House just two days into his presidency to talk about his $800 billion stimulus plan, said, "You can't just listen to Rush Limbaugh and get things done."[2] The comment was leaked and widely reported, and once again elevated Rush even before the administration established the strategy of Limbaugh is the "leader of the Republican Party" bit.

Well before the Obama inauguration, the entire talk radio industry must have seen the return of a Democratic president—a far more liberal one than the Bill Clinton for that matter—as a potential ratings bonanza. Now, to be clear, Sean Hannity, who began talking about "conservatism in exile," Limbaugh, Mark Levin, Glenn Beck, and others almost certainly were not secretly hoping for an Obama victory. The ratings were doing just fine under a Bush presidency, thank you very much. But, one would have to be tone deaf not to see a clear opportunity to be on the offense, rather than (sometimes begrudgingly) defending Bush against the left.

Companies saw new opportunities, bringing new hosts into the fold such as Fred Thompson, a former Law & Order star, presidential candidate and Tennessee senator. He was replacing Bill O'Reilly's show on Westwood One. Joe Scarborough, once MSNBC token conservative host, briefly had a radio run. What began as a simulcast on radio syndication and MSNBC became just an MSNBC program "Morning Joe." Also, popular WABC personality Monica Crowley— coincidently the sister-in-law of Alan Colmes—got a national syndication as did CNN anchor Lou Dobbs, who later went to work for Fox Business. New programs seemed like a decent investment as talk radio surpassed all other radio genres in 2008 in popularity, largely because of the iPod and other forms of listening to music. Also, five of the top hosts, Limbaugh, Hannity, Beck, Ingraham and Savage all signed new contracts in 2008, which means there could be enough of a residual effect for the new shows to get spillover audience before or after the top ranking hosts.[3]

With a Democratic president and Democratic congress, many conservatives feared a return of the Fairness Doctrine. Obama made an appointment to confirm those beliefs, naming Mark Lloyd as the "Diversity Czar" at the FCC, and it was not long before Glenn Beck began talking about Lloyd's paper trail.

Lloyd had said, "The purpose of free speech is warped to protect global corporations and block rules that would promote democratic governance."[4] Beck highlighted Lloyd's 2006 book, "Prologue to a Farce: Communication and Democracy in America." In the book, Lloyd wrote, "It should be clear by now that my focus here is not freedom of speech or press … This freedom is all too often an exaggeration. … At the very least, blind references to freedom of speech or the press serve as a distraction from the critical examination of other communications policies."[5]

Lloyd wanted to implement strict localism requirements on commercial radio stations. This would mean requiring more local programming instead of carrying nationally syndicated shows. This was seen as a potential means of restoring the Fairness Doctrine by stealth. Further, Lloyd had long advocated ownership caps for stations. Lloyd further said, that Venezuela President Hugo Chavez "began to take very seriously the media in his country" by imposing restraints on cable TV and revoking the licenses of more than 200 radio stations.[6]

During the Obama years, talk radio played a vital role in the formation of the Tea Party movement. They railed against Democratic health care bill that eventually. They also were leading advocates for Republicans during the 2010 elections, which led to a new majority in the House.

"I think talk radio helped catalyze the tea party movement. It would be absolutely shortsighted and ignorant of me to think there would be no tea party if there was no talk radio because our history is full of historic populist movements," Michael Harrison of *Talkers Magazine* said. "Populist movements such as the tea party go all the way back to the original tea party in Boston. They didn't have talk radio then. Wouldn't it be just absolute arrogance on my part being a booster and a fan of talk radio to say if it were not for talk radio there would be no tea party. How the hell did the world exist before talk radio if that's the case. The answer is no. There would still be tea parties. And there would still be populist movements."

Talk radio did become more popular and influential, enough so to send much of the left-wing commenteriat into fits. *New York Times* columnist Paul Krugman, blamed Fox News and talk radio for a shooting at the U.S. Holocaust Memorial Museum in Washington.[7] MSNBC's Chris Matthews said, "The activists on radio are not afraid, because they're not afraid of anything. But at some point, if we have violence in this country against our president of any form or attempt, people are going to pay for it, the people who have encouraged the craziness."

Bill Clinton, this time as a private citizen and spouse of the Secretary of State, talked again about how dangerous talk radio can be in a speech to the Center for American Progress.

"This tea party movement can be a healthy thing if they're making us justify every penny of taxes we've raised and every dollar of public money we've spent. But when you get mad, sometimes you wind up producing exactly the reverse result of what you say you are for," the former president said. "Before the [Oklahoma] bombing occurred, there was a sort of fever in America. ... We didn't have blog sites back then, so the instrument of carrying this forward was basically the right-wing radio talk-show hosts, and they understand clearly that emotion was more powerful than reason most of the time."

Rush fought back against Clinton in the pages of *The Wall Street Journal*. "The Obama/Clinton/media Left are comfortable with the unrest in our society today. It allows them to blame and demonize their opponents (doctors, insurance companies, Wall Street, talk radio, Fox News) in order to portray their regime as the great healer of all our ills, thus expanding their power and control over our society."

While Obama eventually signed his landmark health care overhaul bill, the Patient Protection and Affordable Care Act, he did so after more than a year of debate and changes to the legislation, a 2,700 page bill that had become incredibly unpopular with the public, according polls. That is much longer than it should have taken to pass such legislation considering the massive Democratic majorities in the House and Senate.

Talk radio show hosts definitely played a role in helping to make the debate more intense. Hugh Hewitt, Mike Gallagher and Bill Bennett were all key players in the joint effort by the Salem Radio Network and the National Center for Policy Analysis (NCPA) to generate more than 1 million e-mails from 50 states to members of Congress opposing the health care overhaul. In the summer of 2009, SRN and NCPA gathered 1.3 million signatures on the "Free Our Health Care Now!" petition.

Meanwhile, Limbaugh put the number of the Capitol switchboard on his website in March, with the words, Code Red: Click Here for List of Targeted Congressmen." This led to 500,000 calls. The Chief Administrative Office, which handles technology issues for members of Congress, told *The Hill* newspaper there were about 40,000 calls per hour after Limbaugh's call to action.

Laura Ingraham participated in a Capitol Hill rally opposing the health care overhaul. Mark Levin was part of a separate rally at the Capitol in opposition to the Obamacare legislation. Both Ingraham and Levin live in close proximity to Washington.

Finally, the 2010 election. Turnout was key and conservatives had all the energy. People who the mainstream media might have deemed unelectable won Republican primaries in Kentucky, Florida, and Utah after winning a special election in Massachusetts in January and turning two gubernatorial seats over to Republicans in New Jersey and Virginia.

Clearly Rush has been a big player in the age of Obama, as has Hannity and others. But two hosts really emerged as superstars during—and largely because of—the Obama administration and some of the overreaching that occurred.

Glenn Beck and Mark Levin had political shows running for some time, and were writing bestsellers when George W. Bush was in the White House. When Obama came into office, the Tea Party movement emerged with a focus not only on debt and deficits but also on the Constitution and American tradition, a central focus for Levin and Beck.

Beck skyrocketed to the number three spot just behind Rush and Hannity, and became a marketing powerhouse. Levin became an intellectual trailblazer for conservatism—something he had always been but more people really began to take notice faced with an ever expanding government.

## Mark Levin: Chief Justice of the Airwaves

Perhaps no other radio host can speak words that inform, enlighten, crystallize thinking and still be entertaining the way Mark Levin does. While critics have described the program as "anger theater," it is more passion than anger. Levin goes through rants, and throw out terms like "New York Slimes" referring to *The New York Times* and "Hillary Rotten Clinton," referring to the former first lady and secretary of state, and telling know-nothing callers, "get off the phone you big dope." But he also delivers monologues that are quite professorial.

Levin can be most accurately described as a very passionate conservative with a great sense of humor and even greater intellect. His show with 8.5 million listeners became prominent during the Bush years, the program and Levin became a true political force during the Obama administration thanks largely to Levin's book "Liberty and Tyranny," that became a cultural phenomenon and proved that ideas matter. Levin was not a trained broadcaster, or aspiring media star from the beginning. Rather, he was a whiz kid who leaped into the Reagan movement in 1976 and stayed on board through the revolution in the 1980s.

Levin skipped his senior year of high school to go to Temple University, where at the age of 19 graduated Phi Beta Kappa and magna cum laude. Shortly thereafter, he was elected to the local school board, making him the youngest school board member in the state of Pennsylvania at the time. He graduated from Temple Law School at 22, and then became active in politics.[8]

He was a foot soldier for Reagan's effort at the state level in Pennsylvania to rest to the Republican nomination away from incumbent President Gerald Ford in 1976, a losing battle that still saw Reagan come extraordinarily close.[9]

He was then part of the Reagan revolution in 1980, when Reagan won the nomination and trounced Jimmy Carter to become president Levin was deputy assistant Secretary for Elementary and Secondary Education at the U.S. Department of Education, and Deputy Solicitor for the U.S. Department of the Interior before he moved up to the Associate Director of Presidential Personnel and eventually became the Chief of Staff to Attorney General Edwin Meese.

After his career in government, Levin went into private practice and later became the president of the non-profit Landmark Legal Foundation, based in Leesburg, Virginia, where he lives and broadcasts his radio show from. As president of Landmark Legal, he became an enemy of the National Education Association, the nation's largest teachers union, over their questionable funding of political campaigns. He also brought legal action against the Environmental Protection Agency, the Forest Service and other federal agencies regarding federal grants. While many public interest non-profits tend to be press release factories, Landmark Legal was never a publicity hound, working quietly and taking press calls as they came, but hardly ever calling a press conference.

"Landmark Legal Foundation is a great passion of mine because it is a relatively small legal group which has done truly amazing things both before I came here and now that I am here," Levin said. "And we have enormous challenges. Our opponents are much more heavily funded and more numerous."[10]

A fan of talk radio for 30 years, he became a frequent legal analyst, penning op-eds for *National Review* and other publications, and appearing as a guest on the Rush Limbaugh radio show. Limbaugh gave him the name "F. Lee Levin," jokingly after the famous defense attorney F. Lee Bailey. In 2001, the American Conservative Union honored him with the Ronald Reagan Award.[11]

After Hannity reached national syndication, Levin became a frequent guest and occasional guest host. Hannity gave him the name "The Great One," a phrase callers to the show continue to use. Levin took to radio well enough that in 2002, WABC gave him a Sunday afternoon program.[12]

WABC had brought on the increasingly popular Savage Nation for the Monday through Friday 6 p.m. to 9 p.m. slot. But in 2003, Michael Savage had a contract dispute with WABC's sister station KSFO in San Francisco. So WABC dropped Savage from his valued slot as well. It was Levin's gain, who went to five times per week in starting September 2, 2003.[13] Savage's show was quickly picked up by rival WOR, but Savage was not the fit for the New York City market that Levin was. Levin shot to number one in his timeslot in the first 18 months on the air.[14] Still, Levin was only heard by northeastern states in and around the big apple despite broadcasting from his "bunker" in a "non-descript building," which was his Northern Virginia home.

His first book "Men in Black: How the Supreme Court is Destroying America," was released on February 7, 2005, and hit the number three spot on *The New York Times* best-seller list.[15]

His second book was "Rescuing Sprite," a completely non-political book about Levin's family and the shelter dog they rescued, who they named Sprite, as a companion for their dog Pepsi. Sprite's previous owner treated him very poorly and the Levin family nurtured, and became very attached. It turned out that the dog they believed was six or seven years old was actually closer to 11. After about two years, Sprite became sick and was suffering, and had to be put to sleep. The anguish that commonly hits so many families hit the hard-edged Levin very hard. Levin explained that he first began writing an essay about Sprite to deal with the loss. But later, added background to fill in the blanks and it became a book. "I can't describe the depression I felt," Levin said. "I was in agony. I thought maybe if I wrote the story, I could explain to myself what I was going through."[16]

By 2006, his show was nationally syndicated by Citadel Media Networks, breaking into 50 cities, including 17 of the top 25 markets.[17] "We're about to enter a golden age," Levin said. "The 2006 elections leading to 2008, with Hillary Clinton. We'll be bigger than ever, and I can't wait."[18] Like virtually everyone else at the time, Levin believed Hillary Clinton was destined to be the Democratic candidate for president.

While Levin mainly targets liberals, he has been known to go after fellow conservative hosts, namely Savage, his nationally syndicated rival in the 6 p.m. timeslot. For Savage, he refers to "Weiner Nation," using the host's real last name. He once said, "I'm not sure why anyone would want to hear someone have a nervous breakdown every night I'd think it would get tiring," he said of Savage.[19]

Of Joe Scarborough's "Morning Joe" on MSNBC, he called "Morning Schmo." He calls Bill O'Reilly, "The 8 p.m.-er." MSNBC Hardball host Chris Matthews is "Screwball on Screwball." Countdown with Keith Olbermann is "Countdown to No Ratings with Keith Overbite." Even Glenn Beck, who has a 9 a.m. radio show, has been called a "morning back bencher."

House Democratic leader Nancy Pelosi has always been "Stretch Pelosi." Senate Democratic Leader Harry Reid has always been "Harry the Body Reid." Senator Ted Kennedy was the "Cape

Cod Orca," and former President Bill Clinton is "BJ Bill Jefferson Clinton," a reference that BJ stands for something else that Clinton became known for in the 1990s impeachment battle. The American Civil Liberties Union is the "American Criminal Liberties Union." Former Vermont Governor and Democratic National Committee Chairman Howard Dean is called "Dr. Demento Dean." The Rev. Al Sharpton was "Al Not So Sharpton."

Levin called Vice President-to-be Joe Biden "The Dumbest Man in the Senate," and "Plugs Biden." President Obama is "Barack Milhous Nobama." Moderate Republicans are "Repubicans." California Governor Arnold Schwarzenegger was the "Jerkinator." For Senator John McCain, the name was "McLame."

It was Levin who was probably harsher than Limbaugh and definitely harsher than Hannity on McCain during the 2008 primary. He also did not care for former Arkansas Governor Mike Huckabee, whom he called "Hucka-phony." Levin reminded Republican voters of McCain's sins against conservatism—campaign finance reform, support for amnesty for illegal aliens, support for cap and trade legislation and opposition to interrogation techniques such as water boarding to terrorism suspects. All but the interrogation issue was also supported by President Bush. With a moderate Republican against an ultra liberal Democratic nominee Obama, conservatism itself seemed in the wilderness. Long before the primaries were really heated, Levin decided to write a book explain conservatism, which he considered liberty, and liberalism, which he considers a soft tyranny through a heavy taxed, regulated, nanny state.

"Liberty and Tyranny: A Conservative Manifesto" was released in the spring of 2009, months after Obama took office. It came out just a few months after "The Death of Conservatism" by *New York Times* Book Review Editor Sam Tanenhaus, which was incidentally reviewed by the *Times*, and featured in other media.

Levin's book was largely ignored by the *Times* and the rest of the mainstream media. He didn't get an appearance on Today or Good Morning America or Oprah. Not even on Larry King. He made it on Fox News and talk radio, but so do a lot of other conservative authors.

Still the book was a phenomenon. It sold 1.2 million copies, focusing less on contemporary politics than on history and philosophy.[20] Books about Adam Smith, Alexis de Tocqueville, John Locke and Edmund Burke, the American Revolution, and critiques of the New Deal do not typically fly off the shelves. This one did. It remained in the number one spot on *The New York Times* best seller list for months on end, occasionally dropping to number two, before elevating to the top spot again the following week. It also topped the Amazon best seller list. What reviews the book did not get in the mainstream media was made up for on Amazon, where it got more than 2,000 mostly glowing customer reviews.[21]

The book was also a favorite among tea partiers. The crux of the book was that the nation's core values were worth fighting for against the left. He did not use the term liberal (a term going back to Locke that has a more libertarian context) or progressives. Rather he used the term "statists" to describe most Democratic politicians and a modern liberalism philosophy that seeks more power by the state and collective and less by the individual.

To back up the message of his book, he looked for conservative candidates across the United States to challenge the GOP establishment moderates. For him, it was a micro version of the epic Reagan vs. Ford battle of 1976 in House and Senate primaries across America.

The National Republican Senatorial Committee, Senate Republican Leader Mitch McConnell and former GOP presidential nominee McCain among other establishment figures endorsed moderate Republican Governor Charlie Crist for the Florida Senate race—a sure thing. Levin invited Crist's challenger—former state legislator Marco Rubio polling at just 8 percent against the governor—on his show. Levin kept putting him on the air, giving Rubio airtime he wasn't getting elsewhere, and a national fundraising platform. Eventually Rubio surged so far ahead of Crist, establishment Republicans who did not defect sheepishly said they would support the nominee without offering a word of encouragement. Realizing it was hopeless, Crist dropped out of the GOP primary and mounted an independent candidacy. With a credible Democrat in the race,

U.S. Representative Kendrick Meek, Rubio still captured 50 percent of the vote in an astonishing victory and embarrassing defeat for a governor who once had a bright future.[22]

The pattern repeated itself elsewhere when Levin brought long shot candidates onto his program.

McConnell, who built the modern Republican Party in his home state of Kentucky had groomed the state's Secretary of State Trey Grayson for an open Senate seat in 2010. Another sure thing when Levin started to plug ophthalmologist Rand Paul, who's only political experience was campaigning for his father Representative Ron Paul. Paul won the state's Republican primary then the Senate seat, both by wide margins. Levin also backed Mike Lee on his show in his challenge against incumbent Utah Republican Senator Bob Bennett. Lee won the nomination at the state party convention then won the race in November.[23]

Not all were success stories for the general election. Sharon Angle in Nevada lost to Harry the Body Reid. Insurgent tea party candidate Joe Miller beat incumbent Senator Lisa Murkowski in the Alaska Republican primary, but Murkowski managed to keep her seat by running as an independent. There was also Christine O'Donnell—which Republicans and conservatives still debate the wisdom of. O'Donnell upset Delaware's U.S. Representative Mike Castle—a former governor who was considered a lock for the Senate and scared most Democrats out of contesting the seat. O'Donnell was crushed by Joe Koons in November, allowing Democrats to keep the seat.[24]

Levin argued that conservatives shouldn't simply give up on blue states like Delaware, and can perhaps win one day if they are willing to at least compete. While Glenn Back and CNBC host Rick Santelli get most of the credit for the Tea Party movement, Levin certainly helped push it into a more cohesive electoral strategy and prove that conservatism—declared dead barely a year early—can win big.

In 2012, he had yet another number one *New York Times* bestseller, *Ameritopia*. He also sought to steer the Republican Party toward nominating a conservative for president. Though he fell short of blocking Mitt Romney's near inevitable path to the GOP nomination, he and other talkers likely had some sway in the unlikely phenomenon of Rick Santorum, who won a string of upsets on a shoestring budget against the far better financed Romney.

### Glenn Beck: Commentator and Guru

The verdict still is not out on Glenn Beck's Internet-based TV network GBTV that will include his program, similar to the shows he had on Fox News and CNN Headline News. But thus far, Beck has been a marketing genius, and a political one for that matter. He writes at least two books per year, has multiple websites, one magazine, and for the last two years has led rallies in Washington and Jerusalem. He is an activist and a corporation.

As reflected on in the first chapter, Beck is perhaps closest to Rush in terms of reach and influence through multi-faceted means. Limbaugh by comparison has a popular political "Limbaugh Letter," a paid online element to his radio show, and hasn't written a book in almost two decades. Beck, the third most listened to talker on 400 stations, still gets barely half as many listeners as Limbaugh for his radio show. The way in which the two are very different is that Rush has repeatedly said his success is not based on who wins elections or what legislation gets passed, only in rare instances encouraging listeners to call their congressmen and demand something. While Limbaugh used to hit the public speaking circuit regularly, he has never established a large scale rallies such as Beck's "Restoring Honor" and "Restoring Courage" events.

Maybe it could be said that Limbaugh cast a more looming presence over the conservative movement, but Beck works harder at it. Otherwise, they have enough in common, a love for radio at a young age, both started out playing top 40 music, they had messy personal lives of which they both cleaned up, and have most of the same enemies. They also have the same syndicate.

Perhaps Beck's strongest marketing point to stations and to Premiere, a division of Clear Channel, is that he attracts a younger audience, even as talk radio generally attracts an older audience of

40 or over. For a genre that has an overwhelming older male audience, Beck also attracts more females as a percentage of his audience than other hosts.[25]

Beck's influence over the conservative movement might have waned marginally since losing his 5 p.m. show on Fox News. The 2 million he reached on TV is not even half of the 9 million he teaches on the radio. "I guess I'm too stupid to self-edit, so I tell people exactly the way I feel," Beck said. "I truly believe radio is the most powerful medium there is. It's really treated so many times as a bastard child of other mediums. It is the most effective medium, when it's done right, because it reaches right into the listeners and connects with them on a one-on-one level."[26]

Nothing seems to be really stopping Beck's success, success that is even more pronounced when considering his personal story. Beck grew up in rural Mount Vernon, Washington. Tragedy hit his life at age 13 when his mother committed suicide, events that might have led to problems he would have in his young adult life.[27]

It was his mother who helped shape his interest in radio when she gave him a collection of shows that were produced in the Great Depression. Beck, as a child, would imitate the voices he heard on the recordings, and record himself. As a teenager, he got his first radio job when he won a contest to be a deejay for a local AM station. Beck later got a job, at the age of 15, at a Seattle FM station, where he would take a bus to every Friday after school, and broadcast through the weekend. Beck did not go to college and instead was determined to have fame in the radio business, ideally in New York City. He got jobs in Louisville, Kentucky; Houston, Texas; Phoenix, Arizona; and Washington D.C. It was paying off. By age 21, he was earning $70,000.[28]

Beck was mostly a liberal during his days as a deejay, once saying, "I wasn't just pro-choice, I was pro-everything, until I started taking everything off the table and began looking at things and asking if this view was consistent with that view."[29]

He began moving to the right during the Reagan years, or at least becoming more patriotic during his deejay show, such as expressing support for the U.S. bombing of Libya in 1986.[30] But shifting right on the political spectrum did not keep him away from alcohol and marijuana.

By his mid-20s he was making $300,000, and said he was "a scumbag alcoholic with money and modicum of fame?"[31] He recalled to *The Washington Post* that when he worked at a Baltimore station, he fired someone for bringing him the wrong pen as one example of how he had become insufferable.

He had a string of failed morning radio programs. His first marriage failed. After working in some of the biggest markets, he ended up taking a job at a Connecticut radio station.[32]

He said he realized he needed to change after he had too much to drink and blacked out while reading his daughters a bedtime story. When he awoke, they asked him to finish, but he did not remember starting.[33]

So he joined Alcoholics Anonymous. When Joe Lieberman first ran for U.S. Senate in 1988, he and Beck became friends. Lieberman wrote a recommendation letter for Beck to enter Yale divinity school. Beck started the program but did not finish.[34]

Beck's second wife, Tania, agreed to get married on the condition that they find a religion. They converted to Mormonism together. He was motivated to take his radio career in a more meaningful direction than the top 40. After the Connecticut contract expired, Beck in 2000 got a political talk show in Tampa, Florida. It turned out to be the perfect state to be in after the electoral mess of the presidential race between Bush and Gore. Beck was able to reach the number one spot locally.[35]

His national syndication was modest at first.

After the 9/11 terrorist attacks and the beginning of the war on terror, demand for more talk radio programming increased. In 2002, he went into national syndication with just 47 stations. His stated mission was to make listeners "feel goodness from my show and accept me for who I am, flaws and all."[36] Beck moved his operation to Philadelphia, Pennsylvania, as the Glenn Beck Program was being carried 150 stations by 2004, and later to New York. The radio program syndicated through Premiere, reached 400 stations. In 2006, he got a show on CNN's Headline News, part of rebranding

HLN with more talk show hosts in hopes of competing with Fox and MSNBC.[37]

"What amazed me about him is that he was the number-three-rated radio talk show in the country, and he wasn't [on the air] in three of the biggest markets in the country—Chicago, New York and Los Angeles," said Ken Jautz, the Headline News chief that hired Beck. "And we thought that his style, tone and sensibility would work on TV."[38]

Beck pulled in impressive ratings for a network fewer and fewer people had been watching. During his two years on HLN, the shows ratings grew by 200 percent.[39] Still, he was getting only 336,000 viewers, a pittance compared to what he later have.[40]

The National Association of Broadcasters presented Beck with the 2008 Marconi Award for syndicated radio personality of the year, an award that came his way before he really hit superstardom.[41]

In October 2008, he announced he was heading to Fox News, where his program began in January just as newly minted President Barack Obama was taking office. At Fox, he was given more freedom, and often ran with it. In a guest appearance on the morning show Fox & Friends, Beck said Obama had "a deep-seated hatred for white people or the white culture."[42] The comment was in regards to Obama stating that the Cambridge Massachusetts Police "acted stupidly," with regards to an incident where an African-American Harvard professor was allegedly profiled outside his home, even though Obama admittedly did not have all of the information to the incident.

Still, the program concentrated more than any other TV punditry show on American history, what the Founders might have said, and the lineage of the progressive movement of the early 20th Century to both the fascist and communist regimes that would emerge mid-century in Europe. He further drew this to the influences of the radical left in the United States such as the Students for a Democratic Society. And, lest there be any doubt, Woodrow Wilson was the worst president in American history, from Beck's view. He rarely got into such weighty topics on his HLN show. But on Fox, the historical trajectory was demonstrated on his chalk board. While critics persistently accuse him of rewriting history, Beck calls on viewers and listeners to consult primary sources, don't take his work for it, look it up. Beck is hardly a credentialed historian, but to imply that no one else has ever politicized interpretations of history is quite rich. Also, it captured the American public's interest, as 2.4 million viewers generally tuned it, unheard of for a 5 p.m. show. That rivals the audience of Bill O'Reilly and Sean Hannity, the first and second in the Fox primetime line up (and ranked first and second overall in cable news programming).

Beck can be perplexing for conservatives, as he can speak to such true points, but then scatter into what can sometimes be dismissed as a conspiracy theory.

"His on-air weepiness is unmanly, his flirtation with conspiracy theories debilitating, and his judgments sometimes loopy (McCain worse than Obama?) or just plain counterproductive (such as his convoluted charge that Obama is a racist)," wrote conservative intellectual and historian Stephen Heyward. "Yet Beck's potential contribution to conservatism can be summed up with one name: R.J. Pestritto. Pestritto, a political scientist at Hillsdale College in Michigan who has appeared on Beck's TV show several times, is among a handful of young conservative scholars engaged in serious academic work critiquing the intellectual pedigree of modern liberalism. Their writing is often dense and difficult, but Beck not only reads it; he assigns it to his staff. Beck may lack Buckley's urbanity, and his show will never be confused with 'Firing Line.' But he's onto something with his interest in serious analysis of liberalism's patrimony. If more conservative talkers challenged liberalism's bedrock assumptions as Beck does, liberals would have to defend their problematic premises more often."[43]

Though he did not create the Tea Party movement, his commentary was largely credited with the proliferation of Tea Party rallies across the country. In particular, he teamed up with Freedom Works, a conservative grassroots group that helped sponsor Tea Party events.

He also started the 9/12 Project, with the idea of returning to the unity that the country experienced right after the 9/11 attacks.

292

The 9/12 Project revolved around nine principles and 12 values. The Nine Principles are "1.America is good. 2.I believe in God and He is the Center of my Life. 3.I must always try to be a more honest person than I was yesterday. 4.The family is sacred. My spouse and I are the ultimate authority, not the government. 5.If you break the law you pay the penalty. Justice is blind and no one is above it. 6.I have a right to life, liberty and pursuit of happiness, but there is no guarantee of equal results. 7.I work hard for what I have and I will share it with who I want to. Government cannot force me to be charitable. 8.It is not un-American for me to disagree with authority or to share my personal opinion. 9.The government works for me. I do not answer to them, they answer to me." The Twelve Values are 1.) Honesty, 2.) Reverence, 3.) Hope, 4.) Thrift, 5.) Humility, 6.) Charity, 7.) Sincerity, 8. Moderation, 9.) Hard Work, 10.) Courage, 11.) Personal Responsibility and 12.) Gratitude.[44]

The principles and values sort of cross over from political commentator to life coach guru.

In 2009, Beck—already a growing list of *New York Times* best sellers signed a contract with Simon & Schuster to give him profit participation in each new book he wrote for the publisher. Profit sharing is typically a privilege reserved for such bestselling authors as Stephen King.[45] Beck writes fiction and non-fiction, and loves to promote others books.

Beck, again stepping a little outside the political realm, promoted suspenseful political thrillers on his radio and TV show. Beck interviewed more than 40 novelists on his shows, including James Rollins, Vince Flynn, David Baldacci, James Patterson and Brad Thor. "He's our Oprah," Thor said. "God love him, we're very fortunate." Just as a mention by Oprah could propel a book on to the best seller list, the same was becoming true for Beck.[46] Generally Rush, Hannity and others promote non-fiction.

One of Beck's most notable successes came with the ouster of presidential advisor Van Jones. Beck pointed out that Jones was a communist. Jones only said he previously embraced communism in the 1990s, but had a change of heart. Jones also signed a petition in 2004 that said "people within the current [Bush] administration may

indeed have allowed 9/11 to happen, perhaps as a pretext to war."
Jones claimed he did not really believe what he was signing. "Where
is the press on this?" Beck asked. Jones, who had expressed far out
of the mainstream views, was the Green Jobs Czar, the slang title for
special adviser to the White House Council on Environmental
Quality. But *The New York Times*, *USA Today* and the networks had
not done a single story, according to *The Wahsington Post*, which had
done one story.[47]

Beck almost singlehandedly took down a radical working in the
White House, as the message still spread widely enough to be a
tremendous embarrassment to the Obama administration. Jones
resigned over Labor Day weekend 2009.[48]

The whole course of events at least prompted some in the
mainstream media higharchy to be introspective. *New York Times*
Managing Editor Jill Abramson said the paper was "a beat behind
on this story" and that while the Washington bureau was short-
staffed during a holiday week, "we should have been paying closer
attention."[49]

On August 28, 2010, Beck held the "Restoring Honor" rally at
the National Mall in Washington. Hundreds of thousand attended,
stretching from the Lincoln Memorial to the World War II
Memorial. For Beck, the event was not about politics, but restoring
a spirit of serving God. Unlike Tea Party rallies, where political signs
are everywhere, political signs were banned at this event. Sarah
Palin, the 2008 Republican vice presidential candidate, joined him
on the stage, as did Alveda King, the niece of the Reverend Martin
Luther King, Jr. Beck invited more than 200 clergy to attend, in
what he called the "Black Robed Regiment," a reference to pastors
in the Revolutionary War who whipped up opposition to British
colonial rule.[50]

Beck spoke in front of the Lincoln Memorial, and the fact that
August 28, 1963 is when the Reverend King spoke from the same
location was not lost on his many critics, who claimed it was disre-
spectful. Beck said he did not mean to pick the anniversary for the
"I Have a Dream" speech, but thought it was "divine providence"
that it happened that way. "Whites don't own Abraham Lincoln.

Blacks don't own Martin Luther King. Those are American icons, American ideas, and we should just talk about character, and that's really what this event is about. It's about honoring character."[51]

It was big news the following April 2011 that Beck and Fox were parting ways. The ratings by this time had dropped, but he was still getting a very impressive 1.9 million viewers, astonishing for 5 p.m. But the advertising boycott pushed by pressure group Color of Change, a group affiliated with none other than Van Jones, had taken its toll on ad revenue, as several hundred sponsors pulled their commercials from Beck , and a few companies stopped advertising on Fox News because of Beck.[52] His final show aired on Fox on June 30. Under contract, he could not promote his new venture, GBTV, by name on the air. But, he referred viewers to his website repeatedly. GBTV is Internet-based pay TV that is risky and experimental. But, it gives Beck absolute control over his content. "It's my network, so if I want the show to run 2 hours and 15 minutes one night, it will," Beck said.[53]

In a sequel to the "Restoring Honor" rally, Beck was even bolder in 2011, scheduling a "Restoring Courage" rally in Jerusalem to support the state of Israel. Earlier in the year, President Obama called for Israel to return to its pre-1967 borders, though he almost immediately backtracked.

During the rally, Beck said, "In Israel, there is more courage in one square mile than in all of Europe. In Israel, there is more courage in one Israeli soldier than in the combined and cold hearts of every bureaucrat at the United Nations. In Israel, you can find people who will stand against incredible odds, against the entire tide of global opinion, for what is right and good and true. Israel is not a perfect country. No country is perfect. But it tries, and it is courageous."

Beck slammed the international community's hostility to Israel. "The grand councils of the earth condemn Israel. Across the border, Syria slaughters its own citizens. The grand councils are silent," he said. He later added, "The diplomats are afraid, and so they submit. They surrender to falsehood. The truth matters not. To the keepers of conventional wisdom, a sacrifice of the truth is a small price to pay. What difference does it make if we beat up on little Israel? These are the actions of the fearful and cowards."[54]

Beck has never taken himself too seriously, but since changing himself, is a big believer in taking on serious causes.

# NOTES

CHAPTER ONE

1 Glenn Beck's keynote address to the 2010 Conservative Political Action Conference; http://www.youtube.com/watch?v=DHDuHZVhIgM
2 Ibid.
3 Brian Montopoli; "Rush Limbaugh Knocks Glenn Beck; Criticized for 'Reparations' Comment;" CBS News; February 23, 2010
4 Andy Barr; "Mark Levin to Glenn Beck:'Stop Acting Like a Clown;'" *Politico*; February 23, 2010
5 Michael Calderone; "Beck vs. Limbaugh;" *Politico*; September 17, 2009
6 Ibid.
7 Jonathon Martin; "Rush Job: Inside Dems' Limbaugh Plan;" *Politico*; March 4, 2009
8 "Limbaugh the Leader? Obama Chief of Staff Calls Talk Show Host a Barrier to Progress;" Fox News; March 1, 2009
9 Transcript of Rush Limbagh's Address to CPAC; February 28, 2009; http://www.foxnews.com/politics/2009/03/01/transcript-rushlimbaughs-address-cpac/
10 Zev Chafets; "Rush and the Republicans;" *The Virginian-Pilot*; May 24, 2010
11 Ibid.
12 Ibid
13 Interview with Bill Bennett for this book
14 Ibid
15 Brian Stelter; "For Conservative Radio, It's a New Dawn Too;" *The New York Times*; December 22, 2008
16 Fred Lucas; "Conservatives Hail New Media Influence;" CNSNews.com; March 1, 2007
17 2010 Talk Radio Research Project; *Talkers Magazine*
18 Interview with Michael Harrison for this book.
19 2010 Talk Radio Research Project; *Talkers Magazine*
20 David Frum; "Conservative Waterloo; Even if Republicans Win in November, Obamacare is Forever;" *Pittsburgh Post-Gazette*; March 24, 2010
21 David Brooks; "The Wizard of Beck;" *The New York Times*; October 2, 2009
22 Chris Matthews Show; April 18, 2010
23 Patt Morrison; "Patt Morsion Asks: Madame Speaker;" *Los Angeles Times*; June 27, 2009
24 Interview with Michael Harrison for this book
25 Interview with Lee Edwards for this book

CHAPTER TWO

1 Interview with Michael Harrison for this book.
2 "Calvin Coolidge;" The American Experience; Public Broadcasting System;
   http://www.pbs.org/wgbh/amex/presidents/30_coolidge/index.html
3 Richard A. Viguerie & David Franke; "Amserica's Right Turn: How Conservatives Used New and Alternative Media to Take Power;" Bonus Books; 2004; Page 174
4 Ibid.
5 Byron York; "An Unfair Doctrine: Democrats Try Once Again to 'Hush Rush' and Many Others;" *National Review*; July 30, 2007
6 Viguerie & Franke; Page 175
7 Elizabeth Fones-Wolf; "Creating a Favorable Business Climate: Corporations and Radio Broadcasting 1934 to 1954;" *Business History Review*; Summer 1999
8 Timeline of Call-In TV and Radio Format; C-Span; http://legacy.c-span.org/C-SPAN25/timeline_a.asp
9 Barry Gray; "The 25 Greatest Radio Talk Show Hosts of All Time;" *Talkers Magazine*; September 2002; http://www.talkers.com/greatest/8rgray.htm
10 Howard Kurtz; "Hot Air: All Talk All the Time: How the Talk Show Culture has Changed America;" Basic Books; 1996; Page 270-271
11 Interview with Michael Harrison for this book.
12 Kathleen Ann Ruane; "Fairness Doctrine: History and Constitutional Issues;" Congressional Research Service; March 11, 2009
13 Byron York; "An Unfair Doctrine: Democrats Try Once Again to 'Hush Rush' and Many Others;" *National Review*; July 30, 2007
14 "America's Town Meeting of the Air in the Great Depression;" American Studies at the University of Virginia;
   http://xroads.virginia.edu/~1930s/Radio/TownMeeting/TownMeeting.html
15 "Elmer Holmes Davis; Indiana Journalism Hall of Fame; 1974;
   http://indianajournalismhof.org/1974/01/elmer-holmes-davis/
16 Donald Ritchie; "Reporting from Washington: The History of the Washington Press Corps;" Oxford University Press; 2005; Page 66
17 Richard J. Brown; "Hans Von Kaltenborn"; St. James Encyclopedia of Pop Culture; January 29, 2002
18 Ibid.
19 Old Time Radio; http://www.otr.com/kaltenborn.shtml
20 Richard J. Brown; "Hans Von Kaltenborn"; St. James Encyclopedia of Pop Culture; January 29, 2002

21 Minnesota Historical Society; In their Words: Stories from Minnesota's Greatest Generation; Hans von Kaltenborn

22 Richard J. Brown; "Hans Von Kaltenborn"; St. James Encyclopedia of Pop Culture; January 29, 2002

23 Ritchie; Page. 49

24 Ibid.

25 Richard J. Brown; "Hans Von Kaltenborn"; St. James Encyclopedia of Pop Culture; January 29, 2002

26 Ibid.

27 Ritchie; Page 53

28 Ibid; p. 54

29 Hilton Kramer; "Life After Liberalism;" *The American Spectator* December 1994

30 Richard J. Brown; "Hans Von Kaltenborn"; St. James Encyclopedi of Pop Culture; January 29, 2002

31 University of Kansas, History of American Journalism; http:// history.journalism.ku.edu/1930/1930.shtml

32 Brown; St. James Encyclopedia of Pop Culture; January 29, 2002

33 Ritchie; Page 57

34 Brown; St. James Encyclopedia of Pop Culture; January 29, 2002

35 Ibid.

36 Gerald Parshall; "Shockwave;" *U.S. News & World Report*; July 31, 1995

37 Brown; St. James Encyclopedia of Pop Culture; January 29, 2002

38 David Gelernter; "Truman Beats Dewey Again!!!" *The Weekly Standard*; November 15, 2004

39 Neil Conan; "Dewey and Truman;" NPR Weekly Edition; November 7, 2000

40 Ibid.

41 Ibid.

42 Ritchie, Page 68

43 Boake Carter; Radio Days; http://www.otr.com/bcarter.html

44 The Lindbergh Kidnapping; http://www.fbi.gov/aboutus/history/famous-cases/the-lindbergh-kidnapping

45 Ibid.

46 Boake Carter; Radio Days; http://www.otr.com/bcarter.html

47 Douglas Edwards; "Lowell Thomas was Truly the Granddaddy of us All;" *The New York Times*; September 20, 1981

48 "The Press: Loudspeaker;" *Time*; April 13, 1936

49 The Lindbergh Kidnapping; http://www.fbi.gov/about-us/history/famous-cases/the-lindbergh-kidnapping

50 "The Press: Loudspeaker;" *Time*; April 13, 1936
51 Ibid
52 Ibid.
53 Ritchie; Page 55
54 Douglas B. Craig; "Radio Active: Advertising and Consumer Activism, 1935-1947;" *Business History Review*; Autumn 2005
55 Ritchie; Page 55
56 Steven V. Roberts; "What a Rush;" *U.S. News & World Report*; August 16, 1993
57 Neal Gabler; "Decency in the Face of Hatemongering;" *The Boston Globe*; May 26, 2009
58 Evan Thomas, Holly Bailey and Richard Wolfe; "Only in America; Barack Obama is a Niebhur-reading, ESPN Watcher. The Origins of His Troubles with the 'Other' Tag;" *Newsweek*; May 5, 2008
59 Lanny Davis; "White House vs. Fox News Make Sense?" *The Washington Times*; October 26, 2009
60 Douglass McCollam; "A Distant Echo: What Father Coughlin tells us about Glenn Beck;" *Columbia Journalism Review*; January/February 2010
61 Paul Harris; "Glenn Beck and the echoes of Charles Coughlin;" *The Guardian*; February 2, 2011
62 Interview with Michael Harrison for this book.
63 Harris; *The Guardian*; February 2, 2011
64 PBS; The American Experience; Rev. Charles E. Coughlin; http://www.pbs.org/wgbh/amex/holocaust/peopleevents/pandeAMEX96.html
65 The Center for History and New Media; George Mason University; http://chnm.gmu.edu/courses/hist409/coughlin/coughlin.html
66 PBS; The American Experience; Rev. Charles E. Coughlin; http://www.pbs.org/wgbh/amex/holocaust/peopleevents/pandeAMEX96.html
67 Ibid.
68 Jonah Goldberg; "Liberal Fascism: The Secret History of the American Left from Mussolini to the Politics of Meaning;" Doubleday; 2008; Page 138
69 PBS; The American Experience; Rev. Charles E. Coughlin; http://www.pbs.org/wgbh/amex/holocaust/peopleevents/pandeAMEX96.html
70 Goldberg; Page 138
71 Ibid.
72 Ibid; Page 140
73 Ibid; Page 141

74 "Religion: Priest in Politics;" *Time*; December, 11, 1933

75 PBS; The American Experience; Rev. Charles E. Coughlin; http://www.pbs.org/wgbh/amex/holocaust/peopleevents/pandeAMEX96.html

76 The Center for History and New Media; George Mason University; http://chnm.gmu.edu/courses/hist409/coughlin/coughlin.html

77 Ibid; http://historymatters.gmu.edu/d/5111

78 PBS; The American Experience; Rev. Charles E. Coughlin; http://www.pbs.org/wgbh/amex/holocaust/peopleevents/pandeAMEX96.html

79 Ibid.

80 Ibid.

81 Ibid.

82 Eric Boehlert; "Fair and Balanced - The McCarthy Way;" *Salon*; May 26, 2005

83 Ibid.

84 Lee Edwards; "The Conservative Revolution: The Movement that Remade America;" *The Free Press*; Page 16

85 Syracuse University Library; Fulton Lewis Jr. Papers; http://library.syr.edu/digital/guides/l/lewis_f_jr.htm

86 University of Texas Austin; Mike Wallace interview with Fulton Lewis, Jr. February 1, 1958; http://www.hrc.utexas.edu/multimedia/video/2008/wallace/lewis_fulton_t.html

87 Interview with Lee Edwards for this book.

88 Lee Edwards; "The Conservative Revolution: The Movement that Remade America;" *The Free Press*; Page 16

89 University of Texas Austin; Mike Wallace interview with Fulton Lewis, Jr. February 1, 1958; http://www.hrc.utexas.edu/multimedia/video/2008/wallace/lewis_fulton_t.html

90 Radio Days; http://www.otr.com/lewis.html

91 Ritchie; Page 57

92 Radio Days; http://www.otr.com/lewis.html

93 Ritchie; Page 58

94 Syracuse University Library; Fulton Lewis Jr. Papers; http://library.syr.edu/digital/guides/l/lewis_f_jr.htm

95 Radio Days; http://www.otr.com/lewis.html;

96 Ritchie; Page 57

97 Ibid.

98 Ibid; Page 58

99 Ibid.; Page 58-59

100 Syracuse University Library; Fulton Lewis Jr. Papers; http://library.syr.edu/digital/guides/l/lewis_f_jr.htm

101 Don Ritchie; "Reporting from Washington: The History of the Washington Press Corps;" Oxford University Press; 2005; Page 59

102 Ibid; Page 60

103 Ibid.

104 Syracuse University Library; Fulton Lewis Jr. Papers; http://library.syr.edu/digital/guides/l/lewis_f_jr.htm

105 Eric Boehlert; "Fair and Balanced - The McCarthy Way;" *Salon*; May 26, 2005

106 Verne W. Newton; "A Soviet Agent? Harry Hopkins?" *The New York Times*; October 28, 1990

107 "Investigations: Dark Doings;" *Time*; December 12, 1949

108 Ibid.

109 Ibid.

110 Ibid.

111 Ritchie; Page 65

112 Boehlert; Solon; May 26, 2005

113 Richard Bernstein; "Ideas and Trends: Culling History from Propaganda;"

114 Ritchie; Page 66

115 Ibid.

116 Wallace interview with Lewis

117 Boehlert; Solon; May 26, 2005

118 Ibid.

119 Ritchie; Page 65

120 Radio Days; http://www.otr.com/lewis.html

121 Wallace interview with Lewis

122 Ritchie; Page 67

123 Bob Edwards; "Author Neal Gabler Discusses His Winchel Biography;" Morning Edition; National Public Radio; November 8, 1994

124 Ibid.

125 Bernard Weinraub; "He Turned Gossip Into Tawdry Power; Walter Winchell, Who Climbed High and Fell Far, Still Scintillates;" *The New York Times*; November 18, 1998

126 Frank Rich; "He Got the Poop on America;" *The New York Times*; October 23, 1994

127 "Walter Winchell; A Bully in Print;" *The Economist*; February 4, 1995

128 Radio Hall of Fame; http://www.radiohof.org/news/walterwinchell.html

129 Weinraub; *The New York Times*; November 18, 1998

130 *The Economist*; February 4, 1995

131 National Radio Hall of Fame; http://www.radiohof.org/news/walter

winchell.html
132 Robert Taylor; "Mr. and Mrs. America, Meet the Real Winchell;" *The Boston Globe*; October 19, 1994
133 Weinraub; *The New York Times*; November 18, 1998
134 Edwards; November 8, 1994
135 Weinraub; *The New York Times*; November 18, 1998
136 Edwards; National Public Radio; November 8, 1994
137 Howard Kurtz; "Hot Air: All Talk All the Time: How the Talk Show Culture has Changed America;" Basic Books; 1996; Page 292
138 Robert Taylor; "Mr. and Mrs. America, Meet the Real Winchell;" *The Boston Globe*; October 19, 1994
139 Weinraub; *The New York Times*; November 18, 1998
140 "Columny;" *Time*; September 23, 1940
141 Bob Edwards; National Public Radio; November 8, 1994
142 Rich; *The New York Times*; October 23, 1994
143 Edwards; National Public Radio; November 8, 1994
144 Weinraub; *The New York Times*; November 18, 1998
145 Edwards; National Public Radio; November 8, 1994
146 Ibid
147 Weinraub; "He Turned Gossip Into Tawdry Power; Walter Winchell, Who Climbed High and Fell Far, Still Scintillates;" *The New York Times*; November 18, 1998
148 Ibid.
149 Rich; *The New York Times*; October 23, 1994
150 Weinraub; *The New York Times*; November 18, 1998

CHAPTER THREE

1 Viguerie and Franke; Page 51
2 Ibid; Page 50
3 Paul Johnson; "A History of the American People;" Weidenfeld & Nicolson; 1997; Page 556
4 Ibid
5 Viguerie and Franke;; Page 79
6 Terry Eastland; "The Collapse of Big Media: Starting Over;" *The Wilson Quarterly*; Spring 2005
7 Scott Collins; "Crazy Like a Fox: The Inside Story of How Fox NewsBeat CNN;" Portfolio; 2004; Page 89
8 Editorial; "How Media Bias Colors the News;" *Investor's Business Daily*; October 18, 2004
9 Christopher Manion; "Tuned Into Principle;" *American Conservative* February 23, 2009

10 Ibid.
11 Sam Tanenhaus; "The GOP, or Goldwater's Old Party; Why W. is No Surprise;" *The New Republic*; June 11, 2001
12 Manion; *American Conservative*; February 23, 2009
13 Glenn Garvin; "Talk Radio Industry Fears Fairness Law Could Silence Them: Some Talk Radio Fans Fear Democrats Are Ready to Reimpose the Fairness Doctrine, Which Mandates Ideological Balance;" *The Miami Herald*; December 21, 2008
14 Manion; *American Conservative*; February 23, 2009
15 Ibid.
16 Ron Robinson; "Funding Notes;" *National Review*; October 23, 2008
17 Interview with Lee Edwards for this book
18 "Manion Effectively Silencing Critics;" *South Bend Tribune*; January 13, 2000
19 Jane H. Ingraham; "Book Review: People Along the Way;" *The New American*; March 7, 1994
20 Ibid.
21 Lionel Van Deerlin; "The Man from Arizona: A Look at Barry Goldwater and the Conservative Movement is Lengthy and Detailed but Lacks Depth;" *The San Diego Union Tribune*; March 18, 2001
22 Ibid.
23 Ingraham; *The New American*; March 7, 1994
24 "Former FBI Agent Dies;" Associated Press; July 25, 2003
25 Ingraham; *The New American*; March 7, 1994
26 Ibid.
27 Ibid.
28 Ibid.
29 Van Deerlin; *The San Diego Union Tribune*; March 18, 2001
30 "Smoot, 89, Was an FBI Agent;" *San Antonio Express News*; July 27, 2003
31 Fred W. Friendly; "The Good Guys, The Bad Guys and the First Amendment: Free Speech vs. Fairness in Broadcasting;" Random House; 1975; Pages 38, 41, 44-45
32 Ingraham; *The New American*; March 7, 1994
33 Douglas Martin; "Rev. Carl Mcintire, 95: Fiery Fundamentalist Preacher;" *The New York Times*; March 23, 2002
34 Ibid.
35 Dennis McLellan; "Carl McIntire, 95; Firebrand Radio Evangelist;" *Los Angeles Times*; March 23, 2002
36 Friendly; Page 78
37 Richard J. Mouw; "You're Right, Dr. McIntire! In the World of Ecumenical Protestantism, Some Owe Carl McIntire Apology for

Dismissing His Warnings;" *Christianity Today*; May 21, 2002

38 McLellan; *Los Angeles Times*; March 23, 2002

39 Mouw; *Christianity Today*; May 21, 2002

40 Friendly; Page 80-81

41 Ibid; Page 82

42 Ibid; Page 83

43 Ibid; Pages 83-85, 88

44 McLellan; *Los Angeles Times*; March 23, 2002

45 Martin; *The New York Times*; March 23, 2002

46 Friendly; Page 83

47 McLellan; *Los Angeles Times*; March 23, 2002

48 Adam Bernstein; "Evangelist Billy James Hargis Dies; Spread Anti-Communist Message;" *The Washington Post*; November 30, 2004

49 "Billy James Hargis, Televangelist, Died on November 27th, Aged 79;" *Economist*; December 16, 2004

50 Robert McFadden; "Billy James Hargis, 79, Pastor and Anti-Communist Crusader;" *The New York Times*; November 29, 2004

51 Bernstein; *The Washington Post*; November 30, 2004

52 Ibid.

53 Ibid.

54 Ibid.

55 "Religion: The Sins of Billy James Hargis;" *Time*; February 16, 1976

56 Bernstein; *The Washington Post*; November 30, 2004

57 Ibid.

CHAPTER FOUR

1 David Hinckley; "Matter of Trust Scandals of the Public Air, 1959;" *Daily News*; September 28, 1998

2 Ibid.

3 Ibid.

4 "Disc Jockeys: Now Don't Cry;" *Time*; December 7, 1959

5 Interview with Barry Farber for this book.

6 Timeline of Call-In TV and Radio Format; C-Span; http://legacy.c-span.org/C-SPAN25/timeline_a.asp

7 Kurtz; Page 266

8 "The 25 Greatest Radio and Television Talk Show Hosts of All Time;" *Talkers Magazine*; September 2002

9 Interview with Michael Harrison for this book

10 Steve Harvey; "L.A. Then and Now; Local Talk Show Hosts Barbs Hooked Viewers; Bickering TV Talkers Leno, O'Brien and Letterman Have Nothing On the Zany Hosts of 50 Years Ago;" *Los Angeles Times*;

January 24, 2010

11 Joe Pyne; Radio Years;
http://www.radioyears.com/wonn/details.cfm?id=666

12 "The 25 Greatest Radio and Television Talk Show Hosts of All Time;" *Talkers Magazine*; September 2002

13 Joe Pyne; Radio Years;
http://www.radioyears.com/wonn/details.cfm?id=666

14 Ron Williams; "'50s Incident Broke Color Line in City;" *The News Journal*; June 29, 2005

15 Kurtz; Page 266

16 Harry Themal; "Two Guys From Radio Days Gone By;" The News Journal; November 28, 2005 Harvey; *Los Angeles Times*; January 24, 2010

17 "The 25 Greatest Radio and Television Talk Show Hosts of All Time;" *Talkers Magazine*; September 2002

18 Patrick Goldstein; "Yakity Yak, Please Talk Back; Inside the Intense and Screwy World of Talk Radio and the Search for the Next Larry King, Rush Limbaugh, Howard Stern, Gordon Liddy, Whomever;" *Los Angeles Times*; July 16, 1995

19 Joe Pyne; Radio Years;
http://www.radioyears.com/wonn/details.cfm?id=666

20 "The 25 Greatest Radio and Television Talk Show Hosts of All Time;" *Talkers Magazine*; September 2002

21 "The 25 Greatest Radio and Television Talk Show Hosts of All Time;" *Talkers Magazine*; September 2002;

22 Joe Pyne; Radio Years;
http://www.radioyears.com/wonn/details.cfm?id=666

23 Joe Pyne; Radio Years;
http://www.radioyears.com/wonn/details.cfm?id=666

24 Interview with Bob Grant for this book

25 Ibid.

26 Transcript; Rush Limbaugh; January 18, 2008

27 Ibid.

28 "The Top 25 Radio and Television Talkers of All Time;" *Talkers Magazine*; September 2002

29 Interview with Michael Harrison for this book.

30 Bob Grant Online; http://www.bobgrantonline.com/bio.cfm

31 "The Top 25 Radio and Television Talkers of All Time;" *Talkers Magazine*; September 2002

32 Bob Grant Online; http://www.bobgrantonline.com/bio.cfm

33 Kurtz; Page 266

34 Bob Grant Online; http://www.bobgrantonline.com/bio.cfm

35 Ibid.

36 Staff; "Bob Grant to Return to Radio;" Newsmax; August 22, 2007

37 Interview with Bob Grant for this book

38 "The Top 25 Radio and Television Talkers of All Time;" *Talkers Magazine*; September 2002

39 Bob Grant; News Talk Radio WABC; http://wabcradio.com/showdj.asp?DJID=51719

40 Rush Limbaugh; "The Way Things Ought to Be;" Pocket Books; 1992; Page 13

41 Lawrie Mifflin; "Bob Grant is Off Air Following Remarks on Brown's Death;" *The New York Times*; April 18, 1996

42 Anthony Gnoffo Jr.; "Whitman is Cutting Ties to Radio Host Bob Grant Is Biased, Protesting Black Clergy Said. A Past Guest: Whitman Says She was Shocked to Learn That;" *The Philadelphia Inquirer*; October 22, 1994

43 Francis X. Cline; "One Thing's Sure with Bob Grant: It's Not Chicken Talk;" *The New York Times*; October 27, 1994

44 Interview with Bob Grant for this book.

45 Tom Turcol; "Radio's Bob Grant May Challenge Whitman: The Outspoken Conservative is Considering an Independent Senate Bit And He Could Divert Voters She Needs. He Said She Had Broken Faith;" *The Philadelphia Inquirer*; May 4, 1999

46 Cline; *The New York Times*; October 27, 1994

47 Ibid.

48 David Kocieniewski; "Bob Grant or Senate? Talk Show Host Ponders as Whitman Squirms;" *The New York Times*; June 27, 1999

49 Cline; *The New York Times*; October 27, 1994

50 Howard Kurtz; "Radio Daze: A Day With the Country's Masters of Gab: Is America Talking Itself Silly?" *The Washington Post*; October 24, 1994

51 Newsmax; January 16, 2006

52 Interview with Bob Grant for this book

53 Mifflin; *The New York Times*; April 18, 1996

54 Interview with Bob Grant for this book

55 David Hinckley; "WABC Welcomes Back Bob Grant;" *New York Daily News*; August 24, 2007

56 Interview with Bob Grant for this book

57 Mifflin; The New York Times; April 18, 1996

58 "The Top 25 Radio and Television Talkers of All Time;" *Talkers Magazine*; September 2002

59 Brent Baker; "Fewer Conservative Journalists, Disney Appeases Liberals;" Cyber Alert; Media Research Center; June 25, 1997;

http://www.mrc.org/cyberalerts/1997/cyb19970625.asp

60 Sean Hannity; "Let Freedom Ring: Winning the War of Liberty Over Liberalism;" Regan Books; 2002; Page 266

61 Interview with Bob Grant for this book

62 David Hinckley; "Award's Odd Bedfellows: Grant, Dershowitz, Disney;" *New York Daily News*; April 30, 1996

63 Deb Reichmann; "Talk Radio Award to Broadcaster Bob Grant Stirs Controversy;" Associated Press; June 21, 1996

64 Newsmax; January 16, 2006

65 David Hinckley; "WABC Welcomes Back Bob Grant;" *New York Daily News*; August 24, 2007

66 "Talk Radio Award Revoked;" *The Washington Times*; January 17, 2008

67 Bob Grant; News Talk Radio WABC;http://wabcradio.com/showdj.asp?DJID=51719

68 Ibid.

69 Interview with Bob Grant for this book.

70 Kenneth R. Clark; "Barry Farber-Bear in Talk Show Arena;" United Press International; October 5, 1982

71 William B. Falk; "Louder and Louder: Fifteen Years Ago There Were 82 All Talk Stations. Today There are 1,308. A Look At How Talk Radio Has Elbowed Its Way Into Media Prominenc;" *Newsday*; May 29, 1996

72 Dean Johnson; "Boston Radio; Talk Radio's Farber Examines Fabric of Lowell;" *The Boston Herald*; April 17, 1998

73 Interview with Barry Farber for this book.

74 Barry Farber; Talk Radio Network; http://www.trn1.com/farber

75 Barry Farber; "The 25 Greatest Radio Talk Show Hosts of All Time;" *Talkers Magazine*; September 2002; http://www.talkers.com/greatest/9rfarber.htm

76 Interview with Barry Farber for this book.

77 Ibid.

78 Joseph Fried; "A New York Voice Heard Elsewhere;" *The New York Times*; August 14, 2005

79 Interview with Barry Farber for this book.

80 Ibid.

81 Ibid.

82 Maurice Carroll; *The New York Times*; September 9, 1977

83 Fried; *The New York Times*; August 14, 2005

84 Barry Farber; "I Think Reagan is a First Rate President;" *The New York Times*; January 5, 1987

85 Ibid.

86 "Farber Blasts Soviet Policy in Moscow Paper;" United Press International; March 18, 1987

87 "New York Radio Journalist Speaks Mind to Soviets;" The Associated Press; March 18, 1987

88 United Press International; March 18, 1987

89 Barry Farber; "The 25 Greatest Radio Talk Show Hosts of All Time; *Talkers Magazine*; September 2002; http://www.talkers.com/greatest/9rfarber.htm

90 Barry Farber; Talk Radio Network; http://www.trn1.com/farber

91 Fried; *The New York Times*; August 14, 2005

92 Judith Lynn Howard; "Voice of Christian Talk Radio Grows Predominantly Evangelical Programs Gaining Influence;" *The Dallas Morning News*; December 17, 1994

93 James S. Jordan; "Radio Network Founder Marlin Maddoux Dies;" Associated Press; March 4, 2004

94 Howard; *The Dallas Morning News*; December 17, 1994

95 James S. Jordan; "Radio Network Founder Marlin Maddoux Dies;" Associated Press; March 4, 2004

96 Howard; *The Dallas Morning News*; December 17, 1994

97 George Lardner Jr.; "North Criticizes Iran Contra Judge; Defendant Contends Trial is Times to Influence Electorate;" *The Washington Post*; July 14, 1988

98 Perucci Ferraiulo; "Christian Radio is Riding the 'Rush' of Limbaugh;" *Seattle Post-Intelligencer*; December 11, 1994

99 Ibid.

100 Jordan; March 4, 2004

101 Interview with Larry Bates for this book.

102 *Los Angeles Daily News* obituary, September 13, 2008; Retrieved from "George Putnam RIP;" http://michellemalkin.com/2008/09/13/george-putnam-rip/

103 Dennis McLellan; "George Putnam, Longtime L.A. Newsman, Dies at 94;" *Los Angeles Times*; September 13, 2008

104 David Allen; "Legendary TV Anchorman George Putnam Dies at 94;" *San Bernardino County Sun*;" September 12, 2008

105 Interview with Chuck Wilder for this Book

106 Ibid.

107 John Rogers; "Los Angeles TV News Anchor George Putnam Dies;" Associated Press; September 13, 2008

108 Ibid.

109 McLellan; *Los Angeles Times*; September 13, 2008

110 George Putnam Biography, Newsmax, Retrieved from "George Putnam RIP;" http://michellemalkin.com/2008/09/13/george-putnam-rip/

111 McLellan; *Los Angeles Times*; September 13, 2008

112 Roger M. Grace; "George Putnam: The Voice That Keeps Booming;" *Metropolitan News-Enterprise*; January 30, 2003

113 Interview with Chuck Wilder for this book.

114 Rogers; Associated Press; September 13, 2008

115 Grace; *Metropolitan News-Enterprise*; January 30, 2003

116 David Allen; "Legendary TV Anchorman George Putnam Dies at 94;" *San Bernardino County Sun*; September 12, 2008

117 Radio Hall of Fame; http://www.radiohof.org/pioneer/focusonthe family.htm

118 "Focus on the Family: Through the Years;" *The Gazette*; July 20, 2002

119 Mark Barna; "Dobson Quits as Chairman; Founder Will Still Give Radio Address, Write Newsletter;" *The Gazette*; February 28, 2009

120 "Focus on the Family: Through the Years;" *The Gazette*; July 20, 2002

121 Paul Clancy; "Radio Talk Host Interviews Bundy;" *USA Today*; January 23, 1989

122 "Focus on the Family: Through the Years;" *The Gazette*; July 20, 2002

123 Clancy; *USA Today*; January 23, 1989

124 "Focus on the Family: Through the Years;" *The Gazzette*; July 20, 2002

125 Ibid.

126 Ibid.

127 Larry Witham; "Pro-Family Dobson Avoids Partisanship; Politicians Find Impact Impressive;" *The Washington Times*; July 20, 1995

128 Ibid.

129 Grover Norquist; "Dobson and the GOP: The Evangelical Right and the Art of Politics;" *The American Spectator*; July 1998

130 Julia Duin; "NBC Flooded with Calls After Couric's Remarks;" *The Washington Times*; October 16, 1998

131 Ibid.

132 Paul Asay; "Dobson to Air White House Conversation About Miers;" *The Gazette*; October 11, 2005

133 Charles Hurt; "Miers to Face Hostile Queries from Both Sides of the Aisle;" *The Washington Times*; October 12, 2005

134 Pam Zubeck; "Alito's Note to Dobson Debated Thank You Has Backers, Doubters;" *The Gazette*; Mach 2, 2006

135 Radio Hall of Fame; http://www.radiohof.org/pioneer/focusonthe family.htm

136 Neil Boortz Show Web site bio; http://www.boortz.com/news/

entertainment/personalities/boortz-bio/n8Lt/

137 John Kessler; "Hall of Fame Beckons Boortz;" *The Atlanta Journal and Constitution*; September 20, 2009

138 National Radio Hall of Fame; http://www.radiohof.org/talk showhost/nealboortz.html

139 Neil Boortz Show Web site bio; http://www.boortz.com/news/ entertainment/personalities/boortz-bio/n8Lt/

140 The Big Talker; http://www.thebigtalkerfm.com/boortz.php

141 National Radio Hall of Fame; http://www.radiohof.org/talk showhost/nealboortz.html

142 Neil Boortz Show Web site bio; http://www.boortz.com/news/ entertainment/personalities/boortz-bio/n8Lt/

143 Ibid.

144 Drew Jubera; "Boortz Uncorked: Atlanta Radio's Feisty Talk Host Returns to Air, and He's Ready to Cut Loose;" *The Atlanta Journal and Constitution*; March 1, 1993

145 The Big Talker; http://www.thebigtalkerfm.com/boortz.php

146 Jim Galloway; "Political Insider: Boortz vs. Barr on Iraq, and Barr-o-metric Reading from the Blogosphere;" *The Atlanta Journal and Constitution*; May 14, 2008

147 Colin Campbell; "Notes on Talk Radio: The Gospel According to Neal Boortz;" *The Atlanta Journal and Constitution*; May 20, 1992

148 John Kessler; "Hall of Fame Beckons Boortz;" *The Atlanta Journal and Constitution*; September 20, 2009

149 Drew Jubera; "Boortz Uncorked: Atlanta Radio's Feisty Talk Host Returns to Air, and He's Ready to Cut Loose;" *The Atlanta Journal and Constitution*; March 1, 1993

150 Howard Kurtz; Page 267

151 Staff; "Boortz Must Tell WGST His Salary;" *The Atlanta Journal and Constitution*; December 10, 1992

152 Neil Boortz Show Web site bio; http://www.boortz.com/news/ entertainment/personalities/boortz-bio/n8Lt/

153 Miriam Longino; "On Radio: WSB Tasking Boortz and Howard National;" *The Atlanta Journal and Constitution*; December 16, 1998

154 David Simpson; "Man Charged with Murder After Calling Neal Boortz Radio Show;" *The Atlanta Journal and Constitution*; July 2, 2005

155 Mike Gangloff; "Delegates Call for Boycotting Talk Show Host for Tech Stance;" *The Roanoke Times*; May 1, 2007

156 Neil Boortz Show Web site bio; http://www.boortz.com/news/ entertainment/personalities/boortz-bio/n8Lt/

157 John Kessler; "Hall of Fame Beckons Boortz;" *The Atlanta Journal and Constitution*; September 20, 2009

CHAPTER FIVE

1 Brad O'Leary; "Shut Up America: The End of Free Speech;" WND Books; 2009; Page 30-31
2 York; *National Review*; July 30, 2007
3 Friendly; Page 24
4 York; *National Review*; July 30, 2007
5 Kathleen Ann Ruane; "Fairness Doctrine: History and Constitutional Issues;" Congressional Research Service; March 11, 2009
6 Ibid.
7 Friendly; Page 32
8 Ibid.
9 Ibid ; Page 35-37
10 Fred J. Cook; "Radio Right: Hate Clubs on the Air;" *The Nation*; May 25, 1964; http://www.thenation.com/archive/radio-right-hateclubs-Air
11 Friendly; Page 39
12 Ibid; Page 38
13 Ibid; Page 40-41
14 Ibid. Page 40
15 Ibid.
16 U.S. Supreme Court opinion; Red Lion Broadcasting Company, Inc. v. Federal Communications Commission; http://www.yalelawtech.org/wp-content/uploads/RedLion.pdf
17 Stuart Lavietes; "Fred J. Cook, 92, the Author of 45 Books, Many Exposes;" *The New York Times*; May 4, 2003
18 Ibid.
19 Friendly; Page 43-44
20 Thomas W. Hazlett and David W. Sosa, "Chilling the Internet? Lessons from FCC Regulation of Radio Broadcasting;" 4 Mich. Telecomm. Tech. L. Rev. 35 (1998) available at <http://www.mttlr.org/volfour/hazlett.pdf>
21 Friendly; Page 44
22 Ibid.
23 Ibid. Page 50
24 U.S. Supreme Court opinion; Red Lion Broadcasting Company, Inc. v. Federal Communications Commission; http://www.yalelawtech.org/wp-content/uploads/RedLion.pdf
25 Friendly; Page 51-56
26 Friendly; Page 59
27 U.S. Supreme Court opinion; Red Lion Broadcasting Company, Inc. v. Federal Communications Commission;

http://www.yalelawtech.org/wp-content/uploads/RedLion.pdf
28 Ibid.
29 Hazlett and Sosa, <http://www.mttlr.org/volfour/hazlett.pdf>
30 Ibid.
31 Ibid.
32 Katherine Graham; "Personal History;" Knopf; 1997; Page 464

CHAPTER SIX

1 Friendly; Page 193-194
2 Ibid; Page 194-195
3 Interview with Mark Fowler for this book.
4 Ibid.
5 "FCC: End Key Broadcasting Doctrines;" *Facts on File World News Digest*; October 2, 1981
6 Interview with Mark Fowler for this book.
7 Ibid.
8 FCC vs. League of Women Voters; U.S. Supreme Court;
   http://supreme.justia.com/us/468/364/case.html
9 Ibid.
10 Ibid.
11 Ibid.
12 Ibid.
13 Ibid.
14 Kathleen Ann Ruane; "Fairness Doctrine: History and Constitutional Issues;" Congressional Research Service; March 11, 2009
15 York; *National Review*; July 30, 2007
16 Congressional Research Service; March 11, 2009
17 York; *National Review*; July 30, 2007
18 Congressional Research Service; March 11, 2009
19 Reginald Stuart; "Fairness Doctrine Assailed by FCC;" *The New York Times*; August 8, 1985
20 Margaret E. Kriz; "Debate Revived Over Fairness Doctrine;" *The National Journal*; March 14, 1987
21 Thomas W. Hazlett; "Dan Rather's Good Deed: His Critics Should Thank Him for Sinking the Fairness Doctrine;" *The Weekly Standard*; March 21, 2005
22 Peter J. Boyer; "Syracuse Group Appeals Fairness Doctrine Ruling; *The New York Times*; August 11, 1987
23 Staff; "Equal Time Remanded;" *Communications Daily*; September 22, 1986
24 Brad O'Leary; "Shut Up America: The End of Free Speech;" WND

Books; 2009; Page 27

25 Kriz; *The National Journal*; March 14, 1987

26 Mike Mills; "Fairness Doctrine Facing Toughest Test;" *Los Angeles Times*; April 9, 1987

27 York; *National Review*; July 30, 2007

28 Interview with Mark Fowler for this book.

29 John Corry; "Should the Fairness Doctrine be Law?" *The New York Times*; May 24, 1987

30 Merill Hartson; "Former FCC Head Applauds Reagan's Fairness Doctrine Decision;" The Associated Press; June 21, 1987

31 Interview with Mark Fowler for this book.

32 O'Leary; Page 28

33 Brian C. Anderson; "South Park Conservatives: The Revolt Against Liberal Media Bias;" Regnery; 2005; Page 35-36

34 Interview with Mark Fowler for this book.

35 Glenn Garvin; "Talk Radio Industry Fears Fairness Law Could Silence Them; Some Talk Radio Fans Fear Democrats Are Ready to Reimpose the Fairness Doctrine, Which Mandates Ideological Balance;" *Miami Herald*; December 21, 2008

36 Interview with Michael Harrison for this book.

37 Ibid.

CHAPTER SEVEN

1 Margaret Carlson; "An Interview with Rush Limbaugh;" *Time*; October 26, 1992

2 Jay Nordlinger; "A Boswell for Rush;" *National Review* June 7, 2010

3 "Top 25 Greatest Radio and Television Talk Show Hosts of All Time; *Talkers Magazine*; September 2002; http://www.talkers.com/greatest/1rRush.htm

4 Scott McCabe; "Limbaugh, Third Wife Party Ways After 10 Years; The Talk Radio Icon's Legal Troubles are said to be Unrelated;" *Palm Beach Post*; June 12, 2004; and, Lauren Johnson; "Rush Limbaugh Marries Gal Pal Kathryn Rogers in Lavish Palm Beach Ceremony;" *New York Daily News*; June 5, 2010

5 "Top 25 Greatest Radio and Television Talk Show Hosts of All Time;" *Talkers Magazine*; September 2002; http://www.talkers.com/greatest/1rRush.htm

6 "Top 25 Greatest Radio and Television Talk Show Hosts of All Time;" *Talkers Magazine*; September 2002; http://www.talkers.com/greatest/1rRush.htm

7 Rush Limbaugh; "The Way Things Ought to Be;" Pocket Books; 1992;

Page 6
8 Ibid; Page 7
9 Ibid; Page 9
10 Ibid;
11 Ibid; Page 10
12 Ibid; Page 14
13 Carlson; *Time*; October 26, 1992
14 Howard Kurtz; "A Day With the Country's Masters of Gab: Is America Talking Itself Silly;" *The Washington Post*; October 24, 1994
15 Rush Limbaugh; "The Way Things Ought to Be;" Pocket Books; 1992; Page 296
16 "Florida Agency Paying Limbaugh $1 Million to Pitch OJ;" Associated Press; February 10, 1994
17 Pat Riley; "Truth is, Limbaugh Didn't Get Bum's Rush;" *Orange County Register*; August 14, 1994
18 Lara Wozniak; "The Politics of Pizza Get a Rush Job;" *St. Petersburg Times*; April 19, 1995
19 Kathleen Hall Jamieson and Joseph N. Capella; "Echo Chamber: Rush Limbaugh and the Conservative Media Establishment;" Oxford University Press; Page 108
20 Robin Toner; "Politics: On the Air; Radio Talk Show Host Fears For True Conservatism's Fate;" *The New York Times*; February 23, 1996
21 Jamieson and Capella; Page 110
22 Ibid; Page 113
23 Timothy W. Maier; "Limbaugh Learning to Listen Again: Rush Limbaugh Lost Most of His Hearing Because of a Rare Disease, but the Conservative Icon Says He Has Not Lost His Ability to Communicate with His Audience;" Insight on the News; January 28, 2002
24 "Limbaugh Admits Addiction to Pain Medication;" CNN; October 10, 2003
25 Maier; Insight on the News; January 28, 2002
26 Peter King; "Open Mouth, Insert Foot: Limbaugh's Comments on McNabb Aren't Racist, But they are Bonehead;" *Sports Illustrated*; October 1, 2003
27 Ibid.
28 "Limbaugh Admits Addiction to Pain Medication;" CNN; October 10, 2003
29 "Limbaugh: 'I Am No Victim';" CNN; January 14, 2004; http://articles.cnn.com/2003-10-10/entertainment/limbaugh.statement_1_pain-role-models-great-demons?_s=PM:SHOWBIZ
30 Scott McCabe; "Limbaugh, Third Wife Parting After 10 Years; The

Talk Radio Icon's Woes Are Said to be Unrelated;" *Palm Beach Post*; June 12, 2004

31 "Rehab, $30,000 to Keep Limbaugh Out of Court;" CNN; April 29, 2006

32 Bob Orr; "Rush Limbaugh Arrested on Drug Charges;" CBS News; April 29, 2006

33 Michelle Malkin; "Fake Soldier Tale Debunked;" *The Washington Times*; May 26, 2006

34 Ibid.

35 Ibid.

36 Gene Johnson; "Man Charged with Falsifying Military Record;" Associated Press; May 19, 2007

37 Ibid.

38 Transcript; "The Anatomy of a Smear: 'Phony Soldier' is a Phony Story;" The Rush Limbaugh Show; September 28, 2007

39 Ibid.

40 Ibid.

41 Ibid.

42 Thomas Ferraro; "Reid-Limbaugh Spat Raises $2.1 Million for Children;" Reuters; October 19, 2007

43 Mark Levin; "Man of the Year: Rush Limbaugh;" Human Events; January 7, 2008

44 Ferraro; Reuters; October 19, 2007

45 Ibid.

46 Independent Film Channel News Release; "Zogby Poll Finds the Internet Today's Most Trusted News Source;" November 20, 2008

47 Richard Johnson; "Prez Won't Play Rush's Game;" *The New York Post*; May 12, 2010

CHAPTER EIGHT

1 Scott Shepard; "G-man Talk Show 'Hell' for Clintons; *The Denver Post*; May 29, 1994

2 Richard A. Viguerie & David Franke; "America's Right Turn: How Conservatives Used New and Alternative Media to Take Power;" Bonus Books; 2004; Page 183

3 Richard A. Viguerie & David Franke; "America's Right Turn: How Conservatives Used New and Alternative Media to Take Power;" Bonus Books; 2004; Page 183

4 Walter Mears; "Clinton's Love-Hate Relationship with Talk Shows;" Associated Press; June 30, 1994

5 Howard Kurtz; "Hot Air: All Talk All the Time: How the Talk Show

Culture has Changed America;" Basic Books; 1996; Page 298

6 Richard A. Viguerie & David Franke; "America's Right Turn: How Conservatives Used New and Alternative Media to Take Power;" Bonus Books; 2004; Page 183

7 Viguerie & Franke; "America's Right Turn: How Conservatives Used New and Alternative Media to Take Power;" Bonus Books; 2004; Page 183

8 L. Brent Bozell III and Tim Graham; "Whitewash: What the Liberal Media Won't Tell You About Hillary Clinton But Conservatives Will;" Crown Forum; 2007; Page 57-58

9 Ibid; Page 61

10 Ibid.

11 Viguerie & Franke; Page 184

12 Kurtz; Page 299

13 Ibid; Page 291

14 Ibid; Page 300

15 Viguerie & Franke; Page 186

16 Kurtz; Page 301

17 Viguerie & Franke; Page 187

18 J. Jennings Moss; "Some Conservatives Suspicious of Push for Fairness Doctrine;" *The Washington Times*; August 30, 1993

19 Brian C. Anderson; "South Park Conservatives: The Revolt Against Liberal Media Bias;" Regnery; 2005; Page 50

20 Jim Wooten; ABC News; November 4, 1994

21 Robin Toner; "The 1994 Campaign: Broadcaster; Election Jitters in Limbaughland;" *The New York Times*; November 3, 1994

22 Wolf Blitzer; Inside Politics; CNN; May 3, 1994

23 Fred Barnes; "Look Who's Talking;" *The New Republic*; October 31, 1994

24 Ibid.

25 Wooten; November 4, 1994

26 Toner; *The New York Times*; November 3, 1994

27 Ibid.

28 Katherine Q. Seelye; "The 1994 Campaign: The Republicans; With Fiery Words, Gingrich Builds His Kingdom;" *The New York Times*; October 27, 1994

29 Rush Limbaugh Show; October 13, 1994

30 Toner; *The New York Times*; November 3, 1994

31 Ibid.

32 Rush Limbaugh Show; November 10, 1994

33 Kurtz; Page 291

34 Howard Kurtz; "Talk Radio Hosts, Waking Up on the Right Side of

the Bed;" *The Washington Post*; November 10, 1994

35 Richard A. Viguerie & David Franke; "America's Right Turn: How Conservatives Used New and Alternative Media to Take Power;" Bonus Books; 2004; Page 187

36 Kurtz; *The Washington Post*; November 10, 1994

37 David Lawrence; "The President in His Own Words;" *The Miami Herald*; December 11, 1994

38 Edward Epstein; "The Mouths That Roared: They Vilified the President, Sneered at the First Lady, then Led the Charge;" *The San Francisco Chronicle*; December 25, 1994

39 Kurtz; "Hot Air: All Talk All the Time: How the Talk Show Culture has Changed America;" Basic Books; 1996; Page 229

40 Steven A. Holmes; "The 104th Congress: Talk Radio; True Believers Rejoice in Babylon;" *The New York Times*; January 5, 1995

41 Viguerie & Franke; Page 188

42 Newt Gingrich; "To Renew America;" Harper Collins; 1995; Page 210

43 Ibid.

44 Holmes; *The New York Times*; January 5, 1995

45 Howard Kurtz; "The Talkmeisters; Saying All the Right Things;" *The Washington Post*; January 5, 1995

46 Gingrich; Page 210

47 Ibid; Page 210-211

48 J. Jennings Moss and George Archibald; "Clinton Lashes Out at Angry Voices; Radio Hosts Return Barbs in Aftermath of Bombing;" *The Washington Times*; April 25, 1995

49 Howard Kurtz and Dan Balz; "Clinton Assails Spread of Hate Through Media; Americans Urged to Stand Against 'Reckless Speech'; Conservatives Take Offense;" *The Washington Post*; April 25, 1995

50 Moss and Archibald; *The Washington Times*; April 25, 1995

51 Ibid.

52 Associated Press; "Clinton Assails 'Hate' Radio;" *St. Louis Post Dispatch*; April 25, 1995

53 Howard Kurtz; "Hot Air: All Talk All the Time: How the Talk Show Culture has Changed America;" Basic Books; 1996; Page 18

54 Jonathan Alter; "Toxic Speech;" *Newsweek*; May 8, 1995

55 Molly Ivins; "History the Result of Stupidity;" South Bend Tribune; May 17, 1995

56 Associated Press; "Clinton Criticizes Divisive Speech;" *Chattanooga Free Press*; May 5, 1995

57 Ibid.

58 Times Wires; "Liddy: Hate Radio? Aim for the Groin;" *St. Petersburg Times*; April 26, 1995

59 Associated Press; "Clinton Assails 'Hate' Radio;" *St. Louis Post Dispatch*; April 25, 1995

60 Reuters; "Excerpts from Clinton's Comments on Cynicism and the Press;" *The New York Times*; June 25, 1994

61 Mears; Associated Press; June 30, 1994

62 G. Gordon Liddy; "Whitewater, Watergate: Don't Give Up Hillary;" *The Wall Street Journal*; March 11, 1994

63. Howard Kurtz; "Hot Air: All Talk All the Time: How the Talk Show Culture has Changed America;" Basic Books; 1996; Page 18

64 Ibid; Page 241

65 Robert Haught; "Does Clinton Know How Much He's Helped Talk Show Ratings;" *Daily Oklahoman*; July 7, 1994

66 Meredith Oakley; "Secrecy in Foster Case Must End;" *Arkansas Democrat Gazette*; April 24, 1994

67 Ibid.

68 John Freeman; "Liddy Lives and Talks Up to His Reputation;" *The San Diego Union Tribune*; August 5, 1994

69 Howard Kurtz; "Hot Air: All Talk All the Time: How the Talk Show Culture has Changed America;" Basic Books; 1996; Page 18

70 Karen Ball; "New Row Over Foster Death;" *Daily News*; September 15, 1995

71 Interview with Kenneth Starr; *Washington Journal*; C-SPAN; December 10, 1999

72 Karl Vick and David Dahl; "Hiring Lawyer for Clinton Gives Allegation Weight;" *St. Petersburg Times*; May 5, 1994

73 Howard Kurtz; "Hot Air: All Talk All the Time: How the Talk Show Culture has Changed America;" Basic Books; 1996; Page 5

74 Howard Kurtz; "Hot Air: All Talk All the Time: How the Talk Show Culture has Changed America;" Basic Books; 1996; Page 306-307

75 Howard Kurtz; "Hot Air: All Talk All the Time: How the Talk Show Culture has Changed America;" Basic Books; 1996; Page 308

76 Schuyler Kropf; "Media Watchers Say Conservative Talk Radio Losing Appeal;" *The Post and Courier*; July 12, 1998

77 Marc Fisher; "The Hot Talk of Radio; White House Crisis Breathes New Life Into Today's Conservative Mainstays;" *The Washington Post*; February 19, 1998

78 Andrea Adelson; "Talk Radio Copes with Life After Lewinsky;" *The New York Times*; March 15, 1999

79 Ibid.

80 Bob Longino and Miriam Longino; "White House in Crisis: The Public Reacts: Broadcasters Offer Scandalous Feast; The Sex-and Lies Allegations are All the Rage on Radio and TV, Drawing Jabs and Jokes;"

*The Atlanta Journal and Constitution*; January 23, 1998

81 Melinda Henneberger; "The President Under Fire: On the Right; Conservative Talk Radio Finding Cause for Revelry;" *The New York Times*; January 29, 1998

82 Ibid.

83 Ibid.

84 Norma Greenaway; "Radio Ranter Outdoes Himself: Rush Limbaugh Corners the Market on Tastelessnes;" *The Ottawa Citizen*; January 28, 1998

85 Bob Longino and Miriam Longino; *The Atlanta Journal and Constitution*; January 23, 1998

86 Michael L. Rozansky; "On Radio, The Ire Comes Through Loud and Clear;" *The Philadelphia Inquirer*; September 12, 1998

87 Interview with Rush Limbaugh; CNN Late Edition with Wolf Blitzer; March 16, 1999

88 "Cliff Kincaid and Lynn Woolley; "The Death of Talk Radio?;" Accuracy in Media; 2007; Page 48

89 Kurtz and Balz; *The Washington Post*; April 25, 1995

90 Times Wires; "Liddy: Hate Radio? Aim for the Groin;" *St. Petersburg Times*; April 26, 1995

91 Ibid; Times Wires; "Liddy: Hate Radio? Aim for the Groin;" *St. Petersburg Times*; April 26, 1995

92 Kurtz; "Hot Air: All Talk All the Time: How the Talk Show Culture has Changed America;" Basic Books; 1996; Page 267
93"The Top 25 Radio and Television Talkers of All Time;" *Talkers Magazine*; September 2002

94 Steve McKerrow; "'Shoot for the Head' Remark Earns Liddy an Award;" *The Baltimore Sun*; May 18, 1995

95 "The Top 25 Radio and Television Talkers of All Time;" *Talkers Magazine*; September 2002

96 Terry Kellaher; "He Starred in Watergate, He Eats Rats and Liberals;" *Newsday*; May 10, 1995

97 John Freeman; "Liddy Lives and Talks Up to his Reputation;" *The San Diego Union Tribune*; August 5, 1994

98 Ibid.

99 Ibid.

100 Scott Shepard; "G-Man Talk Show a 'Hell' for Clinton;" *The Denver Post*; May 29, 1994

101 Howard Kurtz; "Radio Daze; A Day With the Country's Masters of Gab: Is America Talking Itself Silly;" *The Washington Post*; October 24, 1994

102 John Tierney; "In the Studio with Michael Reagan; On the Inside

Looking Surprised;" *The New York Times*; February 22, 1995
103 Ibid.
104 Kevin Merida; "The Heat of the Son; Michael Reagan's New Book Crashes His Father's Party;" *The Washington Post*; September 5, 1997
105 Tierney; *The New York Times*; February 22, 1995
106 Ibid.
107 Ibid.
108 Jennifer G. Hickey; "Talking the Talk; Michael Reagan;" Insight on the News; February 9, 1998
109 Alison DaRosa; "Younger Reagan Refutes Rumors of Run for Office;" *The San Diego Union Tribune*; November 26, 1991
110 Newsmax Pundits; http://www.newsmaxstore.com/nm/newsmax_pundits.cfm
111 Tierney; *The New York Times*; February 22, 1995
112 Hickcy; Insight on the News; February 9, 1998
113 Ibid.
114 Howard Kurtz; "The Talkmeisters: Saying All the Right Things;" *The Washington Post*; January 5, 1995
115 Tierney; *The New York Times*; February 22, 1995
116 Kurtz; "Hot Air: All Talk All the Time: How the Talk Show Culture has Changed America;" Basic Books; 1996; Page 304
117 Elizabeth Kolbert; "Politics: A Radio Ruckus; Rough Ride for Buchanan on His Very Own Turf;" *The New York Times*; February 24, 1996
118 Jamieson and Cappella; Page 110
119 Merida; *The Washington Post*; September 5, 1997
120 Ibid.
121 Brian Beutler; "Conservatives Also Seek Hastert's Resigation;" The Raw Story; October 2, 2006
122 Michael Medved biography; All American Speakders; http://www.allamericanspeakers.com/celebritytalentbios/Michael-Medved
123 Ross Anderson; "A Matter of Opinion - When Conservative Commentator Michael Medved Found Himself Attacking the Hollywood Elite on Their Own Turf, He Moved to a Radio Pulpit Here;" *The Seattle Times*; June 22, 1997
124 Interview with Michael Medved for this book.
125 Michael Medved biography; All American Speakders; http://www.allamericanspeakers.com/celebritytalentbios/Michael-Medved
126 Ibid.
127 Interview with Michael Medved for this book
128 Anderson; *The Seattle Times*; June 22, 1997

129 Michael Medved biography; All American Speakders; http://www.allamericanspeakers.com/celebritytalentbios/Michael-Medved

130 Interview with Michael Medved for this book

131 Anderson; *The Seattle Times*; June 22, 1997

132 Michael Medved biography; All American Speakders; http://www.allamericanspeakers.com/celebritytalentbios/Michael-Medved

133 Anderson; *The Seattle Times*; June 22, 1997

134 Interview with Michael Medved for this book

135 Ibid.

136 Ben Hartman; "Michael Medved Doesn't Just Support Isaral, He Brings His Listeners to See It;" *Jerusalem Post*; June 2, 2011

137 Ibid.

138 Michael Medved biography; All American Speakers; http://www.allamericanspeakers.com/celebritytalentbios/Michael-Medved

139 Interview with Michael Medved for this book

140 Dave Berg; "Dennis Prager for Senate? California Radio Host Could Knock Out Boxer;" *The Washington Times*; February 19, 2003

141 Dennis Prager; "Moral Absolutes: Judeo Christian Values Part XI;" Townhall.com; May 3, 2005

142 Berg; *The Washington Times*; February 19, 2003

143 About Dennis Prager; http://www.dennisprager.com/pages/bio

144 Ibid.

145 Bob Sokolsky; "Dennis Prager Leaving KABC After 18 Years;" *Press-Enterprise*; November 1, 2000

146 About Dennis Prager; http://www.dennisprager.com/pages/bio

147 Berg; *The Washington Times*; February 19, 2003

148 Michael Granberry; "Mike Gallagher Conservative Radio Talk Show Host Springs From a Democratic Tradition;" *The Dallas Morning News*; August 14, 2005

149 Ibid.

150 Ibid.

151 Ibid.

152 D.L. Stewart; "A National Audience, Conservatively Speaking; Dayton Resident Mike Gallagher Has Become a Powerful Voice in Talk Radio;" *Dayton Daily News*; May 9, 2004

153 Ibid.

154 About Mike Gallagher; http://www.mikeonline.com/about.aspx

155 Ibid.

156 Stewart; *Dayton Daily News*; May 9, 2004

## CHAPTER NINE

1 Howard Kurtz; "Radio Hosts Get Closer to the White House-If Only Physically;" *The Washington Post*; October 25, 2006

2 Ibid.

3 Interview with Michael Harrison for this book.

4 Kathleen Hall Jamieson and Joseph N. Cappella; "Echo Chamber: Rush Limbaugh and the Conservative Media Establishment;" Oxford University Press; 2008; Page 113

5 Ibid; Page 114

6 Ibid.

7 Susan Baer; "GOP Right Unleashes its Wrath on Gore; Conservative Vow Gridlock if He Wins;" *The Baltimore Sun*; November 21, 2000

8 Staff; "Fox's Hannity Tell Pro-Lifers That Terrorists Must be Knocked Out; The TV Personality Spoke Saturday at the Grand Rapids Right to Life's Annual Dinner;" *Grand Rapids Press*; October 21, 2001

9 Staff; "Democrats Continue to Press for 9/11 Intelligence Investigation;" The Bulletin's Frontrunner; May 21, 2002

10 Interview with Sean Hannity; ABC News; Good Morning America; August 20, 2002

11 Joyce Howard Price; "Limbaugh Returns Daschle Attack on Terror War;" *The Washington Times*; December 1, 2002

12 David Firestone; "Daschle Ties Threats to Fervor Created by Radio Programs;" *The New York Times*; November 21, 2002

13 Ibid.

14 Stephen Dinan; "Gore Claims Media Alliance with GOP to Further Agenda;" *The Washington Times*; November 28, 2002

15 Ibid.

16 Staff; "Conservative Media Star Urges Vote; Sean Hannity Spoke About Evils of Liberalism During a Visit to Cornerstone University;" *Grand Rapids Press*; October 27, 2002

17 Steve Carney; "Taking up Battle Stations; Both Sides in the War Debate Have Their Outspoken Outposts in Los Angeles Radio;" *Los Angeles Times*; March 14, 2003

18 Ellen Goodman; "Truth is Casualty of Talk Radio;" *Chattanooga Times Free Press*; March 23, 2003

19 Jeff Daniel; "Demand for Facts Overwhelms Radio Talk; Call-In Hosts Give Way to News Bulletins, and Debate is Toned Down;" *St. Louis Post-Dispatch*; March 21, 2003

20 Paul Farhi; "For Broadcast Media, Patriotism Pay; Consultants Tell Radio, TV Clients That Protes Coverage Drives Off Viewers;" *The Washington Post*; March 28, 2003

21 Jon Ward; "Dueling Rallies Focus on Iraq War; Protester, Backers to March Saurday;" *The Washington Times*; April 9, 2003

22 Joe Hagan; "Hannity: A Fox in the Crowd;" *New York Observer*; August 16, 2004

23 Peggy Noonan; "So Much to Savor: A Big Win for America and a Loss for the Mainstream Media;" *The Wall Street Journal*; November 4, 2004

24 Brian McGuire; "Bush Stuns Conservatives in Choice of Miers;" *The New York Sun*; October 4, 2000

25 Interview with Rush Limbaugh; Hannity & Colmes; Fox News Channel; October 18, 2005

26 Howard Kurtz; "Conservative Pundits Packed a Real Punch;" The Washington Post; *October 28, 2005*

27 *Inter*view with Laura Ingraham; Hannity & Colmes; Fox News Channel; October 11, 2005

28 Richard Miniter; "Laura Ingraham for SCOTUS;" *National Review*; October 6, 2005

29 Howard Kurtz; "Conservative Pundits Packed a Real Punch;" *The Washington Post*; October 28, 2005

30 Dean Barnett; "The Truth About Talk Radio; It Just Provides a Dial Tone;" *The Weekly Standard*; January 23, 2008

31 Julie Hirschfeld Davis; "Bush to Push Immigration Bill at Capitol;" Associated Press; June 12, 2007

32 Peter Wallsten, "Immigration Debate Puts Up Wall in the GOP; Pursue Latino Voters or Please the Party's Base? The Senate Overhaul Bill Reveals a Split on What Political Road is Best for Republicans;" *The Los Angeles Times*; May 27, 2007

33 Ibid.

34 Ibid.

35 Perry Hicks; "Trent Lott Answers Immigration Bill Critics;" *Gulf Coast News*; June 22, 2007

36 Morton Kondracke; "Demagoguery Killed Immigration Debate;" *Roll Call*; July 13, 2007

37 Interview with Michael Medved for this book

38 Hicks; *Gulf Coast News*; June 22, 2007

39 Jim Puzzanghera; "Broadcating; Democrats Speak Out for Fairness Doctrine; The Influence Wielded by Conservative Talk Show Hosts Draws Calls to Reinstate Policy;" *The Los Angeles Times*; July 23, 2007

40 Jim Puzzanghera; "Broadcating; Democrats Speak Out for Fairness Doctrine; The Influence Wielded by Conservative Talk Show Hosts Draws Calls to Reinstate Policy;" *The Los Angeles Times*; July 23, 2007

41 Ibid.

42 Dean Barnett; "The Truth About Talk Radio; It Just Provides a Dial Tone;" *The Weekly Standard*; January 23, 2008

43 Rome Neal; "'Hannitization' of America;" CBS News; December 5, 2007

44 Interview with Sean Hannity; ABC News; August 20, 2002

45 Sean Hannity; "Let Freedom Ring: Winning the War of Liberty Over Liberalism;" Regan Books, 2002; Page 264

46 Rome Neal; "'Hannitization' of America;" CBS News; December 5, 2007

47 Hannity; "Let Freedom Ring: Winning the War of Liberty Over Liberalism;" Regan Books, 2002; Page 264

48 Paul Rolly; "Rolly: Truth Will be the First Casually in Hannity, Anderson Matchup;" *The Salt Lake Tribune*; April 28, 2007

49 Sean Hannity; "Let Freedom Ring: Winning the War of Liberty Over Liberalism;" Regan Books, 2002; Page 264

50 David Hinckley; "Hannity Bring 'Freedom' Concert Back to Six Flags;" *New York Daily News*; July 20, 2006

51 Scan Hannity; "Let Freedom Ring: Winning the War of Liberty Over Liberalism;" Regan Books, 2002; Page 265

52 Ibid.

53 Ibid.

54 Joe Hagan; "Hannity: A Fox in the Crowd;" *New York Observer*; August 16, 2004

55 Fox News Personalities Bio; www.foxnews.com/onair/personalities/sean-hannity/bio/#ixzz1YFjKQxoG

56 Hagan; *New York Observer*; August 16, 2004

57 Sean Hannity; "Let Freedom Ring: Winning the War of Liberty Over Liberalism;" Regan Books, 2002; Page 266

58 James Poniewozik; "10 Questions for Sean Hannity;" *Time*; November 5, 2002

59 Sean Hannity Show Web site bio; www.hannity.com/page/our-team

60 Ibid.

61 Hagan; *New York Observer*; August 16, 2004

62 Sean Hannity Show Web site bio; www.hannity.com/page/our-team

63 Ibid.

64 Fox News Personalities Bio; www.foxnews.com/onair/personalities/sean-hannity/bio/#ixzz1YFjKQxoG

65 Interview with Sean Hannity; ABC News; August 20, 2002

66 Poniewozik; *Time*; November 5, 2002

67 Fox News Personalities Bio; www.foxnews.com/onair/personalities/sean-hannity/bio/#ixzz1YFjKQxoG

68 Hugh Hewitt Biography; All American Speakers; http://
www.allamericanspeakers.com/speakers/Hugh-Hewitt/5510
69 Nicholas Lehmann; "The Wayward Press: Right Hook;" *The New
Yorker*; August 29, 2005
70 Andrew Romano; "The Right: The Next Big Thing? Conservative
Pundit Hugh Hewitt Marries Power of Talk Radio With the Reach of
the 'Netroots.' Watch Out Kos;" *Newsweek*; July 3, 200
71 Lehmann; *The New Yorker*; August 29, 2005
72 Hugh Hewitt; "The Media's Acient Regime; Columbia Journalism
School Tries to Save the Old Order;" January 30, 2006
73 Howard Kurtz; "Laura Ingraham, Reporting for W2004;"
*The Washington Post*; August 30, 2004
74 Jeffrey T. Kuhner; "Ingraham Rips Left's Elites; Talk Host Gains
Popularity with her 'Love Letter' to Americans;" *The Washington
Times*; October 30, 2003
75 Andria Billups; "Radio's 'Power Broker;' Ingraham Sees Hope for
Taking Back Nation;" *The Washington Times*; September 13, 2007
76 Ibid.
77 David Daley; "Woman of the Right; Laura Ingraham Leads New
Breed of TV Pundits: Young, Conservative, Female;" *Hartford
Courant*; March 27, 1999
78 Ibid.
79 Ibid.
80 Stu Bykofsky; "Laura Ingraham: Right on Radio;" *The Philadelphia
Daily News*; September 20, 2007
81 D.C. Denison; "Encounter with Laura Ingraham: Warring with the
Media Elite is There Room on the Radio Dial for Another Brash
Conservative Voice;" *The Boston Globe*, July 13, 2003
82 Ibid.
83 Kurtz; *The Washngton Post*; August 30, 2004
84 Ibid.
85 Bill Hoffmann; "Laura Ingraham Has Cancer;" *The New York Post*;
April 27, 2005
86 Ibid.
87 Howard Kurtz; "Ingraham Speaks Up About Her Silencing on Talk
Radio;" *The Washington Post*; June 17, 2008
88 Ibid.
89 Reliable Sources; "Love, Etc…;" *The Washington Post*; July 30, 2009
90 Amanda Somich-Duganier; "Radio Host Ingraham Brings Her Show
to UNF; The Conservative Talks Politics and Her Concern for
America's Future;" *Florida Times Union*; April 21, 2011
91 Mike Linn; "President Pelosi a Frightful Idea, Ingraham Tells 1,900;"

*Arkansas Democrat-Gazette*; February 17, 2010

92 Kenneth Lowe; "Sorting Out the Effect Massachusetts Election Will Have on Illinois on Feb. 2;" *Herald & Review*; January 21, 2010

93 Savage Nation Radio Show; http://www.youtube.com/watch?v=Mo5w1q4WpNw

94 Savage Nation; http://www.youtube.com/watch?v=ZiRI750v_nA&feature=related

95 Savage Nation Radio Show; http://www.youtube.com/watch?v=Mo5w1q4WpNw

96 Dan Fost; "Savage Talk; A Former Herbalist Has Remade Himself Into the Vitriol-Spewing King of the Bay Area's Drive Time;" *The San Francisco Chronicle*; February 6, 2003

97 Talk Radio Network, Michael Savage Bio; http://www.trn1.com/savage-about

98 Rone Tempest; "Tearing it up; Michael Savage, Once an Angry White Man who Couldn't get the Job he Wanted, is now a Voice of Ultraconservatism. His Popular Radio Talk Show Can be Nasty, and Politically Incorrect. Tough;" *The Los Angeles Times*; March 7, 2003

99 Ibid.

100 Ibid.

101 Ibid.

102 Ibid.

103 Ibid.

104 Tempest; *The Los Angeles Times*; March 7, 2003

105 Ibid.

106 Peter Hartlaub; "MSNBC Gives Bay Talk Jock Own Show; Michael Savage Gets an Hour on Saturday;" *The San Francisco Chronicle*; February 13, 2003

107 Ibid.

108 Dan Fost; "Savage Says He's Sorry - But Stays Fired; Talk Show Host Insists Epithets not Aimed at People With AIDS;" *The San Francisco Chronicle*; July 9, 2003

109 Ibid.

110 Dan Fost; "Savage Says He's Sorry - But Stays Fired; Talk Show Host Insists Epithets not Aimed at People With AIDS;" *The San Francisco Chronicle*; July 9, 2003

111 Ibid.

112 Talk Radio Network, Michael Savage Bio; http://www.trn1.com/savage-about

113 Ibid.

114 Savage Nation Website; http://www.michaelsavage.wnd.com/about-michael-savage/

115 http://www.youtube.com/watch?v=Mo5w1q4WpNw

116 Jacques Steinberg; "Savage Has Syndicator's Support;" *The New York Times*; July 25, 2008

117 Ibid.

118 Robert Selna; "Parents Talk Back to Radio Host; Savages Remarks About Autism Draw Scores of Protesters;" *The San Francisco Chronicle*; July 28, 2008

119 Neal Conan; "Michael Savage Banned in the U.K.;" National Public Radio; May 5, 2009

120 Joe Garofoli and Carla Marinucci; "Britain's Ban of Savage Decried by his Opponents;" *The San Francisco Chronicle*; May 6, 2009

121 Ibid.

122 Carla Marinucci; "Radio Host Savage Seeks Clinton's Help Over Ban in Britain;" *The San Francisco Chronicle*; May 15, 2009

123 Jennifer Harper; "Radio Host Savage Sue Over British Ban;" *The Washington Times*; June 2, 2009

124 Ibid.

125 Interview with Bill Bennett for this book.

126 Kathleen Parker; "When Bill Bennett Listens, People Talk; *Saint Paul Pioneer Press*; April 8, 2005

127 Ibid.

128 Ibid.

129 Walter Williams; "Bill Bennett: A Victim of Idiotic Interpretations;" *Human Events*; October 12, 2005

130 Senator Barack Obama, News Release; September 29, 2005

131 Representative John Conyers; News Release; September 29, 2005

132 Michael A. Fletcher and Brian Faler; "Commentator Defends Radio Remarks; Republicans Join Criticism of Bennett's Talk on Race, Abortion and Crime;" *The Washington Post*; October 2, 2005

133 Ibid.

134 Williams; *Human Events*; October 12, 2005

135 Interview with Bill Bennett for this book.

CHAPTER TEN

1 "2011 Talkers Heavy Hundred;" *Talkers Magazine*; February 25, 2011; http://www.talkers.com/2011/02/25/2011-talkers-heavyhundred-2/#more-2740

2 Tim Madigan; "Are Media Talkers Stirring Up a Hornet's Nest?" McClatchy Newspapers; October 18, 2009

3 Interview with Michael Harrison for this book.

4 Ibid.

5 Howard Kurtz; "Hot Air: All Talk All the Time: How the Talk Show Culture has Changed America;" Basic Books; 1996; Page 287

6 Joe Nick Patoski; "What's Left?" *Texas Monthly*; January 1998

7 Ibid.

8 Tom DeVries; "We'll Talk About That; Can Liberals Do Talk Radio?" *The American Prospect*; March/April 1996

9 Patoski; Texas Monthly; January 1998

10 Ann Coulter; "Slander: Liberal Lies About the American Right;" Random House; 2002; Page 119

11 Patoski; *Texas Monthly*; January 1998

12 DeVries; *The American Prospect*; March/April 1996

13 Ibid.

14 Ibid.

15 Ibid.

16 Patoski; *Texas Monthly*; January 1998

17 Howard Kurtz; "Radio Daze: A Day With the Country's Master's of Gab: Is America Talking Itself Silly?" *The Washington Post*; October 24, 1994

18 Paul D. Colford; "Jerry Brown Gets a Rush Out of Radio; Media: The Veteran Politician is Thriving on 'We the People,' His New Talk Show, Which is off to a Modest Start;" *Lost Angeles Times*; March 2, 1994

19 Ibid.

20 Ibid.

21 Howard Kurtz; "Hot Air: All Talk All the Time: How the Talk Show Culture has Changed America;" Basic Books; 1996; Page 322

22 Deborah Hastings; "Manchild in the East Bay: Now Jerry Brown Wants to Be Mayor of Oakland;" Associated Press; March 2, 1998

23 Staff; "Cuomo Wraps Radio Show for TV Work and Politics;" *Daily News*; July 2, 1996

24 Ellen Dehenport; "Long Ago Left in Dust, Liberal Talk Radio ShowsSigns of Life;" *St. Petersburg Times*; April 8, 1996

25 Ibid.

26 William LaRue; "Radio Mario A Year After the Fall;" *The Post-Standard*; November 6, 1995

27 Staff; "Cuomo Wraps Radio Show for TV Work and Politics;" *Daily News*; July 2, 1996

28 Brian C. Anderson; "South Park Conservatives: The Revolt Against Liberal Media Bias;" Regnery; 2005; Page 44

29 Coulter; Page 119

30 Anderson; Page 44

31 Brad O'Leary; "Shut Up America: The End of Free Speech;" WND

Books; 2009; Page 76

32 Ibid.

33 Cliff Kincaid and Lynn Wooley; "The Death of Talk Radio;" Accuracy in Media; 2007; Page 79-80

34 O'Leary; Page 76

35 Ibid. Page 77

36 Kincaid and Wooley; Page 81

37 Anderson; Page 44

38 Kincaid and Wooley; Page 82

39 O'Leary; Page 77

40 Ibid; Page 78

41 Kincaid and Wooley; Page 82

42 O'Leary; Page 78

43 Kincaid and Wooley; Page 69

44 Ryan Nakashima; "Air America Radio Closing; Filing for Bankruptcy;" Associated Press; January 22, 2010

45 Charles Passy; "Talk Radio: The Big Business of Big Mouths;" *Palm Beach Post*; May 10, 2008

46 Nakashima; Associated Press; January 22, 2010

47 Interview with Michael Harrison for this book.

CHAPTER ELEVEN

1 Jeffrey Gettleman; "Talk Radio Thwarts Tennessee Income Tax;" *Los Angeles Times*; July 23, 2001

2 Richard A. Viguerie & David Franke; "America's Right Turn: HowConservatives Used New and Alternative Media to Take Power;Bonus Books; 2004; Page 181

3 Howard Kurtz; "Hot Air: All Talk, All the Time;" Times Books; 1996;Page 297

4 Ibid.

5 Richard Locker and Paula Wade; "It's Over, No Income Tax: Special Session Adjourns Without Even Voting;" *The Commercial Appeal* (Memphis); November 19, 1999

6 Ibid.

7 Theotis Robinson Jr.; "Failure to Pass Tax Creates Train Wreck;" *Knoxville News-Sentinel*; November 22, 1999

8 John Commins; "Extended Budget Conflict Grinding on Legislators;" *Chattanooga Times Free Press*; June 18, 2000

9 Joyce Howard Price; "Dissonance Over Taxes Heard in Home of Country Music;" *The Washington Times*; June 11, 2001

10 Duren Cheek and Rob Johnson; "Horn Honkers Back in Session;"

*The Tennessean*; May 15, 2001

11 Price; *The Washington Times*; June 11, 2001

12 Ibid.

13 Cheek and Johnson; *The Tennessean*; May 15, 2001

14 Jeffrey Gettleman; "Talk Radio Thwarts Tennessee Income Tax;" *Los Angeles Times*; July 23, 2001

15 Ibid.

16 Ibid.

17 Richard Locker; "Riot Police Block Tax Protesters Threatening Lawmakers at Capitol;" *The Commercial Appeal*; July 13, 2001

18 Richard Locker; "Talk Stays Hot in Wake of Tax Protest at Capitol;" *The Commercial Appeal* (Memphis); July 14, 2001

19 Gettleman; *Los Angeles Times*; July 23, 2001

20 Bonna de la Cruz, Duren Cheek and Rob Johnson; "No-Tax Budget Passes as Protesters Swarm Capitol;" *The Tennessean*; July 13, 2001

21 Rebecca Ferrar and Tom Humphrey; "State Budget OK'd as Angry Mob Roils;" *News-Sentinel* (Knoxville); July 13, 2001

22 Richard Locker; "Talk Stays Hot in Wake of Tax Protest at Capitol;" *The Commercial Appeal* (Memphis); July 14, 2001

23 Tom Humphrey; "Talk Radio is Major Player in Tennessee PoliticalWars Talk Show Stations Reaping Rich Harvest of Political Ads;" *News-Sentinel* (Knoxville); July 19, 2002

24 Jeffrey Gettleman; "Talk Radio Thwarts Tennessee Income Tax;" *Los Angeles Times*; July 23, 2001

25 Andrew Cline; "Tea Party Time;" *National Review*; August 3, 2001

26 Wade Rawlins; "Protesters' Sqall Hits Budget Stall;" *News and Observer* (Raleigh) August, 1, 2001

27 Andrew Cline; "Tea Party Time;" *National Review*; August 3, 2001

28 Scott Mooneyham; "Tax Protesters Gather at Legislature;" The Associated Press; July 31, 2001

29 Wade Rawlins; "Protesters' Sqall Hits Budget Stall;" *News and Observer* (Raleigh) August, 1, 2001

30 Cline; *National Review*; August 3, 2001

31 Christopher Kirkpatrick; "Anti-Tax Hike Protesters go to Raleigh;" *The Herald-Sun* (Durham, N.C.) August 1, 2001

32 Cline; *National Review*; August 3, 2001

33 Mooneyham; The Associated Press; July 31, 2001

34 Ibid.

35 Lynn Vincent; "Total Recall;" *World Magazine*; August 2, 2003

36 Interview with Melanie Morgan for this book.

37 Vincent; *World Magazine*; August 2, 2003

38 Ibid.

39 Interview with Melanie Morgan for this book.

40 Megan Garvey; "Talk Radio Beats Drum for Recall;" *Los Angeles Times*; July 27, 2003

41 Vincent; *World Magazine*; August 2, 2003

42 Megan Garvey; "Talk Radio Beats Drum for Recall;" *Los Angeles Times*; July 27, 2003

43 Vincent; *World Magazine*; August 2, 2003

44. Timm Herdt; "Recall a Blessing for Republican Talk Radio;" Scripps Howard News Service; August 27, 2003

45 Vincent; *World Magazine*; August 2, 2003

46 Ibid.

47 Ibid.

48 Megan Garvey; "Talk Radio Beats Drum for Recall;" *Los Angeles Times*; July 27, 2003

49 Ibid.

50 Brian Lowry; "Tuning In: The Votes Are In and the Winner is Talk Radio;" *Daily Variety*; October 8, 2003

51 John McLaughlin; "Like Christie, Arnold Owes Talk Radio Hit Team;" *The Star-Ledger* (Newark, N.J.) October 15, 2003

52 Timm Herdt; "Recall a Blessing for Republican Talk Radio;" Scripps Howard News Service; August 27, 2003

53 Joe Matthews; "Schwarzenegger Casts Himself as Conservative;" *Los Angeles Times*; August 26, 2003

54 Ibid.

55 Ibid.

56 Interview with Melanie Morgan for this book.

57 Bob Baker and Steve Carney; "Talk Radio is Still in Attack Mode After the Election;" *Los Angeles Times*; October 9, 2003

58 Steve Carney; "Schwarzenegger Owes a Debt to Talk Radio;" *Los Angeles Times*; October 10, 2003

59 J. Freedom du Lac; "Elation Fills the Talk Radio Airwaves;" *Sacramento Bee*; October 8, 2003

60 Joe Garofoli; "'Nutball' No More, Talk Radio Jocks Bask in Their Recall Role;" *San Francisco Chronicle*; October 9, 2003

61 William McCall; "Oregon Mediator Trying to Settle Mexican-American Adoption Fight;" Associated Press; December 9, 2007

62 Interview with Lars Larson for this book

63 About Lars Larson; http://www.larslarson.com/g/about-lars/61.htmlInterview with Lars Larson for this book

64 Interview with Lars Larson for this book

65 William McCall; "Oregon Foster Child Will Not Be Sent to Grandmother in Mexico;" December 13, 2007

66 "Oregon Governor Takes Interest in 2-Year-Old's Mexico Placement;" Associated Press; November 15, 2007

67 William McCall; "Oregon Foster Child Will Not Be Sent to Grandmother in Mexico;" Associated Press; December 13, 2007

68 Interview with Lars Larson for this book.

69 Ibid.


CHAPTER TWELVE


1 Rush Limbaugh Show; Transcript; January 16, 2009

2 Charles Hurt; "Obama's Picture Perfect First Days; Intimate Look at First Family;" *New York Post*; January 24, 2009

3 Brian Stelter; "For Conservatives; It's a New Dawn Too;" *The New York Times*; December 22, 2008

4 Editorial; "Diversity Czar Threatens Free Speech;" *Investor's Business Daily*; September 1, 2009

5 Ibid.

6 Ibid.

7 Frank Gaffney; "Free Speech, But Not For Me? A Case of Selective Outrage;" *The Washington Times*; June 16, 2009

8 Jeffrey Lord; "Mark Levin and the Book That Changed America;" *The American Spectator*; November 9, 2010

9 Ibid.

10 Craig Smith; "Levin: The Recoil to Tyranny;" *Pittsburgh Tribune-Review*; April 18, 2009

11 Mark Levin Show website; http://www.marklevinshow.com/article.asp?id=1261987

12 Ibid.

13 David Hinckley; "Ingraham and Levin Sure to Float ABC's Boat;" *Daily News*; September 27, 2004

14 Mark Levin Show website; http://www.marklevinshow.com/article.asp?id=1261987

15 Ibid.

16 David Hinckley, "Levin Reflects on His Pal Pooch;" *Daily News*; November 6, 2007

17 David Hinckley; "For Levin, Politics is the Name of the Game;" *Daily News*; October 24, 2006

18 Ibid.

19 Ibid.

20 Lord; *The American Spectator*; November 9, 2010

21 Ibid.

22 Ibid.

23 Ibid.

24 Ibid.

25 Brian Stelter; "A Folksy Guy, in Recovery, Is About to Land Millions;" *The New York Times*; November 5, 2007

26 Ibid.

27 David Segal; "The Right & Wrong; Conservative Talker Glenn Beck Puts His Own Failings Upfront;" *The Washington Post*; January 26, 2007

28 Glenn Beck; Biography Channel; www.biography.com/people/glenn-beck-522294

29 Ibid.

30 Ibid.

31 Segal; *The Washington Post*; January 26, 2007

32 Glenn Beck; Biography Channel; www.biography.com/people/glenn-beck-522294

33 Segal; *The Washington Post*; January 26, 2007

34 Glenn Beck; Biography Channel; www.biography.com/people/glenn-beck-522294

35 Ibid.

36 About Glenn Beck; www.glennbeck.com/content/program

37 Glenn Beck; Biography Channel; www.biography.com/people/glenn-beck-522294

38 Segal; *The Washington Post*; January 26, 2007

39 About Glenn Beck; www.glennbeck.com/content/program

40 Segal; *The Washington Post*; January 26, 2007

41 About Glenn Beck; www.glennbeck.com/content/program

42 Glenn Beck; Biography Channel; www.biography.com/people/glenn-beck-522294

43 Steven F. Hayward; "Is Conservatism Dead? Or Just Brain Dead?" *Tulsa World*; October 11, 2009

44 "The 9/12 Project;" "Nine Principles, Twelve Values;" http://www.glennbeck.com/content/articles/article/198/21018/

45 Jeffrey A. Trachtenberg; "New Deal Gives Beck Share in Book Profits;" *The Wall Street Journal*; May 4, 2009

46 Motoko Rich; "For Thrillers, Glenn Beck is Becoming New Oprah;" *The New York Times*; November 5, 2009

47 Howard Kurtz; "Unamplified, Beck's Vice Still Carries;" *The Washington Post*; September 14, 2009

48 Ibid.

49 Ibid.

50 Michael Boorstein; "Beck's Marriage of Politics and Religion Raising Questions;" *The Washington Post*; August 31, 2010.

51 Amy Gardner; "Beck Rally Will be a Measure of 'Tea Party'Strength;" *The Washington Post*; August 26, 2010

52 Brian Stelter; "Beck Uses Last Show on Fox to Allude to His New Venture;" *The New York Times*; July 1, 2011

53 Ibid.

54 Caroline B. Glick; "Glenn Beck's Revealing Visit;" *Jerusalem Post*; August 26, 2011

# INDEX

## ACKNOWLEDGMENTS

There are many people to thank for this book.

I likely also would have determined there are better things to do with my time without the strong support from my wife Basia. Also, I want to thank my mom and my sisters who early on suggested I write a book on American politics.

My agent Don Gastwirth believed in me at times more than I believed in me. Don Bracken of History Publishing Company was extremely encouraging and helpful throughout the editing process of the book and Bob Aulicino designed a cover that not only catches the eye but the spirit of the book as well.

Thanks to CNSNews.com Editor-in-Chief Terry Jeffrey for giving me the OK to do this book and for his enthusiasm about the project. So too, for the entire CNSNews.com staff, a great place to do great journalism, and also thanks to the parent organization, the Media Research Center, which promotes an environment of excellence for all its staff.

A special thank you goes to all of the talk radio hosts who offered their insight for this book. I add that Michael Harrison of *Talkers Magazine* was particularly helpful in steering me in the right direction. He spoke as a radio industry insider to someone who looked at things entirely from a political aspect.

Lastly, I should thank my dog Jake. On many occasions while writing this book he leaped into my lap and attempted to climb onto the key board, or insisted that I toss a dog toy for him to fetch. It was a temporary delay and required some deleting, but probably provided a needed mental break from the writing process. Anyway, I choose to take his actions as his full fledged support, so a special thanks to a special dog.